THE GILA PUEBLO SALADO

Charmion R. McKusick and Jon Nathan Young

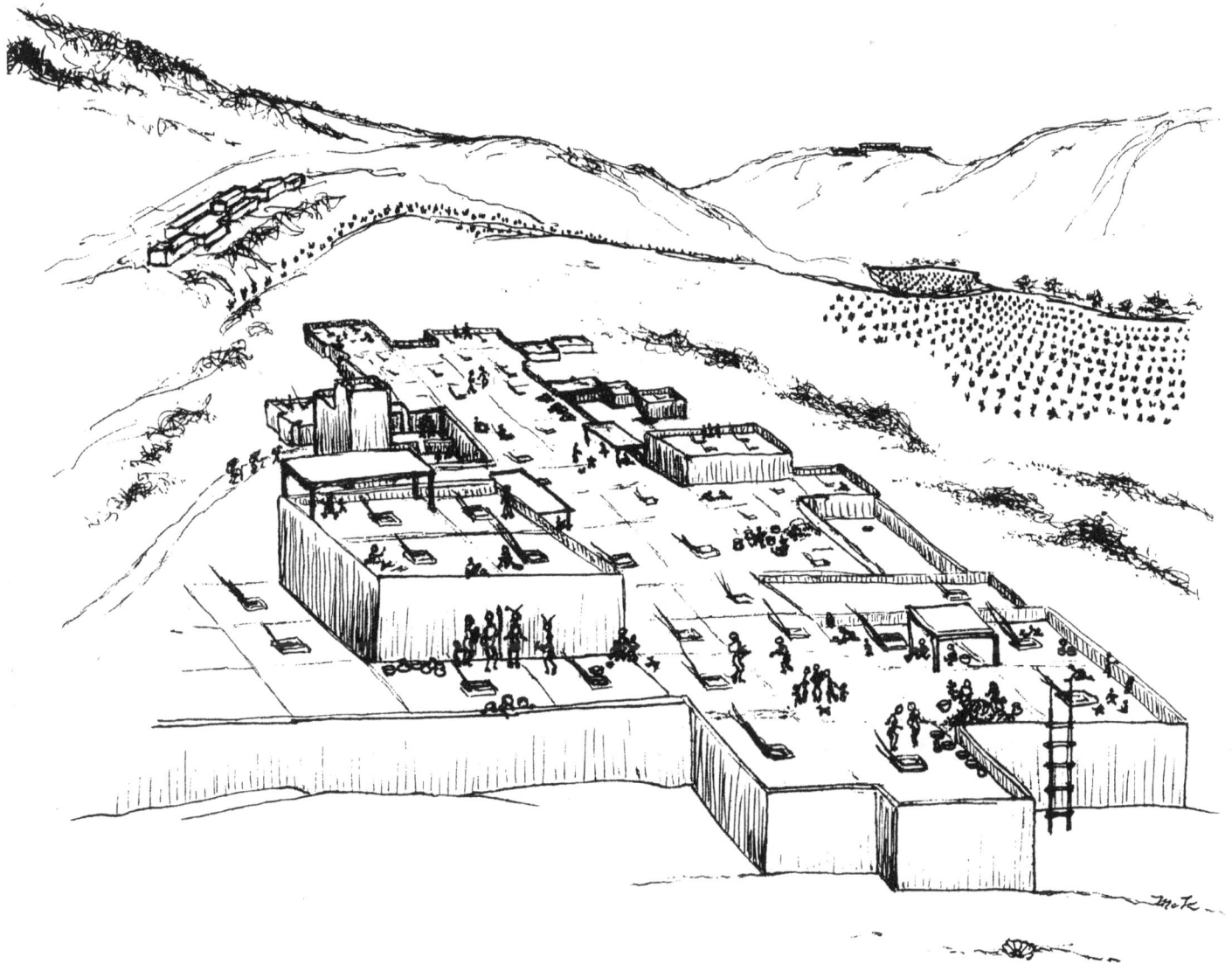

SALADO CHAPTER, ARIZONA ARCHAEOLOGICAL SOCIETY

THE GILA PUEBLO SALADO

Charmion R. McKusick
and
Jon Nathan Young

The Arizona Archaeologist

APRIL 2017   NUMBER 42

This printing of *The Gila Pueblo Salado* is a facsimile of the original 1997 publication, digitally scanned in March 2017 for republication. This is this publication's first appearance as part of the *Arizona Archaeologist* series. It was originally published by the Salado Chapter of the Arizona Archaeological Society in Globe, Arizona, as an occasional paper. Very few changes have been made for this volume:

- A typographical error in a date on page 26 was corrected.
- Because the original camera-ready pages for the original publication were unavailable, this scan was made from a half-tone printed copy. That resulted in some photographs appearing darker than desired and the introduction of minor moiré patterns in some. These have been adjusted to improve their appearance in this volume.
- The original publication's cover has been incorporated in this volume as its frontispiece. Original drawing by Charmion McKusick. Cover adaptation and overall design for this volume by Jim Carlson.

Page numbers in the Table of Contents, List of Illustrations, and List of Tables refer to the numbers shown in the original publication.

Bill Burkett, azarched@azarchsoc.org, *Arizona Archaeologist* Series Editor

© 1997, 2017 Arizona Archaeological Society, Inc.

Published by the Arizona Archaeological Society, Inc.
P.O. Box 9665
Phoenix AZ 85068-9665

www.AZArchSoc.org

ISBN: 978-0-939071-78-4

When new volumes of the *Arizona Archaeologist* are published, members of the Arizona Archaeological Society have the option of receiving a free hardcopy, PDF, or, if available, a Kindle E-reader version. PDF versions of most previous *Arizona Archaeologists* are available to members at any time on the Member-Only page of the Society's website.

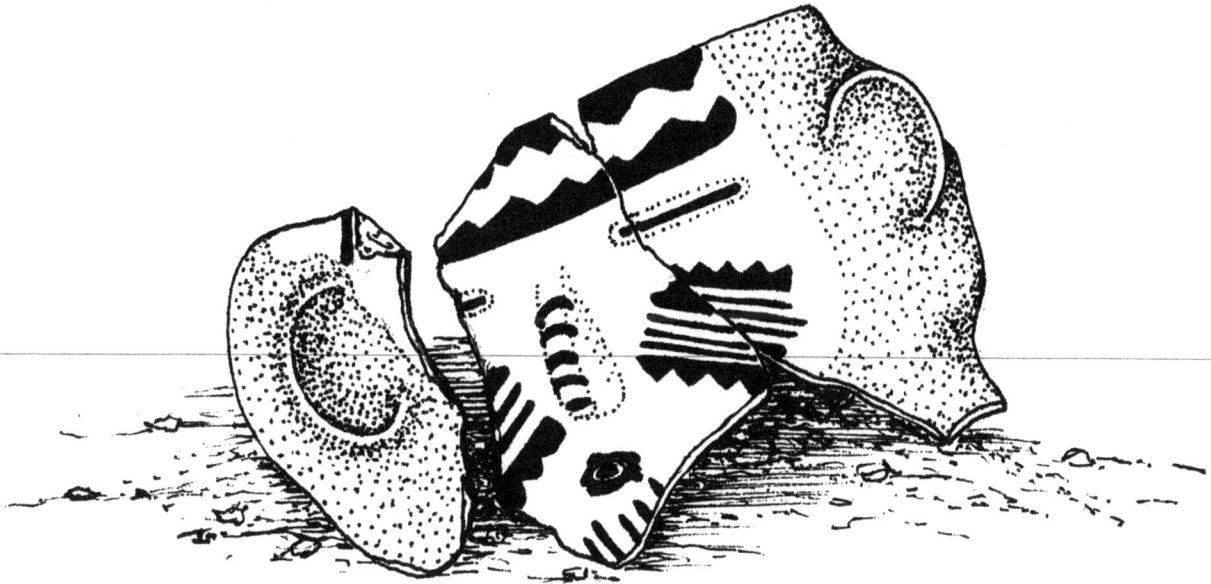

To
Art Thomas
and
Alden Hayes
and to
Gila Pueblo

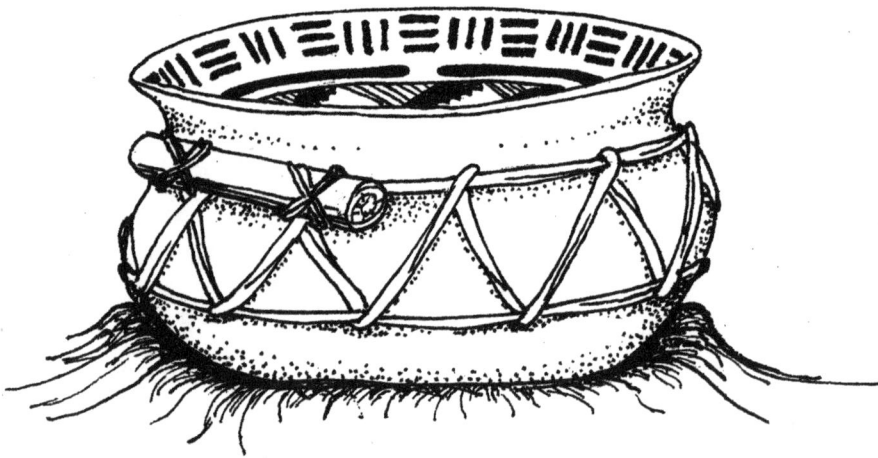

PREFACE

We have shared a deep and abiding interest in the Salado Culture for closer and closer to half a century. Jon's began during the middle 1960's, when Emil Haury and Ray Thompson suggested it as a dissertation subject at the University of Arizona (Young 1967). As soon as he completed his graduate studies, Jon immediately joined the National Park Service and went to work at its Southwest Archeological Center at Gila Pueblo in Globe, Arizona - which is the type-site where the Salado Culture was defined by Harold Sterling Gladwin in the 1920's and 1930's. Charmion already was on the Center's staff, when Jon came on-board in 1967. Charmion traces her interest in the Salado back to 1952, at Point of Pines, when Emil Haury first suggested to her that she begin to focus her research interests in the Salado. We quickly became friends, as well as colleagues. That friendship and collegiality, and the ruminations of a quarter of a century, have led to this publication.

In the fall of 1970, private property lying immediately south and west of Gila Pueblo was subdivided and carved into residential trailer pads. On this land were numerous prehistoric remains contemporaneous with and probably simply an extension of Gila Pueblo itself: The Hagen Site. The developer gave Jon three weeks to salvage as much data as he could. During that period of time, he was able to completely excavate nine rooms, an earth oven, and a burial and to partially excavate eight additional rooms.

Within a relatively short period of time after the completion of work at The Hagen Site, the Southwest Archeological Center was relocated to Tucson, and Gila Pueblo left Federal ownership. It became a branch campus of Eastern Arizona College. Jon went with the Center to Tucson, but Charmion resigned from Federal Service and became a charter member of the faculty of the Gila Pueblo campus. She and her students excavated a total of 13 rooms in the southern portion of Gila Pueblo, proper. The data which Jon recovered from the Hagen Site and which Charmion recovered from Gila Pueblo form the core of this report.

We are grateful to a number of colleagues for their help in the identification of materials and specimens: Richard Ciolek-Torello dated archeomagnetic samples. Joseph Crary shared his survey data regarding settlements in the vicinity of Pinal Creek. Hugh Cutler identified botanical specimens. Bob DuBois dated archeomagnetic samples. Mohomoud El-Najjar analyzed skeletal material. Alan Ferg provided information to us on a variety of subjects, especially with regard to the various materials recovered from Room 111: the human and faunal remains, the matting, and the brass beads. David Jacobs provided information on granary pedestals. Mike Jacobs rummaged through the storerooms of the Arizona State Museum to retrieve bone materials for analysis. Halsey Miller identified mollusk specimens. Phillip Smith transported sherds to the Arizona State Museum for analysis. And Ric Windmiller helped with the analysis of unpainted pottery.

vi

TABLE OF CONTENTS

LIST OF ILLUSTRATIONS

LIST OF TABLES

INTRODUCTION

The people of the Salado Culture were the late-prehistoric Western Pueblo inhabitants of the Roosevelt Basin of east-central Arizona. Their pottery has the largest areal distribution of any Southwestern prehistoric ware. The most famous of their sites are Tonto Cliff Dwellings, near the southern shore of Roosevelt Lake -- and Gila Pueblo and Besh-ba-gowah, just south of Globe (Figure 1).

Most of Gila Pueblo was excavated by Harold Sterling Gladwin nearly three-quarters of a century ago, but the excavational details of only a single room have appeared in print (Shiner 1961a). Subsequent to his excavation, Gladwin rebuilt the ancient pueblo. His reconstruction then served as the physical facilities of his Gila Pueblo Research Center. Later, these same facilities served as the National Park Service's Southwest Archeological Center. And at the present time they are the Globe Branch of Eastern Arizona College.

During the early 1970's, McKusick excavated a total of 13 rooms at the southern edge of Gila Pueblo, proper - Room 98 through Room 110. In 1970, Young excavated a burial, an earth oven, and nine complete rooms. At that same time, he also partially excavated portions of eight additional rooms. Those excavations were immediately south of Gila Pueblo. In an area covering about 75 hectares, there were groups of rooms clustered together into about a dozen small, contiguous-room pueblitos: The Hagen Site. An arroyo bisected the Hagen Site from southwest to northeast. For ease of reference, we have gathered rooms from three of the pueblitos located north of the arroyo - Room 1, Room 2 through Room 6, and Room 7 and Room 8 under the term: North Ruin. Similarly, south of the arroyo, rooms from two separate pueblitos - Room S-1 and Room S-2 through Room S-9, are referred to collectively as: South Ruin (Figure 2).

Gila Pueblo is the type-site for the Salado Culture. It was a major pueblo, consisting of several hundred contiguous rooms. It was bordered by a compound wall on the south, beyond which lay a field house, an extensive burial area, and the Hagen Site. Just across the wash which borders Gila Pueblo on the west there was a block of somewhere between 20 and 40 habitation rooms. Gila Pueblo was a large, nucleated settlement, located at or near the center of a densely populated area. It was one of eight such settlements located along Pinal Creek which, in turn, lay astride the major trade route coming up the San Pedro River from Casas Grandes (Wood 1987:Figure 4).

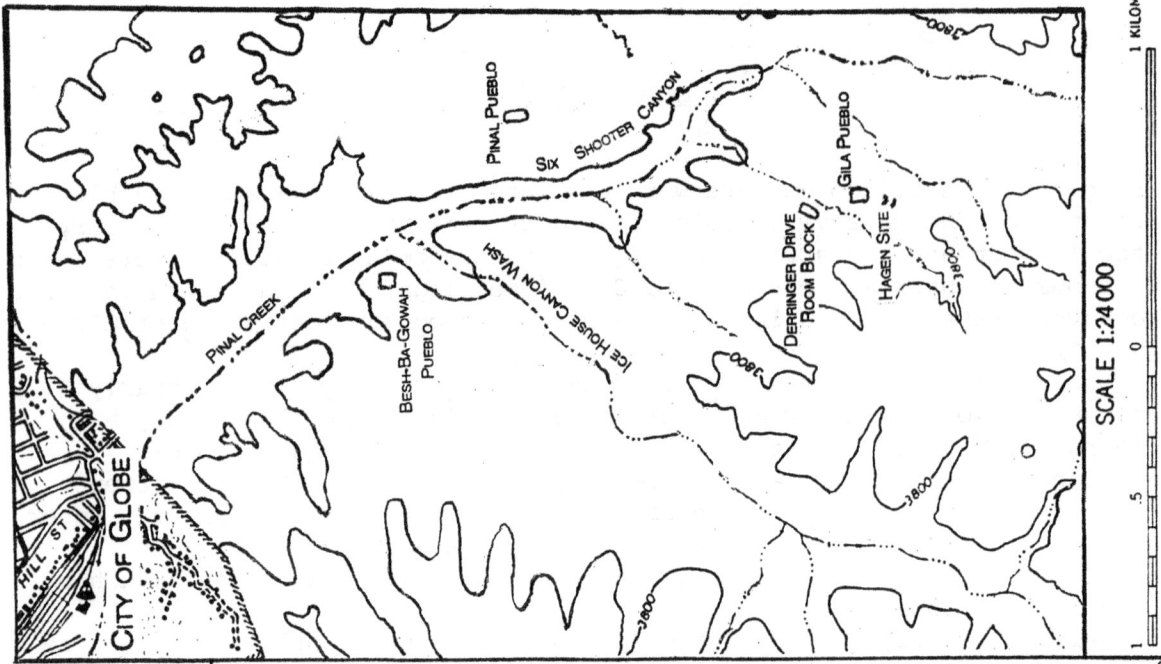

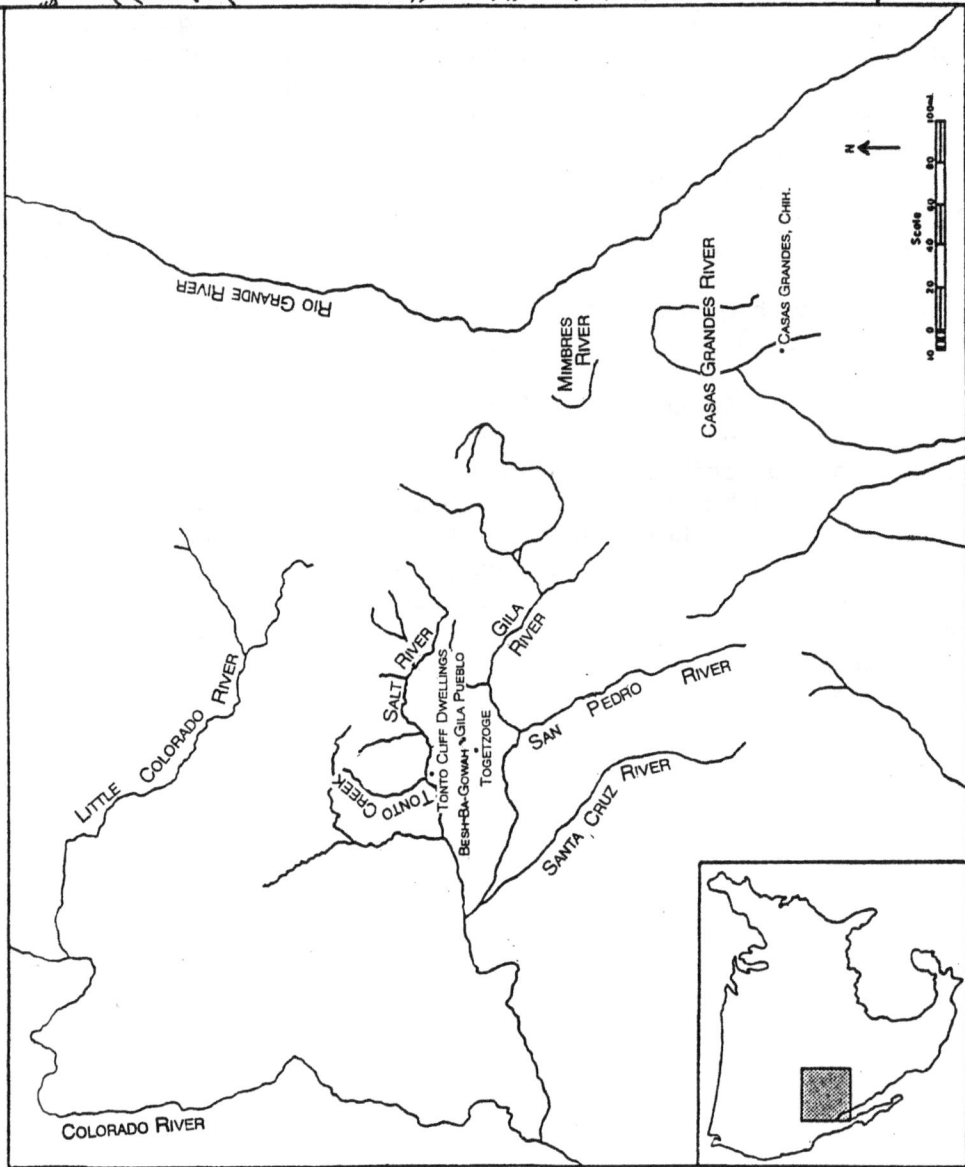

Figure 1, Location Map. Left, general location of Gila Pueblo. Right, detailed map of area. At the time of the Salado occuption, Ice House Canyon Wash and Pinal Creek ran all year. The contour lines indicate the limited arable land in the canyon bottoms adjacent to Besh-Ba-Gowah and Pinal Pueblo. In constrast, Gila Pueblo and its outliers had a broad area available for ditch irrigation farming.

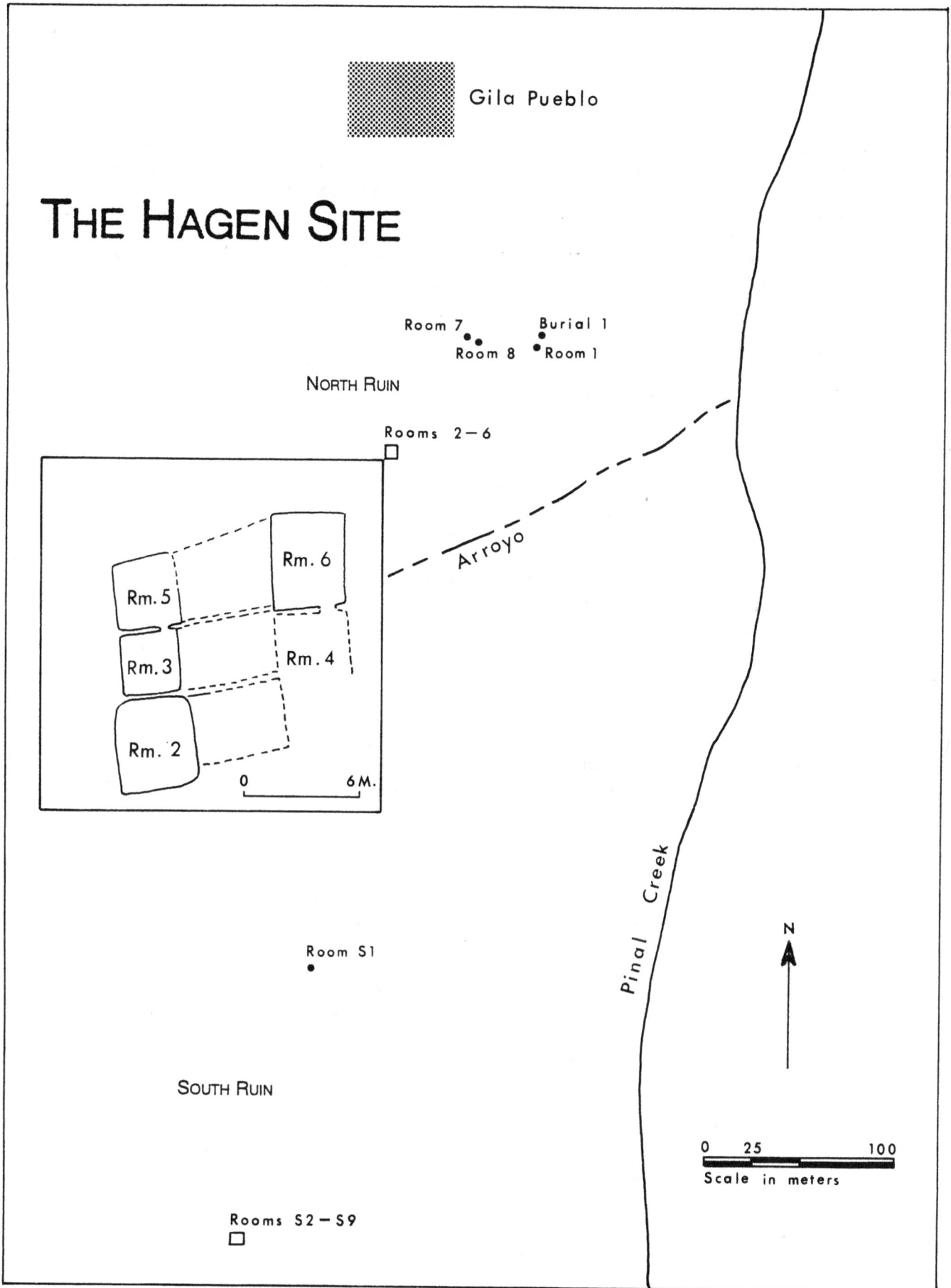

Figure 2. Gila Pueblo and the Hagen Site.

THE GILA PUEBLO SALADO NEIGHBORHOOD

Gila Pueblo is located in the foothills of the northern slope of the Pinal Mountains. There are two local drainages. The westernmost, Pinal Creek, carries the waters from Sixshooter, Ice House, and Kellner Canyons to the Salt River. Water from Ranch Creek joins Gilson Wash to flow eastward to the San Carlos River and thence to the Gila. Until 1929, when miners at the Old Dominion broke into an underground river, the streams in Kellner, Ice House, and Sixshooter Canyons ran the year around and had fish in them. Before that time, the water table in Kelner Canyon lay only three or four feet below the surface of the ground (Blalack 1954). Almost certainly it was equally abundant and as readily available in the other canyons. Chinese laborers, who came to the area with the railroad in the 1890's, settled in upper Sixshooter Canyon and supplied the residents of Globe with vegetables from their irrigated farms just as did Carmen Blalack in Kellner Canyon. The early settlers of lower Ice House Canyon found abandoned, aboriginal, stone-lined irrigation ditches in the canyon. They appropriated these ancient ditches, cemented their bottoms, and promptly pressed them back into service. And vegetables were raised there also, until the bottom dropped out of the water table as it drained into the shafts of the Old Dominion Mine. Three reservoirs still were in use in the 1950s. One was in upper Kellner Canyon, another at the juncture of Kellner and Ice House Canyons, and the third in upper Sixshooter Canyon. All three were located on mounds which were greatly elevated above the surrounding terrain, and all well may have been aboriginal in origin. Bandelier recorded prehistoric irrigation systems on Ranch Creek and Gilson Wash more than a century ago (Crary et al 1992:Figure 4, Lange and Riley 1970:102).

Gila Pueblo and the Hagen Site lie at an elevation of about 3,800 feet -- on a gently sloping terrace south of Pinal Creek. This location on the western flank of Sixshooter Canyon places them squarly in the Upper Sonoran Life Zone. The last frost of the year generally occurs there about 7 May and the first of the fall about 31 October. Annual precipitation in the foothills south of Globe averages about 16 inches, but both winter and summer rains fluctuate widely from year to year.

The area is ideal for the efficient gathering of wild foods. It is possible to travel a short distance to lower altitudes in order to take advantage of the beginning of a given harvest of fruits or nuts and then to follow the harvest up the Pinal Mountains over a period of weeks, as fruits ripen at ever-higher altitudes.

Gila Pueblo and the Hagen Site lie in a dense cluster of subsistence and habitation sites ranging between 20 and 70 sites per square mile. This cluster includes Besh-ba-gowah and its outliers, Pinal Pueblo, Gila Pueblo and its outliers, and a scattering of smaller sites. To the east are similar high density clusters at the Gap, Bar-F Bar, Ranch Creek, Cutter, and Gilson Wash Sites (Crary et al 1992:Figures 4 and 5).

The Gila Pueblo Salado were on a historic trail running along Pinal Creek which was used by Woosley in 1864 (Crary et al 1992:Figure 4) and on a major, prehistoric trade route which was in use from ca. A.D. 1100 to 1450 (Wood 1987:Figure 4).

METHODS

PHOTOGRAPHS, MAPS, AND PROFILES

The Hagen Site, although a salvage project with severely limited time constraints, was dug in a straightforward manner with photographs of the floor features in place. Gila Pueblo, however, was quite different. The constant presence of extraneous students, vandals, and antiquities purveyors made it impossible to leave any artifacts in place, even for a few minutes. This continual thievery made it necessary to broadside each level, mapping-in and removing all artifacts from sight as soon as they were unearthed. As a result, the usual room photographs could not be made. Instead, each natural level was represented by a detailed map. Three representative room profiles follow which are offered in order to compensate for the lack of room photographs (Figures 3 and 4).

STUDENT HYPOTHESES TO BE TESTED

The Eastern Arizona College students who participated in the excavation of the southern end of Gila Pueblo raised the following questions and formulated hypotheses which they hoped to test by excavation:

1. Harold Sterling Gladwin was the principle excavator of Gila Pueblo. His work in the late 1930's led him to speak about multiple killings and the destruction of Gila Pueblo by fire. Irene Vickery excavated the nearby Besh-ba-gowah in the late 1930's. Her work there led her to believe that Besh-ba-gowah had been destroyed several times by fire. The students wished to learn if any evidence of fire and killings was present in the study area.

2. Vickery found telephone-pole-sized beams broken and twisted like toothpicks. She interpreted these as evidence of earthquakes. The students wished to determine if there were any evidences of earthquakes in the study area.

3. Given that Gila Pueblo is a large settlement, the students wished to learn if there was any evidence of social-political-religious organization in the study area.

4. The students hypothesized that crops grown at Gila Pueblo would parallel those recovered from Upper Tonto Ruin.

5. Given that Gila Pueblo is a large settlement, the students hypothesized that evidence of trade activities, perhaps even as far afield as Casas Grandes in Chihuahua, should be present.

ROOM 105 PROFILE

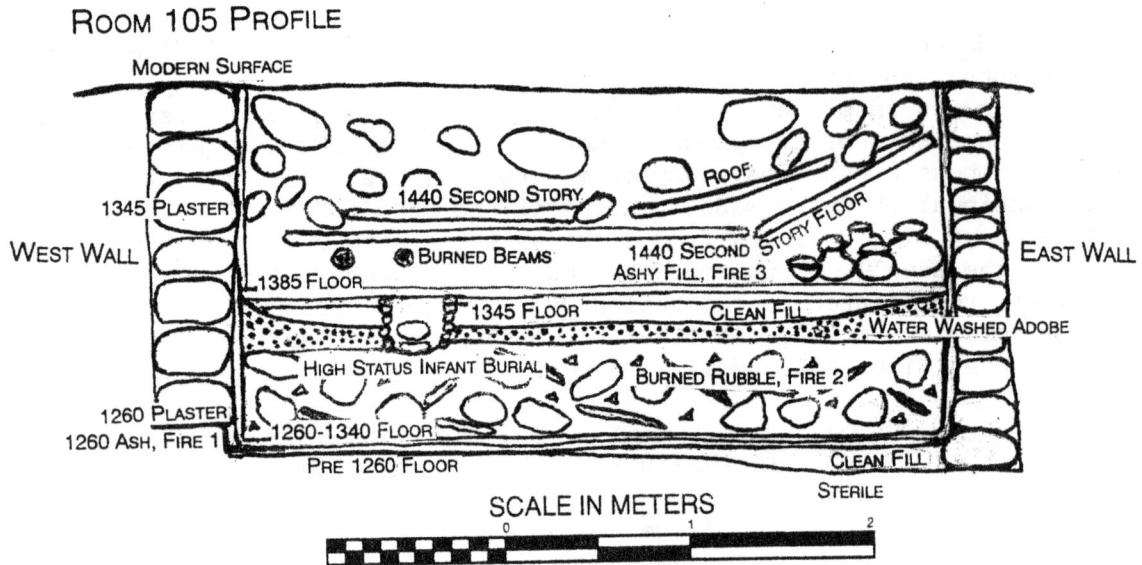

Figure 3. Gila Pueblo, Room 105 Profile.

This is a west-to-east profile of the southern portion of Room 105. The walls of this rooom were built, and then the original ground surface on the west side of the room was removed to fill in the depression on the east side of the room. This provided a level surface which was plastered to form the original floor. Wall plaster covered the exposed sterile underlying the west wall. Following the ca. 1260 First Fire, a new coat of plaster was applied to the walls, covering a layer of ash at the base. The remainder of the floor was swept clean, repaired, and continued in use until the earthquake and conflagration of the ca. 1340 Second Fire.

The two story section of the pueblo suffered the greatest damage in this catastrophe. Apparently, stone fell from the top of the second story wall, sending large chunks of the second story roof crashing through the second story floor to the gound floor below.

During the period the pueblo remained unoccupied, these chunks of roofing and flooring and the burned bones of the former inhabitants were covered by a lens of adobe washed from the still-standing walls. When the pueblo was rebuilt ca. 1345, the floor was leveled with clean fill, and new plaster was applied to the walls and floor.

About 1385 the pueblo underwent a major remodeling, marked by the addition in this room of three granary platforms. A sub-floor infant burial was made after 1385.

The final destruction of Gila Pueblo in ca. 1440 was followed by the Third Fire, which brought about the collapse of the second story roof and floor. This destruction was much less complete, with the roofs falling mostly intact. While the ground floor access to Room 105 was through the ground floor of Room 101, the second story of Room 105 was accessed through a hatch in the roof. The ladder was placed on a base of adobe 14 cm. thick. Second story roof supports were placed on the second story floor above the roof supports in the room below, and were anchored with a basal ring of adobe.

ROOM 98 PROFILE

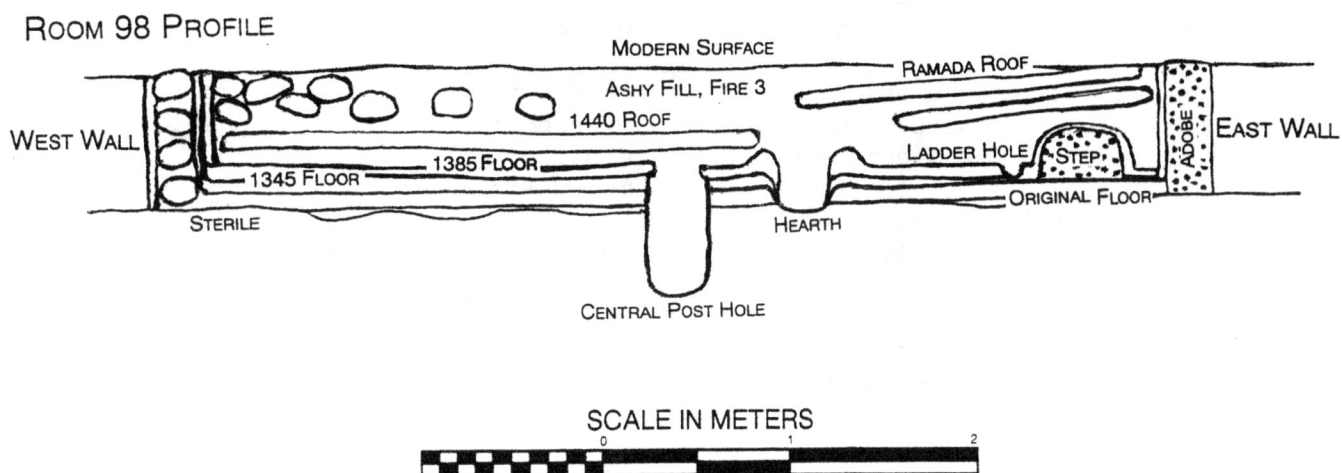

SCALE IN METERS

ROOM 106 PROFILE

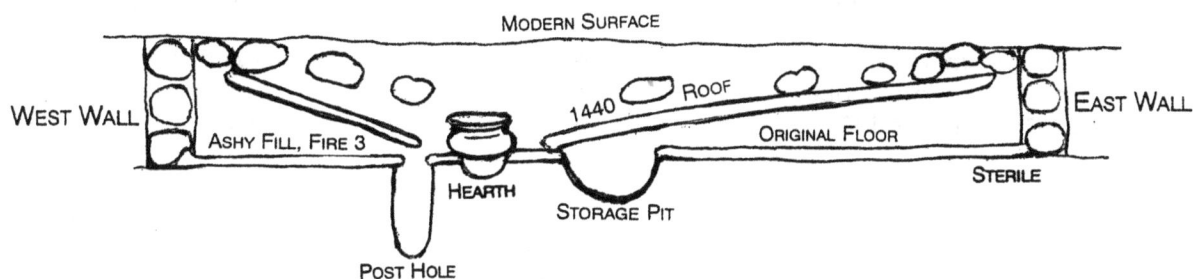

Figure 4. Gila Pueblo, Room 98 and Room 106 Profiles.

The west-to-east profile passes through the middle of Room 98, which is part of a four-room adobe suite built after 1325 but before 1340. The west wall is the already-existing stone wall of Room 99. The ca. 1340 Second Fire burned the roof, but did little other damage. During the 1345 reconstruction, the ashy fill was leveled, and the walls and floor were newly plastered. The roof and roof-top ramada fell, mostly intact, following the the Third Fire. Eventually, the walls, both stone and adobe, collapsed, melted, or both into the fill covering the roof.

The west-to-east profile of the middle of Room 106, represents the very late rooms attached to the south end of the pueblo. Again, the roofs fell mainly intact following the Third Fire, with the rather insubstantial walls gradually falling into the room. It is possible that the walls extended up only about a meter, and were topped by a jacal construction similar to that of the field house immediately to the south.

8

RESULTS OF TESTING OF STUDENTS' HYPOTHESES

1. The students found that Gladwin and Vickery were correct in their descriptions of killings and fires. The Salado occupation of Gila Pueblo suffered not one but three episodes of killing and burning.

2. The students found that Vickery was correct in her interpretation of an earthquake-caused destruction. The layer of rubble profiled in Figure 3, which coincided with The Second Fire, is quite different from the lesser destructions which accompanied The First and Third Fires. In addition, it was found that there is a major fault, the Miami Fault, south of both Gila Pueblo and Besh-ba-gowah. It is the continuing action of this fault which has produced the excellent clay from which the Salado redwares are made. A branch of this fault, the Patrick's Dairy Fault, is just west of Besh-ba-gowah. Residents of the canyon area south of Globe are still experiencing recurring minor to moderate earthquakes ranging up to 5.5 on the Richter Scale.

3. The excavation of a ceremonial/redistribution complex indicated a probable moiety system, with hereditary leadership plus a possible hunting/raiding leader with achieved status. The finding of high status female functionaries was a complete surprise!

4. The crops grown at Gila Pueblo were the same as those recovered from Upper Tonto Ruin. However, cotton proved to be much more important than expected, paralleling material recovered from Antelope House in northern Arizona.

5. Trade in and trade out proved to be much more important than expected. Trade with Casas Grandes, Chihuahua, was indicated by pottery forms, shell specialities, and copper bells. Further, the remains of two scarlet Macaws were recovered from the post-1400 burial of a high status female at nearby Pinal Pueblo. The trade picture provided by this excavation demonstrates that Gila Pueblo was part of an active network of commerce rather than just a cultural backwater.

ARCHITECTURE AND CONSTRUCTION SEQUENCE

HAGEN SITE

At the Hagen Site, we completely excavated an earth oven and nine rooms. Eight additional rooms were partially excavated (Table 1).

Table 1. Hagen Site Structural Features.

	Completely Excavated	Partially Excavated	Interior Dimensions	Archeomagnetic Dates
NORTH RUIN				
Room 1	X		4.3 m by 3.6 m	A.D. 1385+21
Room 2	X		4.3 m by 4.0 m	
Room 3	X		3.1 m by 3.0 m	
Room 4		X		
Room 5	X		3.5 m by 3.3 m	
Room 6	X		4.5 m by 3.9 m	A.D. 1400+47
SOUTH RUIN				
Room S-1	X		4.7 m by 4.2 m	
Room S-2	X		3.4 m by 3.0 m	
Room S-3		X		
Room S-4		X		
Room S-5		X		
Room S-6	X		3.4 m by 3.2 m	
Room S-7		X		
Room S-8		X		
Room S-9		X		A.D. 1430+47
Earth Oven	X		Depth: 45 cm Diam.: 95 cm at top 50 cm at bottom	

Rooms. Rooms were contiguous. Wall lengths of individual rooms varied from three meters to five meters. Floor space covered 10 square meters to 20 square meters. Floor plans were rectangular. None were square, but some were nearly so, especially the smaller ones. The long axis of most was approximately north-south. Walls were courses of large, irregular, unmodified cobbles laid in masses of local orange, clayey-soil mortar. Occasionally, the lower portion of interior walls was faced with a liner of stone slabs. The tallest wall remnant was 75 cm in height. House walls butted at corners, but did not interlock. They varied in thickness from 25 cm to 50 cm. Interior walls had a layer of plaster, which varied in thickness from 15 mm to 25 mm.

In most rooms, roofs were supported by a centerpost. In several instances, exotic items were found resting on the bottom of centerpost holes; there was an opal plaque in Room 2 and a **Conus** tinkler in Room 3. All rooms contained postholes in the floor in various locations other than the center. These additional posts tended to occur in corners or fronting the midportions of walls, but no pattern was readily apparent; some were quite shallow, no more than 5 cm. in depth, and seemed to be butt rests, rather than true postholes. The butt of a juniper post was at the bottom of the central posthole in Room 2. Elsewhere in that structure and in nearby Room 6 were fragments of ponderosa pine and juniper posts and roofing timbers.

Three doorways were found: one in the wall between Room 3 and Room 5, one in the wall between Room 4 and Room 6, and one in the north wall of Room S-6 (Figure 5). All three doorways occurred near one end of short-axis, east-west walls. At the North Ruin, both doorways were near the eastern end of walls; while at the South Ruin, the door was near the western end of a wall. Doorsills were from 10 cm. to 15 cm. above the floors of their respective rooms. The doorway between Room 4 and Room 6 was in such an advanced state of deterioration that it yielded no additional information. The doorway between Room 3 and Room 5 is T-shaped (Figure 6).

Floors were cut from 15 cm to 30 cm into sterile soil or, occasionally, trash. Although previous descriptions of Salado houses note that floors are covered with a layer of puddled adobe, none of the Hagen Site floors were finished in this fashion. All were simple walking surfaces. Immediately below them was sterile soil.

Each of the nine completely excavated rooms contained at least one hearth; three had two hearths each, and one had four (Table 2). Four of the 15 hearths were plugged. Only Room 5 had no open hearth. Sizes and shapes

Table 2. Hagen Site Hearths.

	Open	Possibly Plugged	Plugged	Totals
NORTH RUIN				
Room 1	1			1
Room 2	2			2
Room 3	2		2	4
Room 5			1	1
Room 6	1	1		2
Room 7	1			1
SOUTH RUIN				
Room S-1	1			1
Room S-2	1			1
Room S-6	1			1
TOTALS	10	1	4	15

Figure 5. Hagen Site, Room S-6 Doorway.
     Looking north, interior width 35 cm., Western Archeological and Conservation
Center negative no. 63,242.

Figure 6. Hagen Site, Room 3 Doorway.
     North wall, looking north.

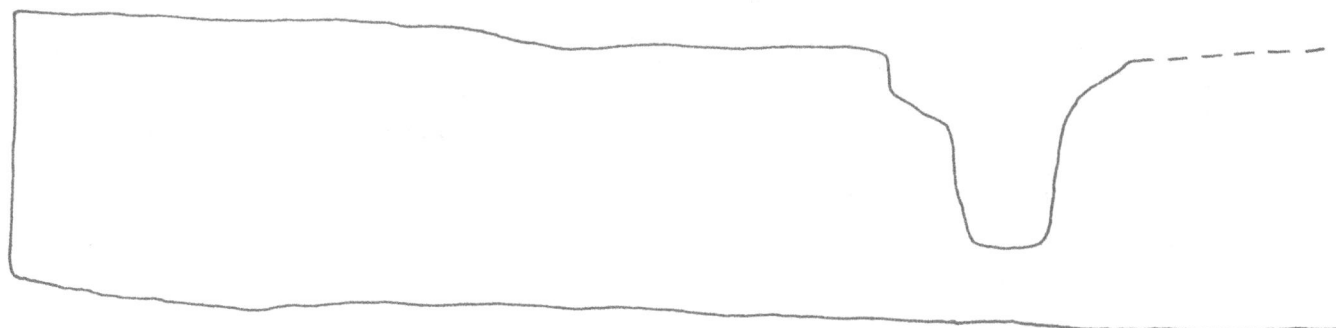

0   50   100
Scale in centimeters

varied, but most hearths had a circular-basin shape, were between 25 cm and 30 cm in diameter, and were about 10 cm in depth. One had a diameter of 60 cm. Another was split-level: one half was about 20 cm deep and the other, 25 cm. Several were lined with clay. Hearths were located from 50 cm to 160 cm from the nearest wall, which usually was a long-axis wall. Seven occurred in rooms which still had portions of doorways present in the walls. Five of the seven were directly opposite the doors. Several hearths had large, hemispherical, granite firedogs in or near them.

Running the length of the entire north wall -- a short-axis wall -- in Room 5, was an earthen benched carved out of sterile soil. It was 50 cm deep and varied in height between 20 cm and 30 cm. In nearby Room 2, there may have been a similar bench along the south wall. It was several centimeters in height and a meter in width.

Various possible indications of rebuilding occurred in most of the rooms at the Hagen Site. In Room 2, Room 6, and Room S-6; for example; the floors in use at the time of abandonment lay 5 cm. to 15 cm. above earlier floors. Room 3, Room 5, Room S-6, and; perhaps; Room 6 each had one or more plugged hearths. Room 2, Room 6, Room S-1, Room S-2, and Room S-6 had various numbers of shallow, butt-rest depressions in their floors, which may have indicated the use of posts to shore sagging roof timbers. Auxiliary posts near the centerpost and another major roof support post in Room 3 also may have represented shoring activities.

At the time it burned, Room 5 may have been used primarily for storage. It was the only completely excavated room at the Hagen Site which lacked an open hearth. It contained many more pottery vessels, especially brownware, than most other rooms; but shell, worked bone, and most types of stone artifacts were absent or poorly represented (Table 3).

The material content of the other rooms at the North Ruin does not present as clear a picture. But Room 2 seemed to contain more than its share of awls, axes, shaft tools, and mescal knives. It also had a disproportionate number of ornamental and religious objects: fetishes, paints, lightning stone, and plaque. Room 3, with its two open and two plugged hearths, contained more than half of all of the firedogs recovered. But only two of the 93 pottery vessels from the site were in this room. Room 6 had more manos than most of the other rooms at the Hagen Site combined. With several notable exceptions, few items of material culture come from South Ruin rooms. The exceptions are choppers, hammerstones, cores, and used flakes, especially cores and used flakes in Room S-1 and choppers in Room S-6.

Earth Oven. In the southernmost corner of the excavated portion of the South Ruin was a depression which was 45 cm in depth and which measured 95 cm in diameter at the surface and 50 cm in diameter at the base. Its wall sloped gently inward from top to bottom, and it was not plastered. It appeared to have been filled intentionally with large cobbles and other stones, some of which were fire-cracked. After it was abandoned, a later room may have been built over it. A meter to the west of the oven was a deposit of orange clay. Perhaps the oven began as an excavation for clay.

Table 3. Material Content of Completely Excavated Hagen Site Rooms.

	NORTH RUIN						SOUTH RUIN			TOTALS
	Rm. 1	Rm. 2	Rm. 3	Rm. 5	Rm. 6	Rm. 7	Rm. S-1	Rm. S-2	Rm. S-3	
STONE ARTIFACTS										
Abraders		2	1		2					5
Arrowheads	1				1					2
Axes		11	2		3	1				17
Choppers		1	1		2		2		6	12
Cores	1	4			1	1	9	3		19
Fetishes		2			1					3
Firedogs	2	1	5		1					9
Flaking Anvils	1		3		3	2				9
Grinding Bases	2	3	2	2		1	1			11
Hammerstones	3		1		2	1	3	3	2	15
Lid						1				1
Lightning Stone		1								1
Manos	5	7	2	4	13	4	1	2		38
Mescal Knives		9	3	3	6	1	1		1	24
Metates	2			2	2					6
Paint Pigments		2		1		1				4
Pecking-Polishing Stones			1			1	1			3
Plaque		1								1
Pottery Anvil						1				1
Scrapers	1				1		2			4
Scraper Plane		1								1
Shaft Tools		2								2
Shavers					1	1				2
Tool Reject							1			1
Unclassified Objects	2	3	2		1	1	1			10
Used Flakes	3	7	1		2	1	10	2	1	27
POTTERY VESSELS										
Painted Wares	7	4	2	11	11	1				36
Redware		2		2	1	1				6
Brownwares										
Plain	5	2		14	10	2				33
Corrugated	3	4	1	4	2	2	2			18
BONE AWLS		4	1							5
SHELLS	1	2	2		1					6

Archeomagnetic Dates. We have archeomagnetic dates for hearths in three
Hagen Site rooms:

North Ruin
Room 1: A.D. 1388+21
Room 6: A.D. 1400+47

South Ruin
Room S-9: 1430+47

GILA PUEBLO PROPER

Dating the Building Sequence. Figure 7 illustrates the prehistoric and
modern ground plans of Gila Pueblo. Both the Salado floor plan and Gladwin's
reconstruction are oriented to the North Star. During the Salado occupation,
Gila Pueblo had a constricted entry from the northwest. The plaza was
divided into two halves, like that at Besh-ba-gowah. We wonder if this
formal division of the plaza in these Salado communities is not a regional
variation of the division of other Western Pueblo communities into two
distinct halves -- at Kinishba, for example, and at Grasshopper -- where one
half of the village lies on one bank of a major arroyo and the other half of
the village lies on the opposite bank. We further wonder if this formal
division of the plaza is not a precursor to or a reflection of the
present-day moiety division that is so visible in the village plans of
today's Rio Grande Pueblos.

The two rooms in Figure 8 were excavated by Gladwin. They appear in
stabilized form bordering the south side of the east-west sidewalk which runs
along the south wall of today's Gila Pueblo. In Figure 7 they are the two
large rooms marked: Original. Immediately south of the more easterly of the
two rooms lay a storage pit, shaped like an inverted, truncated cone and
lined with slabs of Pinal schist. Sometime between A.D 1225 and 1260, the
block of rooms illustrated in Figure 9 was built. It served as a ceremonial
and redistribution center. This complex, which incorporated the earlier two
rooms and storage pit, centered on Room 110. It was surrounded by storage
rooms, including the row of rooms west of Room 110 and the room south of Room
111, which remain unexcavated. The storage pit lay directly below the
northern roof support post of Room 105. In order to give an adequate footing
for this post, the slabs which lined the pit were removed and stacked flat
one upon the other to provide a stone foundation. The roof support post
rested directly upon this base. Between Room 110 and Room 105 was a
rectangular, floor-level aperture which was filled at all periods of
occupation with a wooden construction that is interpreted by a Hopi informant
as a permanent slat altar. Presumably, puppets were manipulated through
openings in the screen by a person or persons concealed in Room 105 during
dramatic presentations accompanying the yearly ceremonial calendar.

With its central hearth, the only ground floor room in the excavated
portion of this complex which can be demonstrated to have been living
quarters at this period is Room 103. Rooms 101, 105, 110, and 111 all were
two-story in height from the time of their original construction to the end
of Salado occupation. There was no hatch opening between the ground floor
and second floor of Room 110, only a foot-square aperture for the escape of
smoke. The ceremonial room probably was illuminated by small clerestory

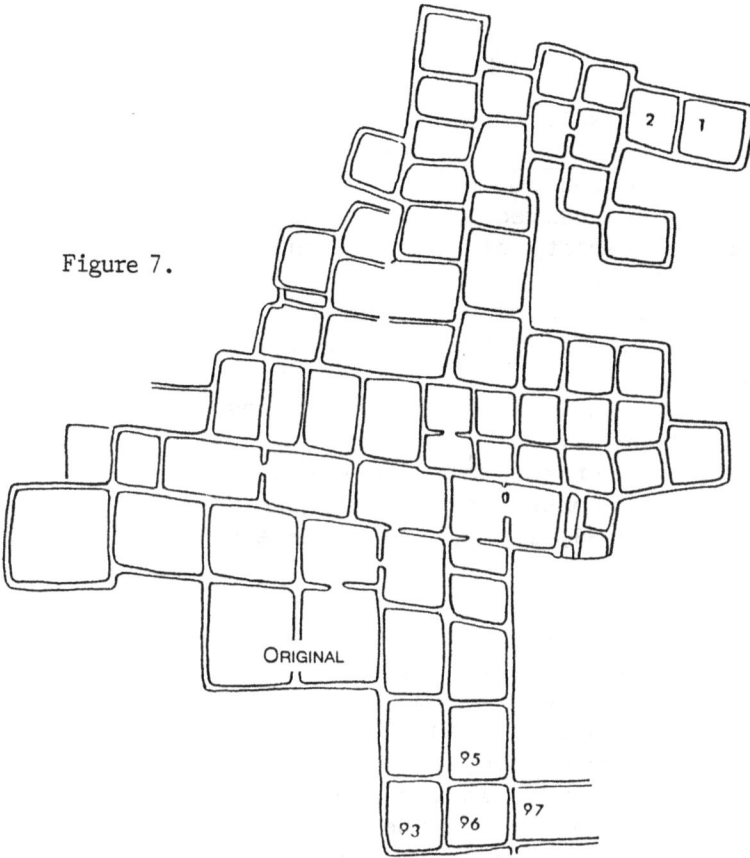

Figure 7.

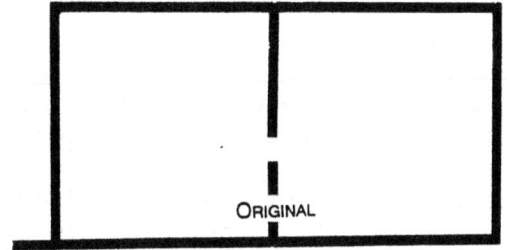

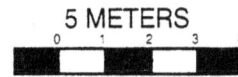

STORAGE PIT

N

5 METERS

Figure 8.

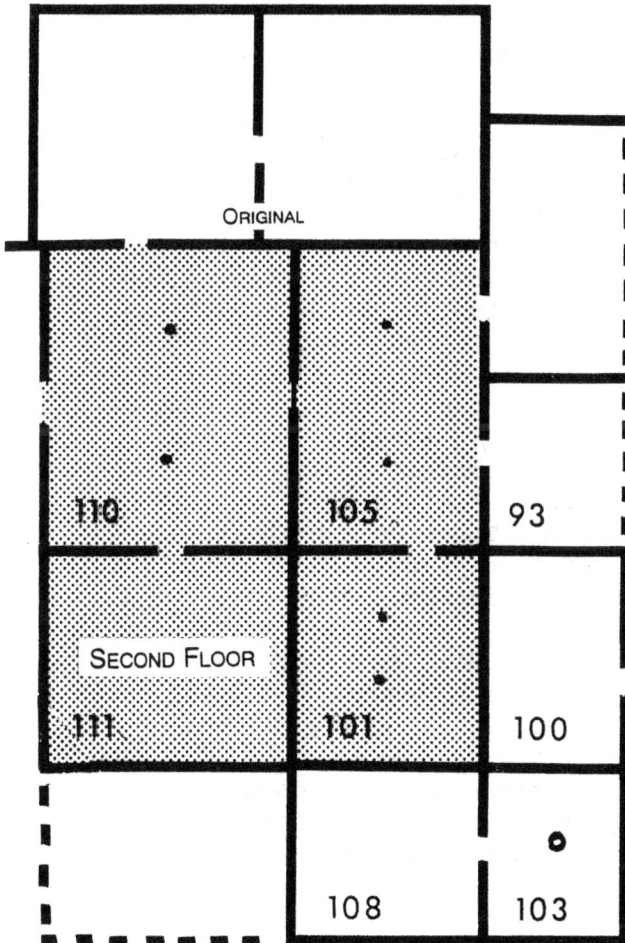

Figure 9.

Figure 7. Gladwin's Sketch of Gila Pueblo.
    Southwest Archaeological and Conservation Center Library. Gladwin dug only to the ca. 1440 level. The walls were more nearly square and the walls more even in width near their original bases.

Figure 8. Gila Pueblo, Original Southern
                                                    Limit.
    This extramural storage pit underlay the north post hole of what was to be Room 105.

Figure 9. Gila Pueblo, Ceremonial/
                            Redistribution Complex.
    Only the central and east portions of the Ceremonial/Redistribution Complex are shown. The western rooms of this complex remain unexcavated. The four shaded rooms were two stories high.

windows located high in the north wall or west wall or both. The second floor of Room 110 appears to have been an area where hides were worked on and arrow shafts were produced. The second floor of room 105 was a workroom for the production of pigments; that above Room 101 served as a storage area for raw, unspun cotton. There also was a large quantity of cotton along the northern wall of the second floor of Room 111.

Room 100 is the only room excavated by Gila Pueblo College which had an exterior doorway. The floor surface in this room had not been leveled nor had it been plastered. There was no hearth in its floor, nor were there ladder holes. Fragments of refuse bone found in it suggest that it was used for dressing small game such as hares and rabbits.

Within the next quarter of a century another row of rooms was added, including Room 96 (Figure 10). A ground-level portal, or roofed work area, was constructed against the south wall of Room 96; it appears to have been used in conjunction with Room 100 (Figure 11).

This Developmental Period of the Salado occupation of Gila Pueblo was terminated at A.D. 1260 by a fire that burned the entire southern complex that has been excavated to date: the First Fire. The portal also burned. This fire was cleaned-up very well, and the rooms continued to be used in the same manner as when they were originally constructed. The fire is considered to have been caused by an attack, rather than by accident, because a thin, triangular, white, chert arrowhead was found embedded in the ash line between the wall and floor plaster that was in use at the time of the fire. Apparently the attackers entered Room 110 and fired an arrow which glanced along the floor, penetrating the wall plaster of the northern portion of the east wall behind the two looms that were situated there. The shaft probably was consumed in the fire, and the point was not noticed during the subsequent clean-up.

The late William Underwood, a commercial pothunter who supported his large family partly by digging Salado sites on private land on shares for the owners, came by the Gila Pueblo excavation regularly to observe progress and to relate his experiences in digging Salado sites. He was very surprised to see this point and similar ones that were associated the unburied bodies of individuals who died immediately before a Third Fire in A.D. 1440. In the thousand Salado burials that Underwood had excavated in the general vicinity of Globe; he had found only small, side-notched, concave-based arrowheads -- usually made of obsidian. In his mind, he associated these thin, triangular, chert points with the Armer Complex in and around the northeastern edge of Roosevelt Lake. Joe Crary (1989), who has conducted extensive cultural resources surface surveys throughout our area of concern, told us that he has seen these same points at Bead Mountain and suggests that they may have been special-purpose points associated with raiding. These Bead Mountain points left behind by the intruders are quite distinctive. They are thin, have very fine flaking, and have no side notches or basal notches. They look for all the world like Christmas tree effigies.

Gila Pueblo seems to have survived the First Fire as a working village organization, but there are tantalizing hints in the record that the village may have suffered a loss of personnel at this time. The original hearth in Room 103, for example, never was used again. The room was cleaned-out after the fire and was used only for storage during the next eight decades. The archeomagnetic data from this hearth has given us a precise date for the Fire. We were able to confirm this date with radiocarbon data from matting

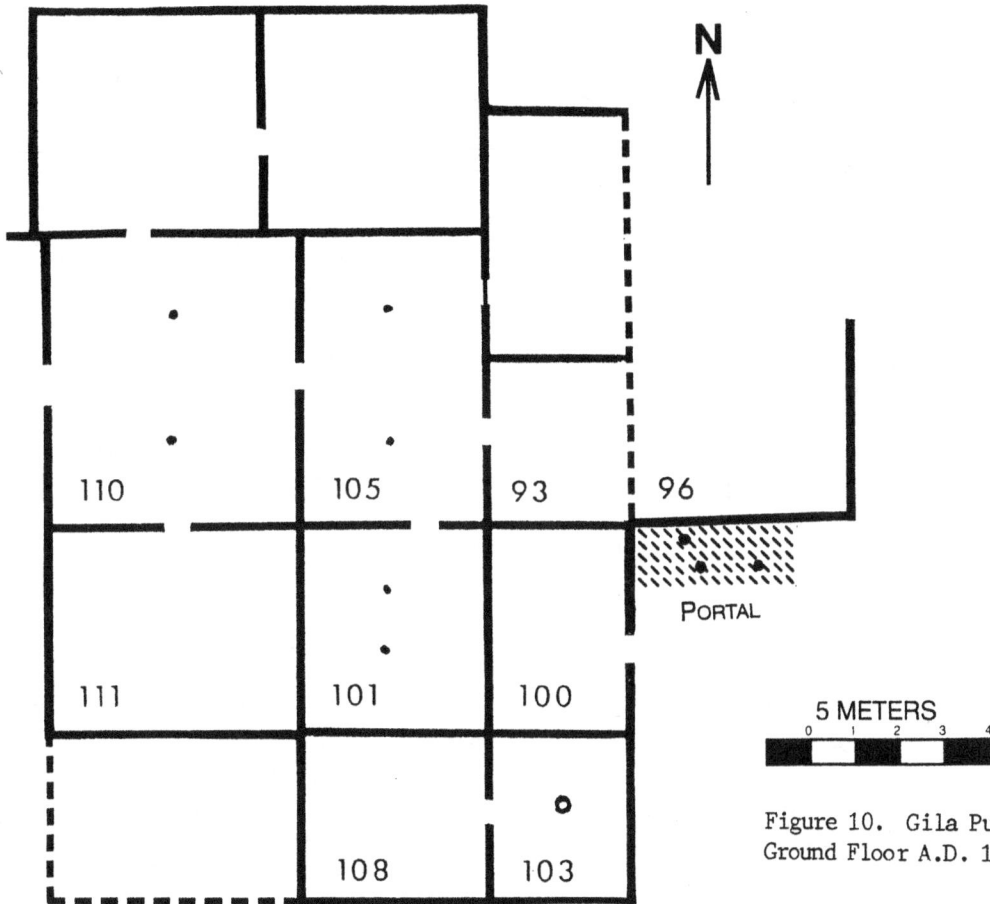

Figure 10. Gila Pueblo Portal Ground Floor A.D. 1260.

110 105 93 96

PORTAL

111 101 100

108 103

5 METERS
0 1 2 3 4

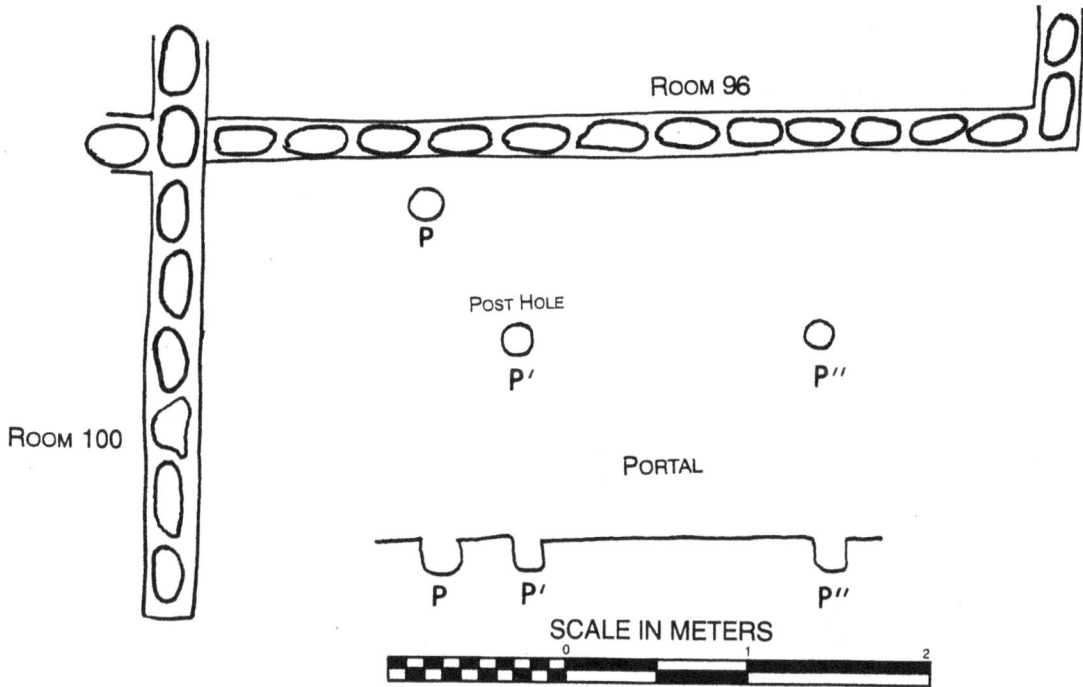

ROOM 96

ROOM 100

P

POST HOLE
P′

P″

PORTAL

P P′ P″

SCALE IN METERS
0 1 2

Figure 11. Plan and Cross-Section of Portal.
A ground floor doorway opened from Room 100 to the exterior at this time. The first use of Room 100 appears to have been for dressing small game. The floor was unsurfaced and without features.

recovered from Room 111. The portal never was rebuilt; perhaps it had provided easy access to the roof one time too many! There is no evidence that ground-level portales ever were built again, after the attack that accompanied the First Fire.

Shortly after A.D. 1325, Room 99 and Room 102 were built (Figure 12). This date is an estimate based upon the number of layers of plaster on walls and floors prior to The Second Fire, which occurred in about A.D. 1340, and on the subfloor presence of Fourmile Polychrome, which began to be manufactured about A.D. 1325, and the presence of Pinto Polychrome, which ceased to be produced about A.D. 1350 (Wood 1987:165, 168). Room 99 was the main living area, Room 100 was a secondary living area, and Room 102 was used for storage. We never had the pleasure of meeting Harold Sterling Gladwin in person, but he was extremely helpful to us by telephone. He told McKusick that Room 99 conformed in every respect to rooms he excavated in the older, main body of the pueblo. The original hearth was rectangular. Against the inside of the east wall was a raised mound of adobe; it was trapezoidal in shape and served as a bottom step for the entrance ladder. The ladder's poles were braced against the bottom of this step, slanting above the hearth and resting against the west side of the roof hatch.

The northeast corner of Room 99 does not bond with the southeast corner of Room 96, it merely touches it. Whereas the walls of the rooms are made of stream cobbles stuck together with gobs of mud, the wall extending to the east of this corner is not nearly so substantial. It is built with few rocks and consists mostly of adobe that has been reinforced with grasses and horizontal branches. It appears to have been built to serve as a compound wall.

Sometime between A.D. 1325 and A.D. 1340 a complex of four rooms (Room 98, Room 104, Room 109, and an unexcavated room), was abutted to the east side of Rooms 99 and 102 (Figure 13). The walls are of unsupported adobe, rather than of stone. The roofs in this unit also are different from those of the other rooms. The roofs in the masonry-wall portions of the pueblo were made of reeds covered with 10 cm of adobe. The roofs in this adobe-wall block of rooms were covered with sticks, grass, and cholla stems, over which was spread an even thicker layer of adobe.

At the time of its construction, Room 104 was the main living area. It had a roof-support post, oval hearth, and ash pit. In the northwest corner was a sump to collect water, which leaked through the rather informally constructed roof. Room 109 had a roof-support post, but the only unusual floor feature in Room 98 during this period of occupation was a large, clay-lined storage pit (Figure 13). Shortly after this group of rooms was built, an earthquake took place which cracked the shell of the pueblo and left it open to attack from without. At least two persons were within the south portion of the pueblo at the time of the quake. A youth took shelter beneath the Pinal schist lintel of the doorway between Room 99 and Room 100. An adult male took shelter in the west doorway of Room 110. Both individuals were trapped in the doorways, pinned more by falling roof members than by falling rock. It appeared to us that both could have been freed, had time permitted. Unfortunately for them, the pueblo was burned before they could be rescued: The Second Fire. Additional unburied, burned bodies lay upon the wreckage. The fire was so intense that the brain of the victim trapped in Room 110 was carbonized within the skull. In order to have been able to kill the survivors and burn the pueblo before these victims could be rescued, the attackers must have come from nearby.

19

Figure 12. Gila Pueblo Circa A.D. 1325

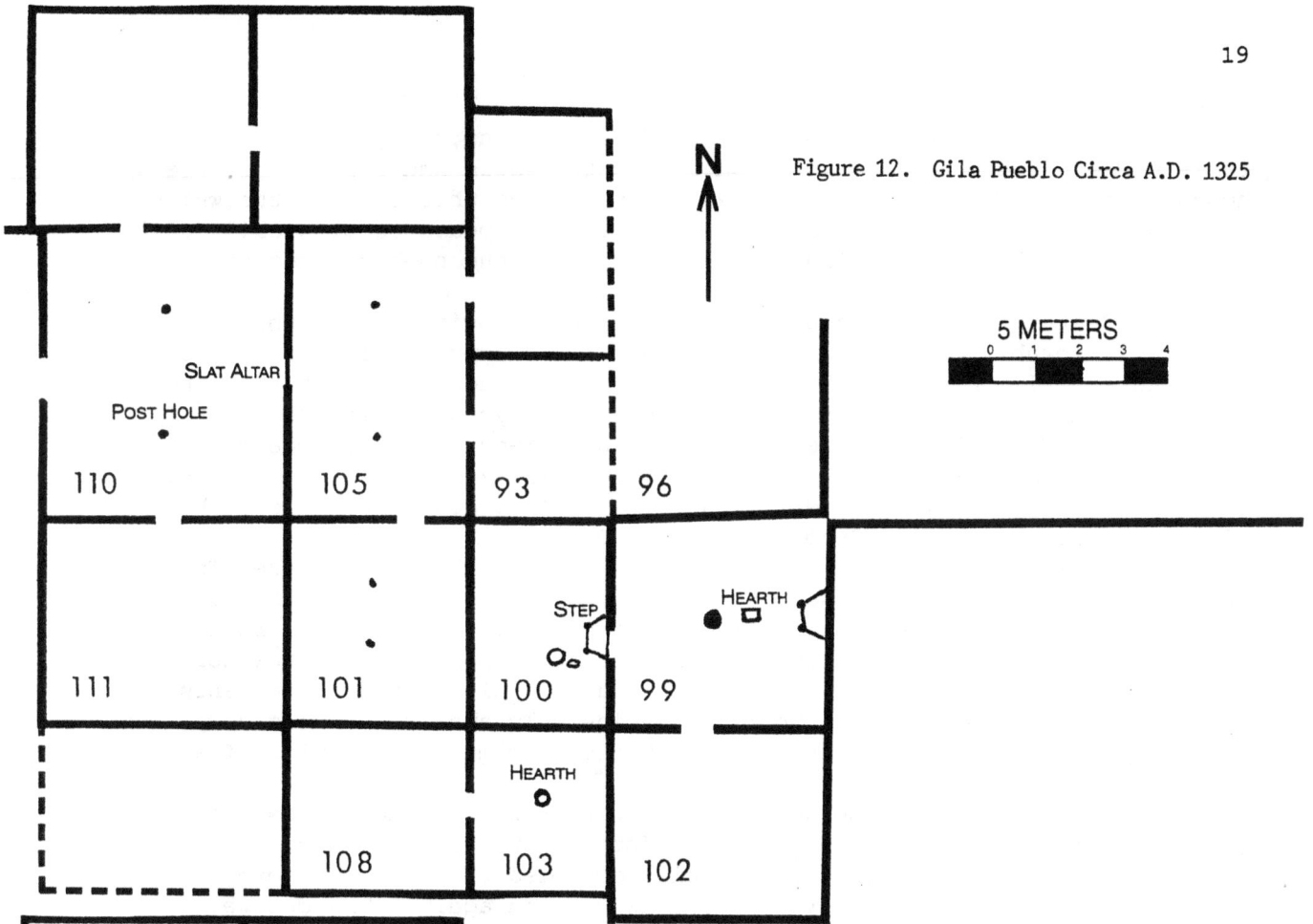

5 METERS

SLAT ALTAR
POST HOLE
110   105   93   96
STEP   HEARTH
111   101   100   99
HEARTH
108   103   102

Figure 13. Gila Pueblo Circa A.D. 1340

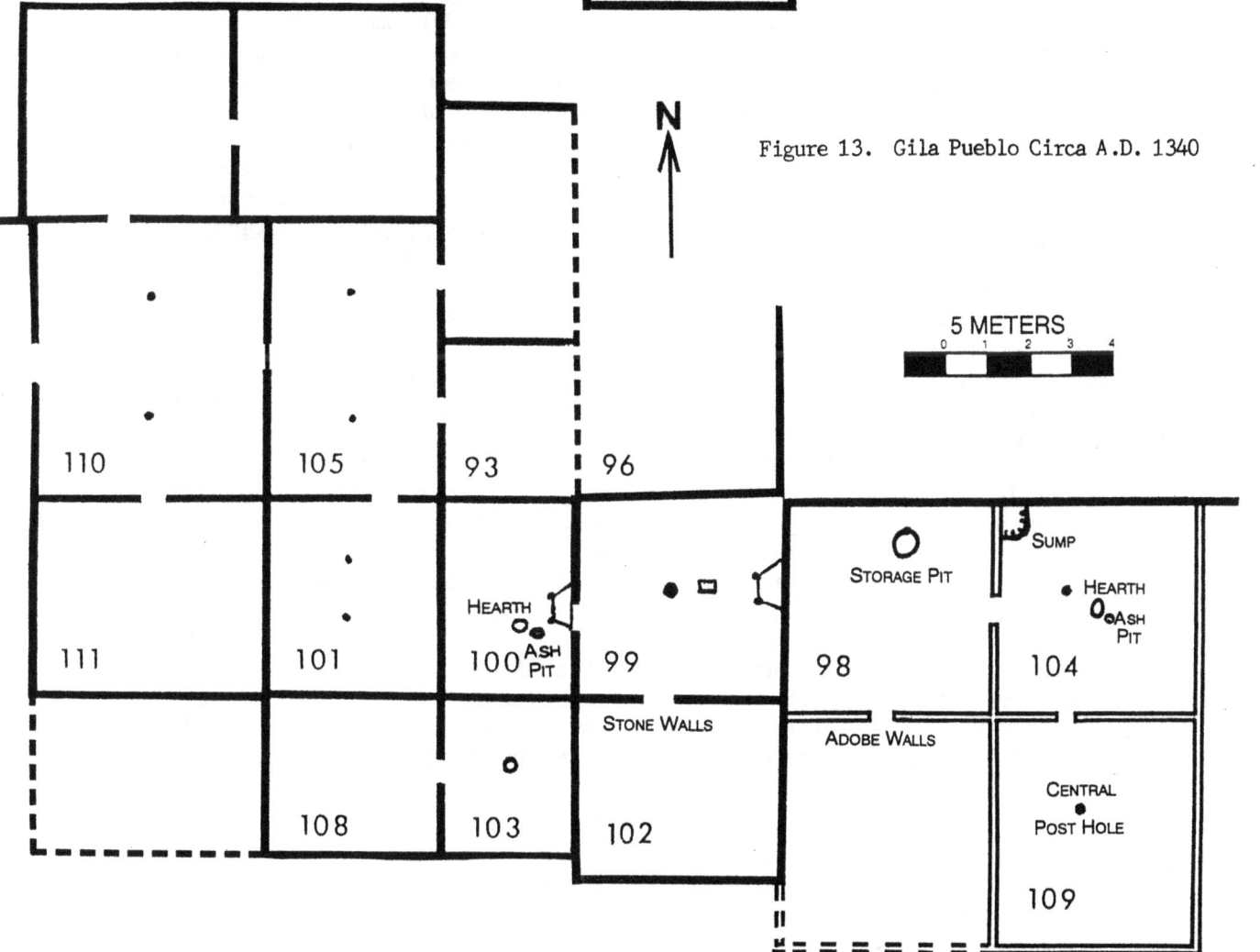

5 METERS

110   105   93   96
STORAGE PIT   SUMP
HEARTH   HEARTH
ASH PIT
111   101   100   99   98   ASH PIT   104
ASH PIT
STONE WALLS   ADOBE WALLS
CENTRAL
POST HOLE
108   103   102   109

The earthquake brought down the roofs and second story floors of all rooms. The unprotected plaster washed down the walls and over the rubble and human remains. The plaster formed a lens which was thicker near the walls than in the centers of the rooms. This gave the appearance of sterile soil, and is the level to which Gladwin's excavation of the pueblo seems to have extended.

The depth of plaster washed off the walls following the earthquake compared favorably with the amount washed off the unprotected walls in the five years following McKusick's excavation. This suggests to us that the pueblo was unoccupied and unroofed for about five years following the earthquake and the Second Fire. Tree-ring specimens from Gila Pueblo cluster at two dates: A.D. 1345 and A.D. 1385 (Smiley 1951:20). The reconstruction of the pueblo probably coincides with the A.D. 1345 building period, which places the earthquake and Second Fire at A.D.1340.

Figure 14 illustrates the changes made by new inhabitants after The Second Fire. Whereas life had continued with few architectural changes after the First Fire, after the Second Fire rooms were put to uses different from those for which they originally were constructed. For example, the north wall of Room 100 collapsed. Instead of rebuilding it, the new occupants built a new wall, which made the room considerably smaller. The stub of the original wall formed a bin, which at that time became an extension of Room 93.

Fragments of human bone were covered with earth in the process of leveling the rubble within the rooms to form a new floor surface. The portions of the two skeletons which still occupied the doorways were plastered over, and these doorways were never used again. The doorway between Room 103 and 108 was closed at this time, and Room 108 became a living area with a hearth (Figure 15). Similarly, Room 101 was now equipped with a hearth and ashpit. Room 100 did not have a hearth during this period. From the refuse found within, it appears to have been used as a workroom, at least partially for the production of flaked stone artifacts.

The slat altar in Room 110 was rebuilt over the remains of the old one, with no attempt to recover the beautiful objects which lay buried there -- such things as a beautifully-incised Oliva shell, Glycymeris maculata pendants, and a murex (Hexaplex brassica) trumpet. In Room 105, roof support-posts were banked with adobe, both on the ground floor and on the floor above. A new clay floor was installed. Upon this surface three cobbled pedestals were built, apparently to serve as dry, rodent-proof, bases for large, bee-hived-shaped granaries made of wicker and covered with clay. The northernmost granary in Room 105 contained burned squash and corn on the cob. These pedestals measured 94 cm by 106 cm, 70 cm by 77 cm, and 103 by 99 cm. A smaller granary-pedestal occupied the northwest corner of Room 102. Lincoln and Jacobs (1990) report that these pedestals were found both extramurally and intramurally in the Tonto Basin during the Roosevelt Platform Mound Study. At sites with a small number of rooms, pedestals were extramural. In sites with larger number of rooms, pedestals were intramural. In this respect, Gila Pueblo is similar to the platform mound sites.

Although he did not attempt to explain their use, Fulton (1934) describes rock and adobe platforms found in several Texas Canyon sites. Tuthill (1947:27-29) describes seven extramural pedestals from Compound II at the Tres Alamos Site, a 12-room, Tucson Phase compound. Excavation reports

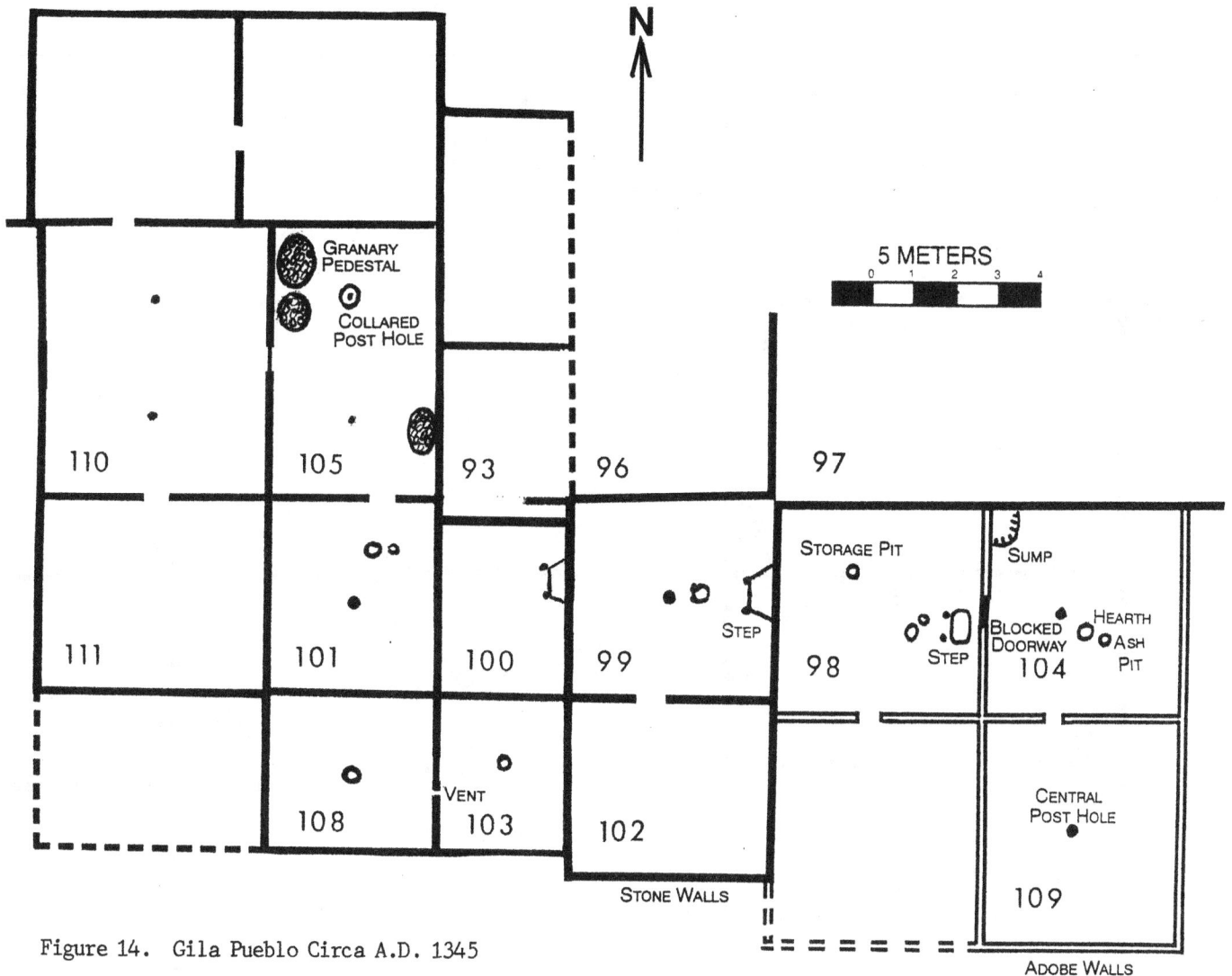

Figure 14. Gila Pueblo Circa A.D. 1345

also note the presence of pedestals at Casa Grande (Spears 1973:17). More than six decades ago, Cosgrove and Cosgrove (1932:21-22, Plate 15b) documented the occurrence and distribution of similar prehistoric granaries throughout southwestern New Mexico and Sauer and Brand (1930:435, 439, 440) did the same for southeastern New Mexico. Similar granaries still are in use by the Pima (Castetter and Bell 1942:183).

Room 98 now had a smaller, deeper storage pit than previously. A free-standing adobe bottom step was supplied for a ladder which extended above a typical, round hearth and ashpit. Room 104 had a new roof-support post, hearth, and ashpit, but retained the sump for water collection.

The destruction by earthquake and fire was most serious in Room 110 and its surrounding cluster of two-story rooms. This was partly caused by the nature of construction: rounded creek cobbles laid in gobs of mud. The earthquake brought the walls down more completely in a few moments than in the hundred or more years between the end of the Salado occupation and the early historic reoccupation of Gila Pueblo. The adobe rooms suffered little damage beyond the loss of their roofs to the fire. Apparently the stick-and-grass reinforcements in their walls made them more resistant to

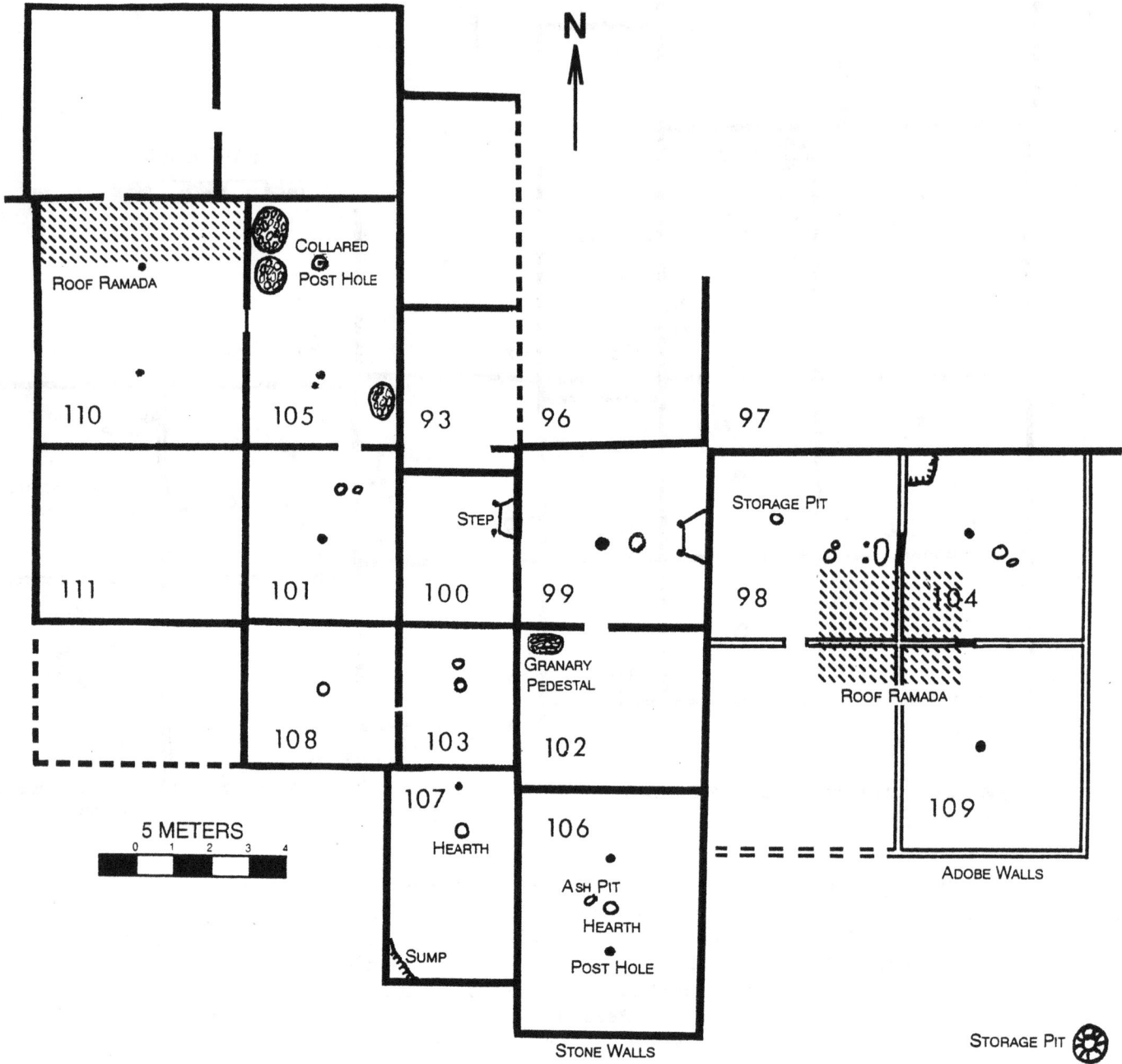

Figure 15. Gila Pueblo After A.D. 1400

damage by quake than were the stone walls. Another factor in the destruction centering on Room 110 was probably the presence of large quantities of flammable corn and cotton stored there.

A major period of renovation took place about A.D. 1385. The doorway between Room 110 and Room 111 was blocked. Also at this time Room 106, with its two roof-support posts, hearth, and ashpit, was built. Figure 15 illustrates the area after A.D. 1400. The circular hearth in newly-built Room 107 has a raised clay edging which, in turn, supported a large Tonto Polychrome bowl that was placed over it. A sump in the southwest corner of the room served to collect water which leaked into the room.

Room 97 probably dates from this period. Shiner (1961:6, Figure 2) dug for six and a half meters without finding the masonry wall he expected. It is our guess that in the beginning Room 97 probably had been a passageway between the pueblo and the compound wall and that later the area was partitioned into living quarters. The room may have been extraordinarily long or may have been partitioned with an adobe or jacal wall which left no obvious traces. Shiner (1961:7, Figure 2) mentions sub-floor burials of infants and a young child. Burials beneath the room floors all date from the period after A.D 1385 and to perhaps as late as A.D. 1440.

Typical Gila Pueblo construction included a massive, central, juniper roof support post, upon which rested an east-west beam. Upon this beam rested north-south juniper poles: four inches in diameter and spaced on 16-inch centers. These poles were covered with a layer of Phragmites communis reeds. And on top of these was about four inches of adobe. Second story roof support posts were anchored at their bases by collars of adobe. Adobe berms, six inches in height and width and hemispherical in section, rimmed hatchways and prevented rain waters from running into rooms. The outside walls of the pueblo extended about 30 inches above the roof level, forming a balustrade. This may have served a defensive purpose or simply may have served to keep puppies and toddlers from falling from roof tops. Figure 16 through Figure 20 are detailed floor plans for various of the Gila Pueblo rooms at various points in time.

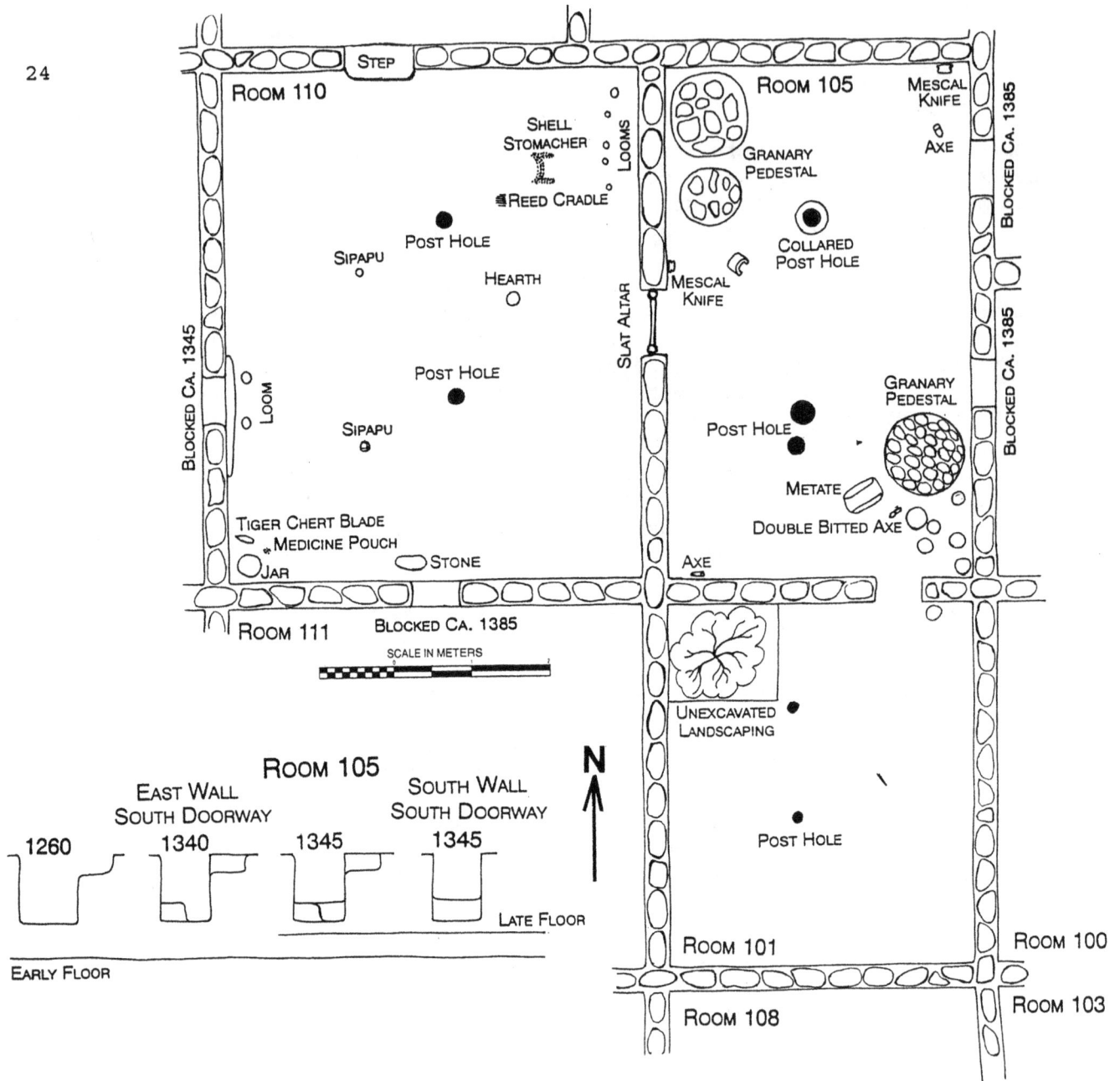

Figure 16. Floor Detail; Rooms 101, 105, and 110.

These three rooms, plus unreported Room 111, formed the central core of the Ceremonial/Redistribution Complex. Originally, Room 110 had the slat altar on the east wall and doorways on the other three walls. At 1340, all ceremonial artifacts were attached to or in front of the slat altar. By 1440, ceremonial artifacts were distributed in foci in several residential units as well. The most conspicuous change in Rooms 105 and 110 was the development of mirror-image balance. Looms were balanced northeast and southwest in Room 110; granary pedestals were balanced northwest and southeast in Room 105. One stepped up into Room 105 from the south, and down into Room 110 from the north.

A stone of unknown purpose was plastered into the floor of Room 110 near the blocked south doorway. The object next to the door of Room 101 was a 40 cm. selenite crystal. The second story of Rooms 101 and 111 contained a large amount of cotton in the boll remaining from the previous year. The second floor of Room 101 also yielded fragments of Tonto Polychrome human and quail effigies, and an heirloom saucer made from the side of a St. Johns Polychrome bowl.

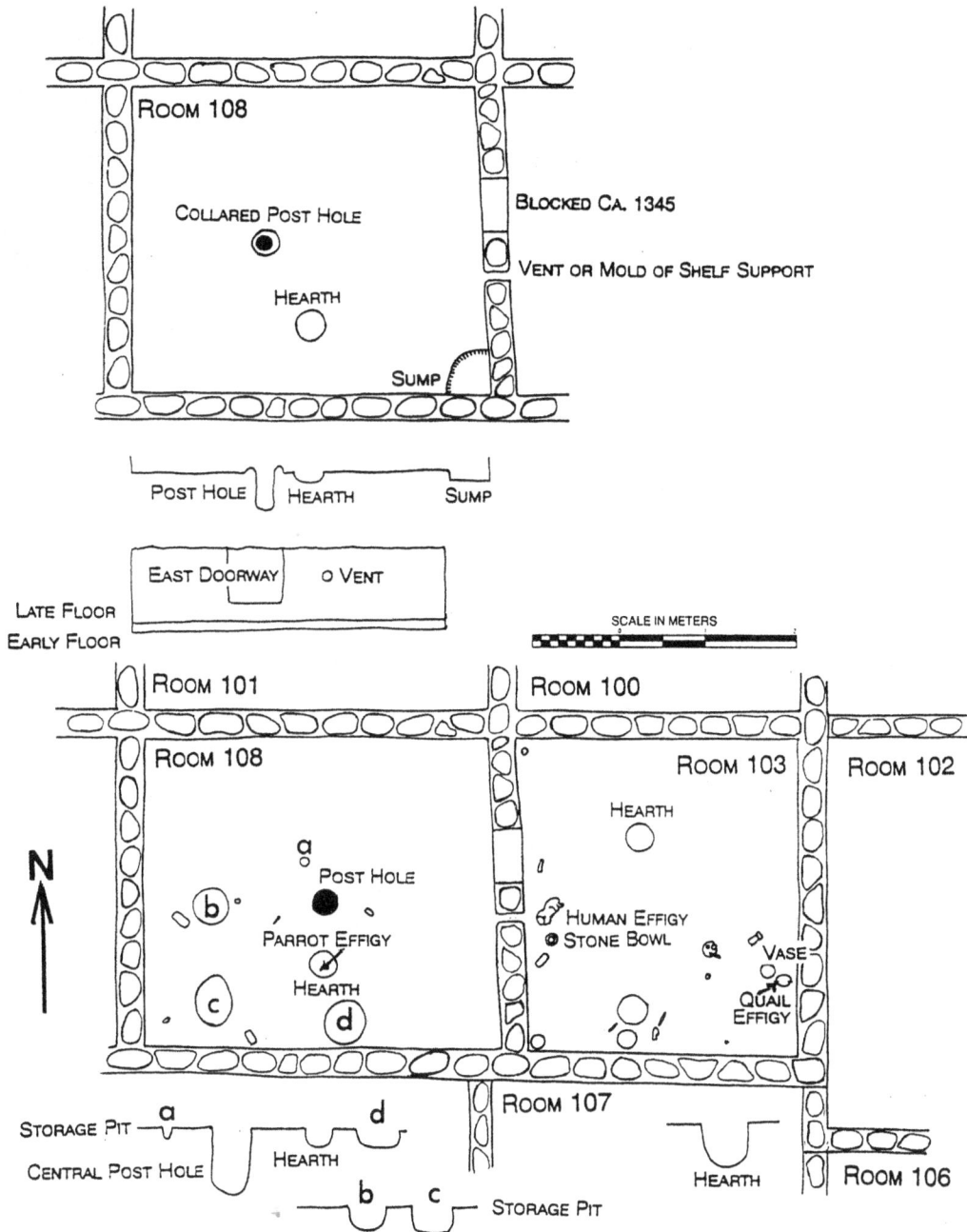

Figure 17. Floor Detail; Rooms 103 and 108.
Above, Structure at 1340. Below, Structure at 1440.

Rooms 103 and 108 originally may have been one long room which was later divided by a crooked, rather poorly-constructed wall. The hole through the wall to the south of the doorway may be the mold of a pole which supported the end of a shelf or shelves, rather than a vent. Room 103 was a storeroom serving Room 108 until the destruction of 1340. By 1440, both rooms seem to have been foci of ceremonial artifacts, with a plainware parrot effigy smashed in the hearth and a turquoise pendant in the southwest corner of Room 108. In addition to utilitarian artifacts, Room 103 contained Tonto Polychrome human and quail effigies; a stone bowl or censer; a Gila Polychrome bowl which held an antler tine, a red concretion, and a ball of ash; a Red-line Tonto vase filled with ash; and a packet of ground malachite wrapped in white cotton cloth.

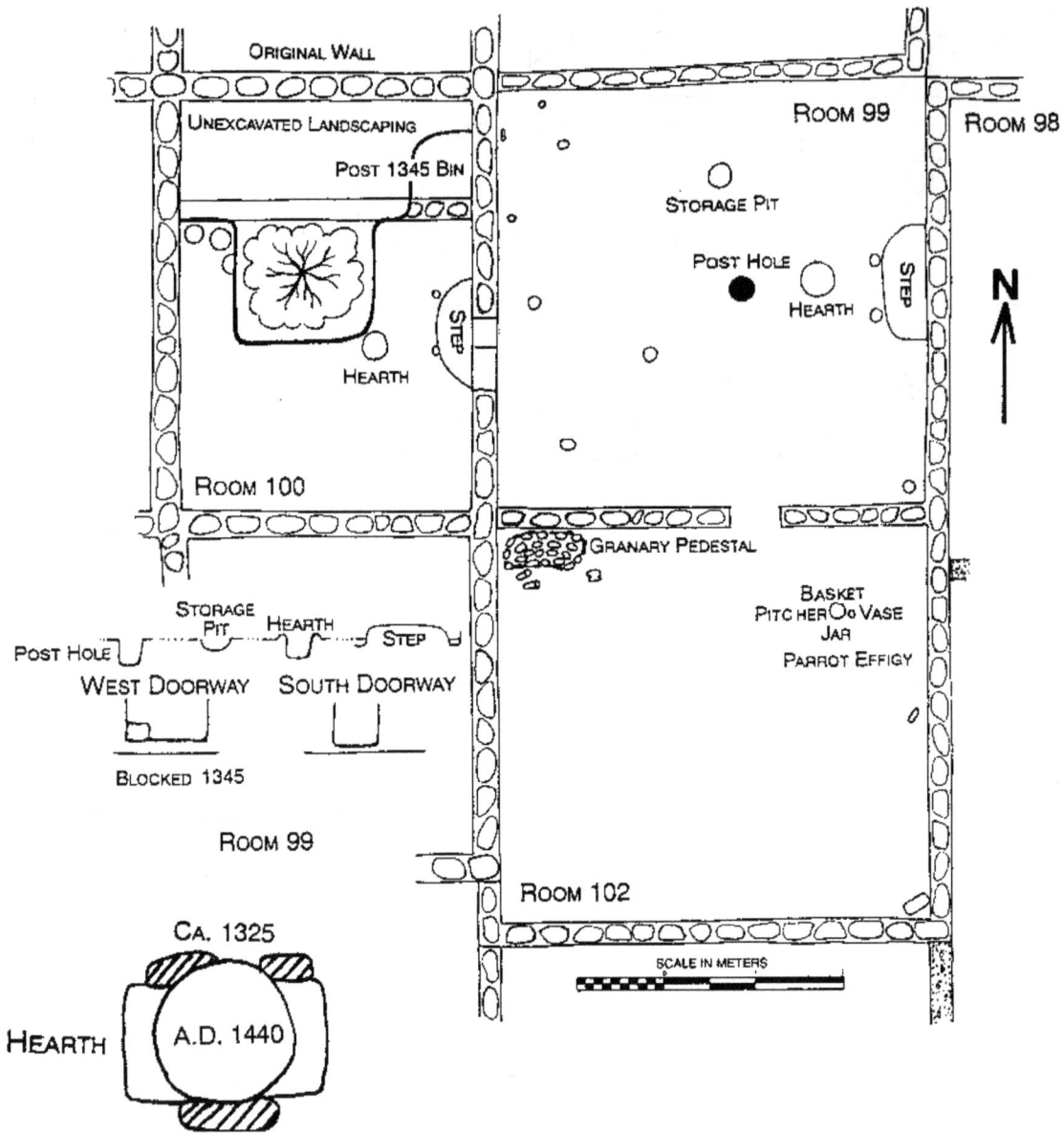

Figure 18. Floor Detail; Rooms 99, 100, and 102.

Only the southern portion of Room 100 was excavated to preserve established landscaping. During the destruction of 1340, the original wall fell except for a low stub at the base. A new wall was built to the south of it, leaving the original wall to form a bin which now served the room to the north.

About 1325, Rooms 99 and 102 were constructed, and Room 100, formerly a small game dressing room, served as a second storage room for Room 99. Later, it was provided with a hearth and hatch, and became a dwelling. The raised step served both the base of the ladder and the doorway into Room 99. A young man took shelter in this doorway during the earthquake of ca. 1340. When the pueblo was reoccupied in 1345, his skeleton was plastered over, and Room 100 was permanently separated from Room 99.

The original hearth of Room 99, built ca. 1325, was rectangular with its long axis east to west, and basalt fire dogs. The hearth in use at 1440 was round, built above and within the early hearth.

The granary platform in Room 102 was built rather late, perhaps during the 1385 general remodeling. An heirloom Gila Polychrome basket jar with handle broken off and ground smooth, a Tonto Polychrome vase, a Chupadero Black-on-white pitcher with an annular base, and fragments of a Tonto Polychrome effigy jar also were located in this storeroom.

SHINER'S ROOM

ROOM 99

ROOM 98

a

b

CENTRAL POST HOLE

c

HEARTH

STEP

STORAGE PIT

ROOM 98
A.D. 1340

a   b   c

POST HOLE   STORAGE PIT

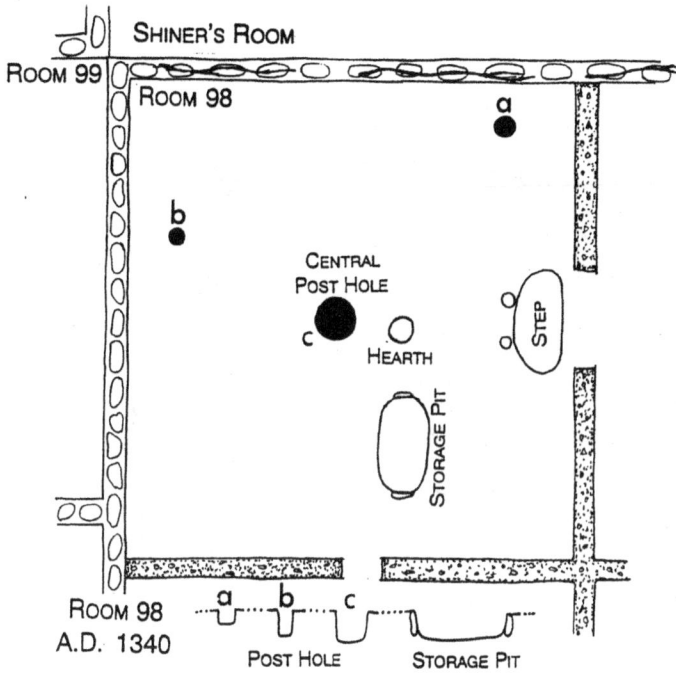

Figure 19. Floor Detail, Rooms 98, 104, and 109.
   The north wall of this suite is shared with Shiner's Room. It is an insubstantial horizontal branch-reinforced construction which may have originally been a compound wall. Suite walls were of unreinforced adobe. The oval storage pit was lined with clay. Roofing at both destructions was as informal as the north wall and included cholla branches and small sticks instead of the standard beams and reeds found elsewhere.

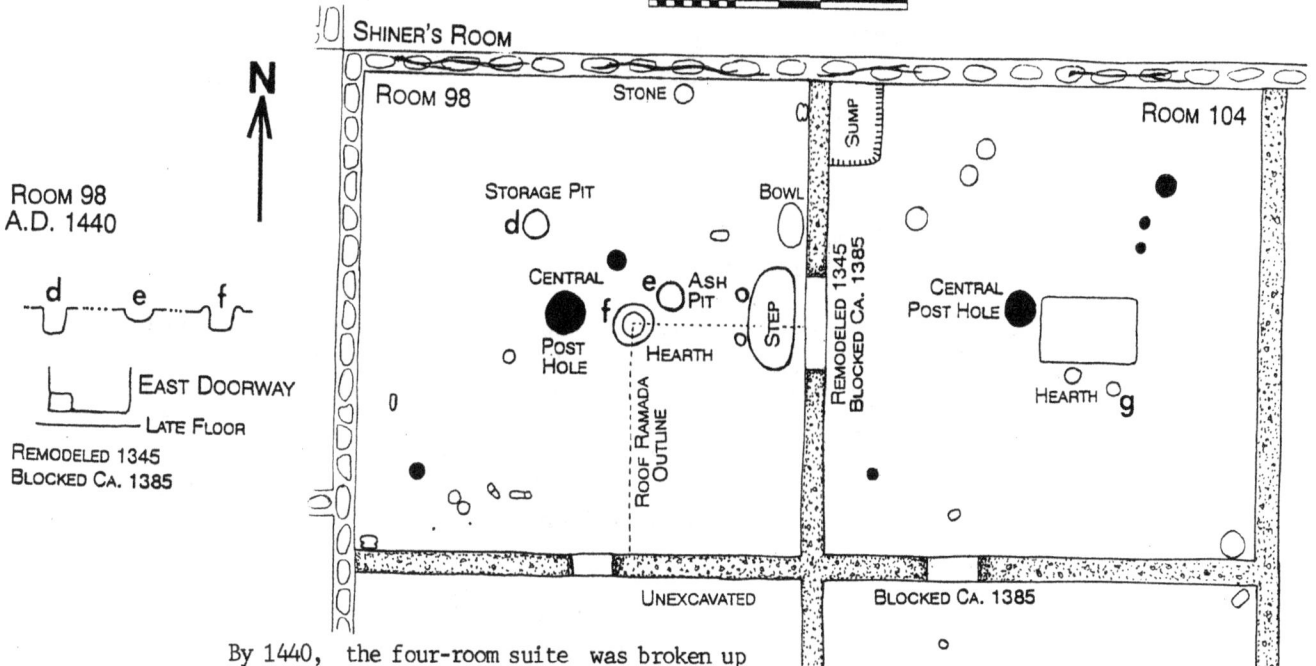

SCALE IN METERS

SHINER'S ROOM

ROOM 98

STONE

SUMP

ROOM 104

N

ROOM 98
A.D. 1440

d   e   f

EAST DOORWAY

LATE FLOOR

REMODELED 1345
BLOCKED CA. 1385

STORAGE PIT

d

CENTRAL POST HOLE

e   ASH PIT

f

HEARTH

BOWL

STEP

ROOF RAMADA OUTLINE

REMODELED 1345   BLOCKED CA. 1385

CENTRAL POST HOLE

HEARTH   g

UNEXCAVATED

BLOCKED CA. 1385

CENTRAL POST HOLE

ROOM 109

By 1440, the four-room suite was broken up into at least three separate units. Storage pit "d" in Room 98 contained the neck bones of a Small Indian Domestic Turkey, an apparent sacrifice to Tlaloc. The greenstone sphere against the north wall is a manuport which may represent the local equivalent of Chalchihuitlique, consort of Tlaloc. The oval Tonto Polychrome bowl north of the step is of a type which appeared in high status burials at Pinal Pueblo. Gila Pueblo may have survived a little longer than Besh-Ba-Gowah and Pinal Pueblo.

The rectangular area in Room 104 is a depression bearing the imprint of successive layers of matting, and may have been a loom work area. A cooking jar stood on a warming pit (g) next to the hearth.

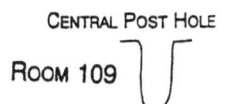

CENTRAL POST HOLE

ROOM 109

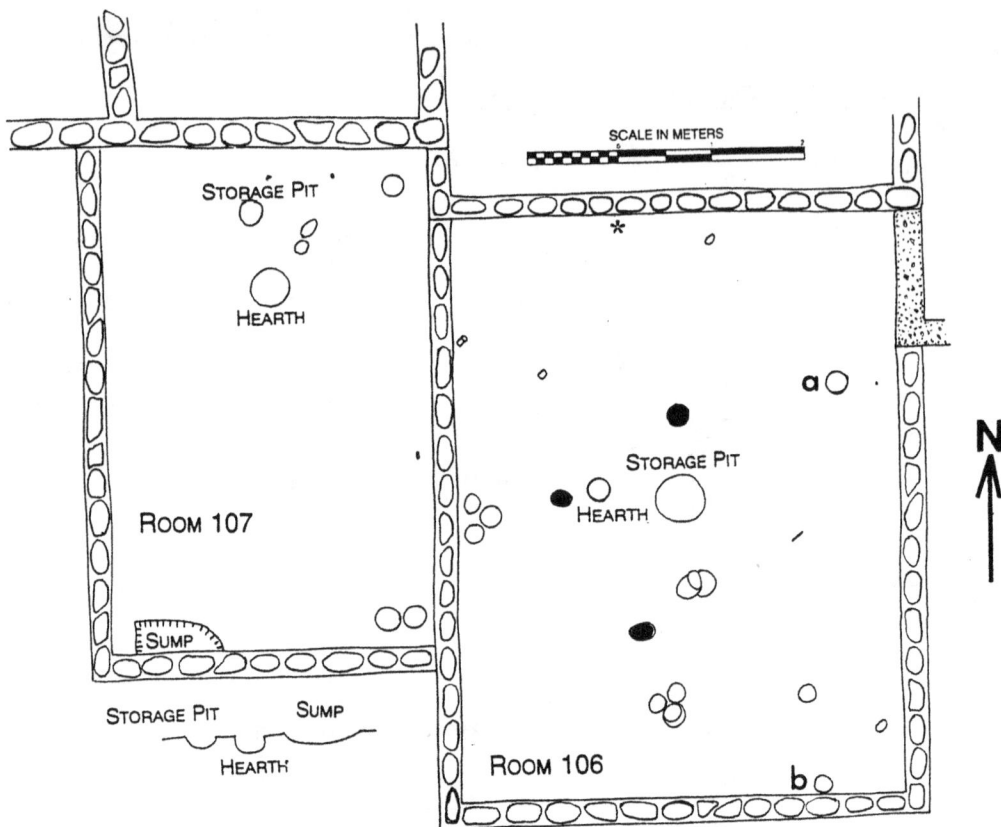

Figure 20. Floor Detail; Rooms 106 and 107.

The hearth in Room 106 held a very large late Gila Polychrome bowl with a recurved rim. Presumably this vessel was lifted by a wooden bar handle on each side secured by a rawhide harness which circled the bowl above and below the lateral bulge, laced together on the diagonal. The Heard Museum in Phoenix has an historic Zuni bowl the same size and shape which is harnessed in this manner. A corrugated jar (a) held limonite. Other artifacts included a shell trumpet (*), glycymeris bracelets, a small glycymeris pendant, and a quartz crystal found with a double-bitted ax. A jar placed against the south wall (b) was filled with burned corn. Pottery from this room bore a repeated diagonal-line/zigzag design which is characteristic of Besh-Ba-Gowah.

The storage pit in Room 106 was covered with a large, rounded sherd lid, and contained a 3/4 grooved ax. Room 107 was the last room built in this section of Gila Pueblo. Both Room 106 and 107 were built with a minimum of rock, and may have had lower than usual or jacal upper walls. A compound wall enclosed the area south of these rooms. The present paved parking lot destroyed the field house, but is outside the south boundary of the pueblo.

The storage pit south of Room 109 is representative of other extramural storage pits at Gila Pueblo and Besh-Ba-Gowah.

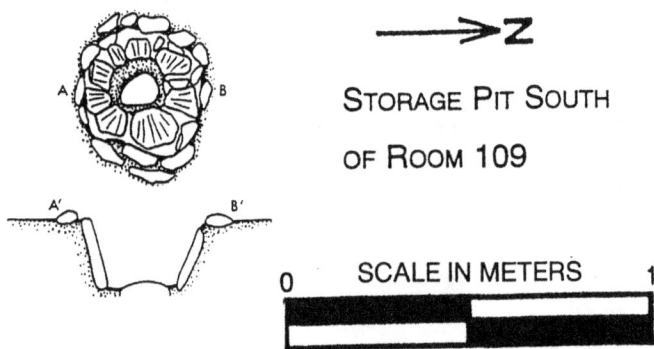

STORAGE PIT SOUTH OF ROOM 109

POTTERY

HAGEN SITE

Ninety-four whole or restorable vessels and 999 sherds were recovered at the Hagen Site (Table 4).

Table 4. Hagen Site Pottery Types.

	Whole Vessels	Sherds
PAINTED WARES		
Gila Polychrome	21	200*
Tonto Polychrome	15	19
Unclassified Salado Polychrome		1
Gila Black-on-red		7
San Carlos Red-on-brown	1	12
Unclassified Red-on-brown		2
Tucson Polychrome?		4
Unclassified White Mountain Redwares		8
REDWARE	6	159
BROWNWARES		
Tonto Brown	18	129
Gila Plain	13	384*
Unclassified plainware	2	28
Tonto Corrugated	16	24
Point of Pines Indented Corrugated	2	16
Unclassified corrugated		6
TOTALS	94	999

*includes one reworked into disk

Slightly more than half of the collection were plain or corrugated redwares. About two out of every five whole vessels were painted in two or more colors. The remaining small fraction, six whole vessels, were slipped red but otherwise unpainted.

Painted Wares. All but one of the 37 whole painted vessels were Salado polychromes. The Hagen Site specimens differed in no significant manner from previous descriptions of Gila Polychrome and Tonto Polychrome (Haury 1945; Young 1967, 1982). Twenty-five out of 30 Gila Polychrome vessels were bowls, and five of the six Tonto Polychrome specimens were jars.

Both the largest and the smallest painted vessels were Gila Polychrome bowls. The largest was recurved, 370 mm to 400 mm in diameter and 200 mm in height. There appeared to be little relationship between size and shape, but hemispherical bowls were about twice as numerous as recurved bowls.

With the exception of Pinto Polychrome, most Salado vessels had one or more thick framing-lines, often referred to in the literature as "life lines," incorporated into their design motif. The Hagen Site specimens were no exception; 90 percent have life lines. In every instance but one, these life lines were broken. The single exception, the unbroken life line, was not always complete. It first was painted in the usual fashion with the two ends left unconnected. Later, a line of black paint was drawn between the two ends linking them. But the connecting bar was not as wide as the two ends it joined, leaving a conspicuous set of paired notches in the upper and lower borders of the life line (Figure 21).

According to Haury (1945:65, fn. 136) Gila Black-on-red, "a companion type of Gila Polychrome in the Upper Salt, in the Gila from Globe east and in the Tucson areas," does not occur in the Salt River Valley. Nor is any reported from the Tonto Cliff Dwellings (Steen and others 1962). No whole Gila Black-on-red vessels were recovered from the Hagen Site, and only seven of the 253 sherds are that type. Los Muertos, the Tonto Cliff Dwellings, and Gila Pueblo all were occupied during the later portion of the Salado developmental sequence. And the latter two are pure Salado sites. If Gila Black-on-red is a Salado type, it must belong earlier in the sequence or have a restricted area of distribution or both. If it is not a Salado ware, perhaps it was produced by closely related Western Pueblo neighbors living in the vicinity of the Mogollon Rim.

Not a single sherd of Hohokam painted pottery was found at the Hagen Site, and none was recovered at Tonto Cliff Dwellings. When we mentioned this Albert Schroeder some years ago, he replied that decoration on Hohokam pottery had practically ceased in the Civano Phase, after A.D. 1300. Furthermore, Sacaton Phase decorated ware occurs only rarely in the Salado area.

All whole painted vessels came from the North Ruin. Most were on the floors of rooms, especially Room 5 and Room 6 (Table 5). One Gila Polychrome bowl accompanied the single burial encountered.

Redwares. At the Hagen Site, slipped redware pottery occurred with much less frequency than the painted wares or the unpainted brownwares. Only six of the 94 whole vessels and 159 of 999 sherds were redware. In 1937, Colton and Hargrave used the term "Tonto Red" to describe redware found in the Tonto Basin. The original definition was broad. During the intervening years it has become increasingly inclusive. In 1962, Pierson placed obliterated corrugated material within the definition and Steen (p. 17) brought so many brownwares under it that his Tonto Red from the Upper Ruin at Tonto Cliff Dwellings "is more commonly brown than red." In the analysis of Hagen Site ceramics, plain brownwares were divided into three groups: 1) Gila Plain, 2) unclassified plainware, and 3) a new type: Tonto Brown. A second new type -- Tonto Corrugated -- was established for oblitered-corrugated brownware. Only slipped redware pottery was classified as Tonto Red.

Even with the unslipped plain and textured wares removed from consideration, the slipped Tonto Redware from the Hagen Site covered a broad spectrum of diversity. A few sherds, between five and ten percent of the total, closely resembled Salado Redware. Their soft, unpolished exteriors were covered with a raspberry red wash or slip that tended to be fugitive.

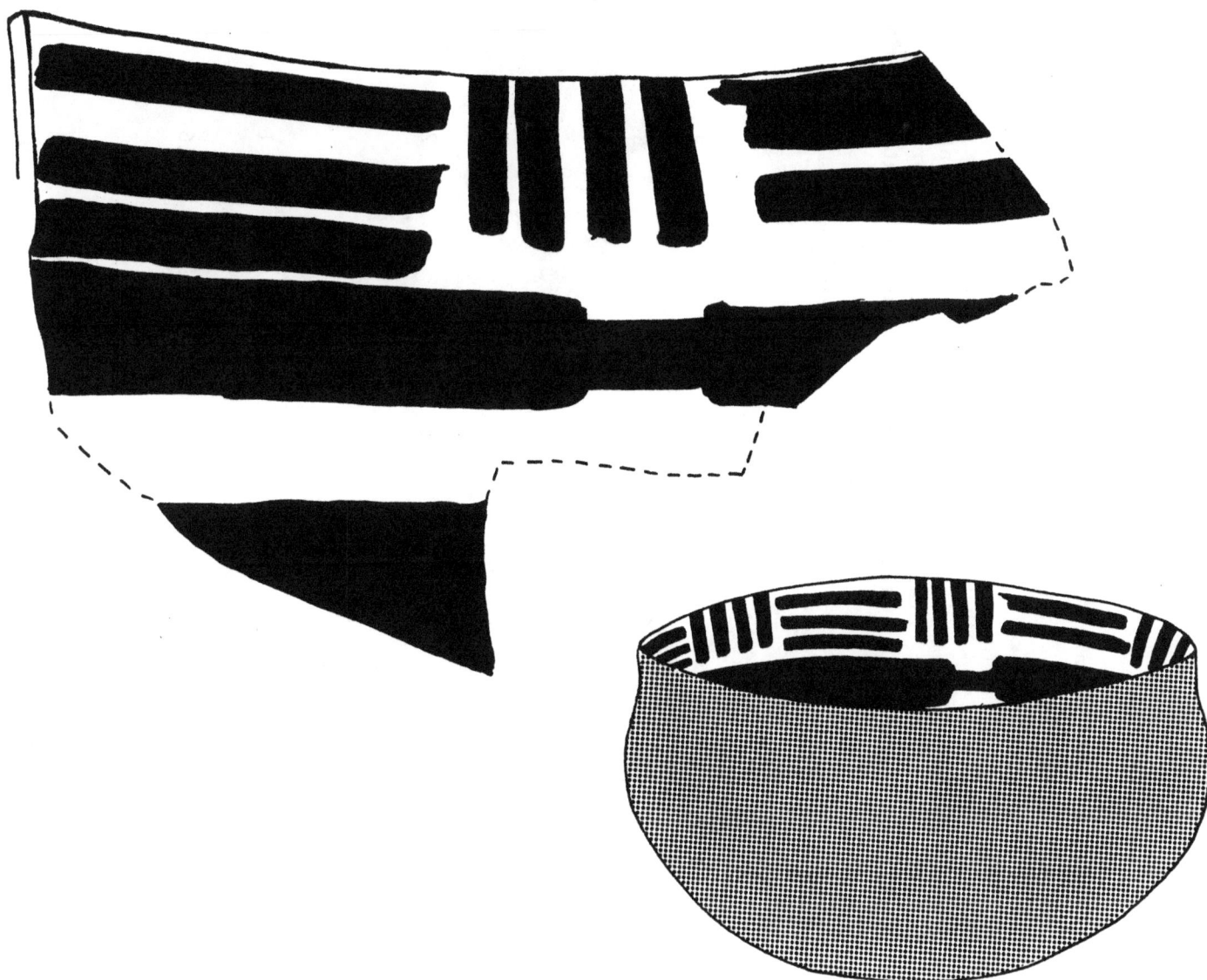

Figure 21. Atypical Life Line.
 Gila Polychrome Bowl, Hagen Site, Room 3; ca. 275 mm in diameter, ca. 145-150 mm in depth.

At the opposite end of the Tonto Red spectrum, many specimens resembled Gila Red and Salt Red -- although the Tonto Red vessels tended to be less carefully done. Their surfaces, for example, were noticeably more irregular and bumpy and less polished. The lack of care in the smoothing and finishing of surfaces is a dominant characteristic of Tonto Red, which basically is undecorated Salado Polychrome with a less careful finish. Of the six whole Tonto Red vessels from the Hagen Site, three were bowls and three were jars. Two of the bowls had smudged interiors, and two of the jars were bird effigies (Figure 22).

All of the whole redware vessels were found at the North Ruin. In Room 2 a bird effigy was near the centerpost, and smudged bowl was in the fill. The other smudged bowl was on the floor of Room 5, near the east end of the

Table 5. Hagen Site, Room Association of Whole Vessels

	San Carlos Red-on-Brown	Gila Poly-chrome	Tonto Poly-chrome	Gila Plain	Tonto Plain	Unclas-sified Plain-ware	Tonto Red	Point of Pines Indented Corru-gated	Tonto Corru-gated	TOTALS
NORTH RUIN										
Room 1	1	4	2	2	2	1			3	15
Room 2		4		1	1		2		4	12
Room 3		2						1		3
Room 4			1							1
Room 5		10	1	5	8	1	2		4	31
Room 6		9	2	4	6		1		2	24
Room 7		1		1	1		1		2	6
SOUTH RUIN										
Room 1								1	1	2
TOTALS	1	30	6	13	18	2	6	2	16	94

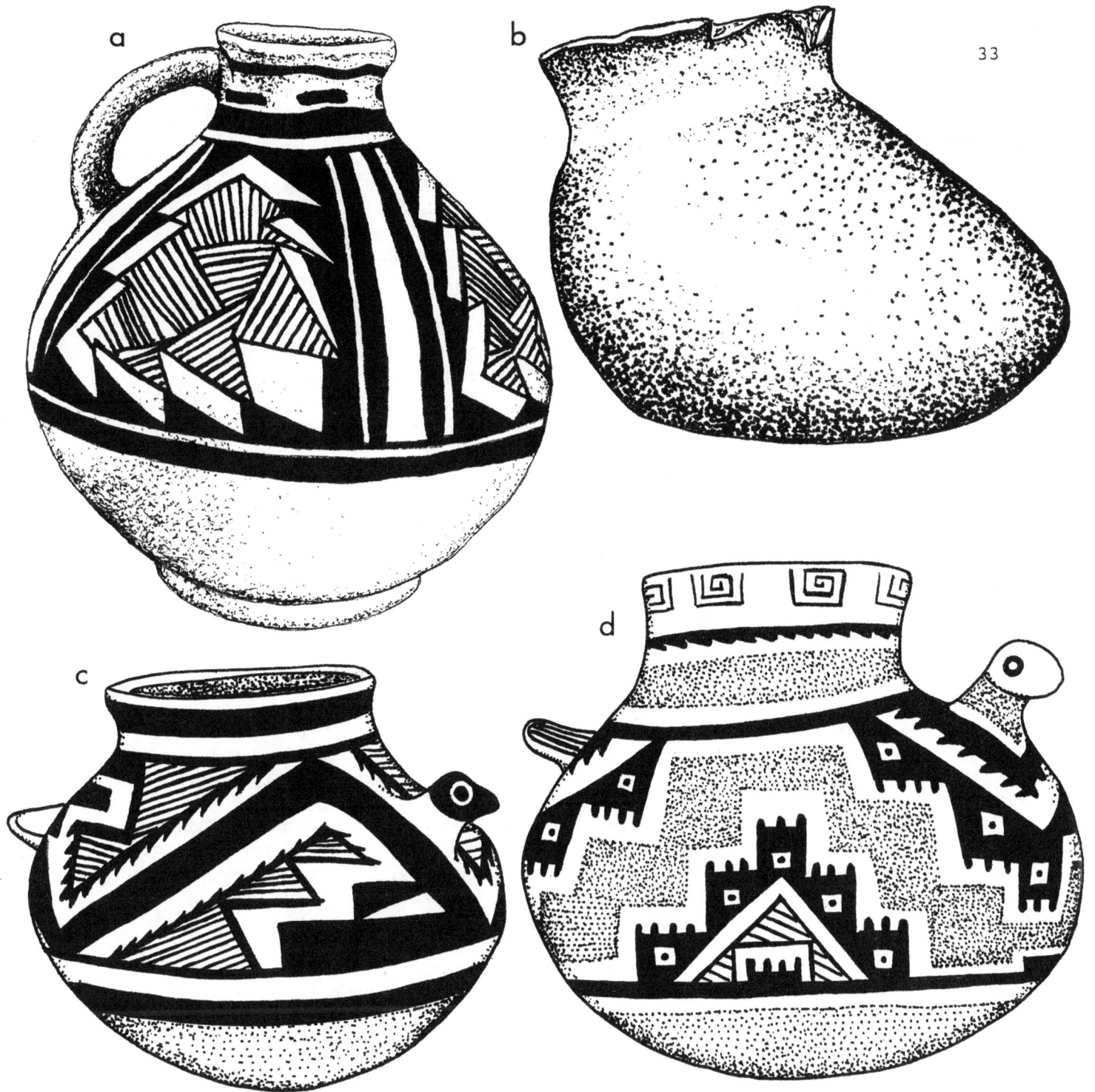

Figure 22. Chupadero Black-on-white Pitcher and Bird Effigy Vessels.
a. Intact Chupadero Black-on-White pitcher with annular base, Room 102, floor, Gila Pueblo. After Helga Teiwes photo, Arizona State Museum Negative No. 64440.
b. Tonto Red Jar, 195 by 164 mm; Room 2, Hagen Site; Southwest Archeological and Conservation Center catalog no. S2039/47. This form is considered ceremonial by some authorities. A smaller boot-shaped "duck" pot was recovered from Room 99 at Gila Pueblo. Another plainware "duck" pot, this one with wings, was recovered from the second floor of Room 110 at Gila Pueblo. This vessel, the size and shape of a partly inflated football, was filled with shelled corn. Both Gila Pueblo vessels date ca. 1440.
c. Gila Polychrome Quail? Effigy Jar, second floor, Room 105, Gila Pueblo, ca. 1340, the only effigy found relating to the original occupation of Gila Pueblo.
d. Tonto Polychrome Quail? Effigy Jar, floor, Room 103, Gila Pueblo, ca. 1440. All painted effigy jars from the 1440 level were Tonto Polychrome.

bench, and a third bowl was **on** the bench, near its west end. A bird effigy jar was in Room 6. The third jar was on the floor of Room 7.

Brownwares. The brownware utility pottery from the Hagen Site was more numerous than the painted and redware materials combined. Fifty-one brownware vessels were recovered: 33 plain and 18 corrugated. None were bowls. They showed a strong affinity both to the Hohokam wares to the west and southwest and to the pottery of other Western Pueblo peoples to the north and northeast. Thirteen were Gila Plain, two were unclassified plainware, and two were Point of Pines Indented Corrugated. The remaining brownware vessels were about equally divided between two types that have not been described previously: Tonto Brown and Tonto Corrugated.

Tonto Brown. This description is based primarily upon 18 whole or vessels recovered from the North Ruin of the Hagen Site. Throughout most of the aboriginal Southwest, pottery is made from relatively long, thin ropes of moistened, tempered clay. The vessels are built by coiling the clay rope in an upward spiral. Adjacent coils are welded by pinching, and vessels walls are scraped to a uniform thickness. This method of manufacture is characteristic of the Anasazi, Mogollon, Western Pueblo, and their descendants: the modern Pueblos.

Techniques used by Pima and Hohokam potters to build their vessels differ somewhat from the Puebloan tradition. Pima clay coils are thicker than those of the Pueblo and usually shorter in length. Often it takes two or three Pima clay rolls to make a single circuit of the vessel. Adjacent rolls are pinched together and vessel walls may be scraped, but coils are welded and walls are brought to a uniform thickness primarily by means of a paddle and anvil. A smooth, round stone with a convex surface is held against the inner wall of the vessel while a wooden paddle is slapped against the exterior surface.

Elements of both the pueblo and the Pima traditions are found in Tonto Brown. Construction coils are relatively thick, varying from 15 mm to 30 mm in width when flattened to form vessel walls. In general there appears to be a direct relationship between coil thickness and size of vessel. Firing was in an oxidizing atmosphere; colors vary from reddish-brown to black. Temper is quartz particles whose size varies from medium to large. Mica is present and is especially noticeable as float on vessel surfaces. Walls, especially those of large vessels, are weak and crumbly. Surfaces tend to have a rough, coarse, bumpy feel and appearance. This is due to a number of factors. Individual particles of temper often are quite large in size and noticeably project above the vessels surface. Exterior surfaces frequently are scored as occasionally are interior surfaces. The brush marks are most noticeable in the vicinity of vessel necks and usually are horizontal. Often, little attention was paid to filling-in junctures between successive coils, resulting in a rippled surface. In many instances interior surfaces, especially of large vessels, are covered with a series of anvil impressions. The interior surfaces of at least some of the vessels received varying amounts of scraping, which removed any evidence of paddling.

Jar sizes range from relatively small to quite large. Wall thickness varies from 7 mm to 16 mm, with a mean of 9 mm. Shapes are globular, with bases running a gamut from almost flat through round to slightly pointed. Most rims are slightly outcurved; a few are vertical. One medium-sized vessel is a bird effigy. It is boot-shaped and had a slightly flattened loop handle and is the only vessel with a handle recovered at the Hagen Site. Two of the the Tonto Brown jars from Gila Pueblo proper are boot-shaped, rudimentary bird effigies. A third is a full-fledged parrot effigy, with head and tail and wings modeled in the round. Diameter and height usually are about the same measurement on any given vessel. The smallest are about 200 mm. The larger vessels have dimensions of up to about 600 mm. Rim diameters are about 150 mm on smaller jars and as great as 320 mm on the largest specimen. All were found on the floors of North Ruin rooms: Room 1 (1), Room 2 (2), Room 5 (8), Room 6 (6), and Room 7 (1).

Tonto Brown appears to be closely related to the contemporaneous Gila Plain and Verde Brown. Each is a regional manifestation of the plainware tradition in late-prehistoric central and southern Arizona. We have not made a detailed comparison among the three types but have a general impression that Tonto Brown is less carefully built and finished than Gila Plain. The only major difference we noticed is that all 19 Tonto Brown whole vessels from the Hagen Site are jars. Jars predominate but bowls occur regularly in both Gila Plain and Verde Brown. We expect to find fairly well-defined and mutually exclusive areas of distribution for the three types: Gila Plain in the broad river valleys of south-central Arizona's Hohokam, Verde Brown in the Sinagua's Verde Valley, and Tonto Brown in the Tonto Basin and the immediately adjacent, rugged, dissected upland areas occupied by the Salado.

Tonto Corrugated. Except as noted below, the 16 whole or restorable Tonto Corrugated vessels conform to the Tonto Brown type description. The most obvious difference between Tonto Brown and Tonto Corrugated is the presence of partially-obliterated, indented corrugations on the exterior of the latter. The horizontal corrugations are altered into a series of diagonal ridges, a practice which first occurred at least as early as Pueblo II in Anaszi sites: "in making the indentation the potter forces up a ridge of clay in front of the thumb. Since the depressions are staggered the ridges are also, with the result that a series of ridges sweep diagonally from rim to base with such prominence as to be more evident than the horizontal corrugations" (Hayes 1964:49, Figure 29 g-i).

Tonto Corrugated jars tend to be somewhat smaller than Tonto Plain, and none have flat bases. All of the Tonto Corrugated vessels recovered at the Hagen Site appear to have been built from long, thin coils of clay rather than from short, flat rolls. And none of the Tonto Corrugated interiors have anvil marks. Such marks may have been removed by scraping. The 16 vessels were on the floors of North Ruin rooms: Room 1 (4), Room 2 (4), Room 5 (4), Room 6 (2), and Room 7 (2).

Reworked Sherds. Two reworked-sherd disks were recovered. One, a piece of Gila Plain jar, was about 65 mm in diameter. Its edge was ground smooth, and a hole, 7-8 mm in diameter, was drilled in its center. It was found in the fill of Room 6. The other disk, 35 mm in diameter, was a Gila Polychrome bowl fragment. Its edge had not been ground, and there was no central perforation. It was in Room 5.

GILA PUEBLO PROPER

There were no sherds of Gila Black-on-Red at the Hagen Site, but they do occur at Gila Pueblo and at Besh-ba-gowah in small numbers. Gila Pueblo proper had a more complete sampling of the Salado Redware series and other contemporaneous painted wares (Table 6). The beginnings of the Salado Polychromes at Gila Pueblo occurred subsequent to the building of the ceremonial/redistribution complex, but before the construction of Room 99. Only black-on-white painted sherds underlay the complex, and they date to before A.D. 1260. The portal area south of Room 96 yielded sherds of Pinto Black-on-Red, Pinto Polychrome, and Fourmile Polychrome bowls. There also were parts of the bulbous necks of two, small polychrome jars -- which we believe are early Gila Polychrome. These sherds date between about A.D. 1260 and A.D. 1325. Pinto Black-on-Red and Pinto Polychrome appear at Chodistaas in the Grasshopper region between A.D. 1263 and A.D. 1300 (Reid et al. 1992:212; White and Burton 1992:217), which lends strength to the postulation that they had a rather late and brief popularity.

By A.D. 1340 Gila Polychrome was the dominant painted type -- with such forms as small, hemispherical bowls and jars and a bird effigy. Whereas Gila Polychrome was present at Gila Pueblo about A.D. 1325, it did not appear at Grasshopper until about A.D. 1350 (Reid and Whittlesly 1992:224, 225, 229).

After A.D. 1400 Gila Pueblo pottery was typified by a large amount of Gila Polychrome in hemispherical bowl forms; bowls whose rims are flared; large, flat bowls whose rims are recurved; jars; and a form that looks for all the world like a basket with a strap handle (Figure 23c). It is our belief that these strap-handled vessels are ceremonial in nature and that they demonstrate Mexican influence. Even more common at this time was Tonto Polychrome: large bowls with recurved rims; large jars with flat shoulders; jars; a beaker; and effigy jars in the forms of humans, birds, and a quadruped. There also were large bowls with recurved rims which combined both Tonto Polychrome and Gila Polychrome design elements and layouts on a single vessel. Other painted wares occurring after A.D. 1400 at Gila Pueblo included: Gila Black-on-Red, Gila White-on-Red, San Carlos Red-on-Brown, and Jeddito Black-on-Yellow.

Table 6. Gila Pueblo Pottery Count

B = Bowl Sherds, J = Jar Sherds, Min. = Miniature, x = Presence, unwashed, no count.

	Room 98	Room 99	Room 100	Room 101	Room 102	Room 103	Room 104	Room 105	Room 106	Room 107	Room 108	Room 109	Room 110
Tonto Brown	x	250 B. 3446 J.	39 B. 969 J.Min. B.	x		4616 J.	x	x	x	4557	x	x	x
Corrugated	x	9 J.		x	x	63				27			x
Obliterated	x	1 B. 154 J.	32			231		x					
Indented		43 J.	172			14			x				
Plain Red		230 J.	57			324			x	130			
Salado Red		25		Min. B.		5							
Pinto B/R		7 B.	12 B.										
Gila B/R						x				15			
Salado W/R		3 J.											
Snowflake? B/W	x			x									
Chupadero B/W					pitcher								
Jeddito B/Y							4						
Polished Orange						5 B.				1			

Gila Pueblo Pottery Count, Continued

B = Bowl Sherds, J = Jar Sherds, x = Presence, unwashed, no count.

	Room 98	Room 99	Room 100	Room 101	Room 102	Room 103	Room 104	Room 105	Room 106	Room 107	Room 108	Room 109	Room 110
Pinto Polychrome	x												x
Gila Polychrome	x	162 B. 26 J	650 B.	x	x	x		x	x	630 B. 107 J			
Tonto Polychrome	x	8 B. 6 J	x	x	x		x	x	x	820 J.	x		x
Gila Inside/ Gila Outside			14 B. .5 bwls			31 B.				34 B.			
Gila Inside/ Tonto Outside			37 B. .5 bwls							38 B.			
Tonto Inside/ Gila Outside			37 B.			14 B.				1 B.			
Tonto Inside/ Tonto Outside													
Misc. Salado Poly.		144											
St. Johns Polychrome		1 B.		2 B.		1 B.				5 B.			
Fourmile Polychrome	x	8 B.					3 B.	x		10 B.			x
San Carlos R/Br	x	9 B. 7 J	1 B.			6 J.	10 J.	x		27 J.			
Smudged										56 B.			

Figure 23. Miscellaneous Gila Pueblo Ceramic Forms, Ca. A.D. 1440

a. Tonto Polychrome human effigy, Room 103. The feet have been broken off, and the sharp edges ground smooth. Since the jar would no longer remain upright without feet, the rim was drilled above the ears for suspension. The ears are pierced for ornamentation, but no earrings were found.

b. Tonto Polychrome beaker, ground floor, Room 110.

c. Gila Polychrome heirloom basket form, Room 102. The handle has been broken off and the broken edges ground smooth.

d. Pottery miniatures found on rooftops with the remains of small children. Most are crude, apparently made by children, but the small jar has the imprint of an adult fingertip forming the interior depression. Scale: X 1.

STONE AND MINERALS

Table 7 is a listing of the minerals recovered from the Gila Pueblo proper excavations and Table 8, a tabulation of stone artifacts. The descriptions which follow primarily are details of the stone artifacts from the Hagen Site. The Gila Pueblo stone artifacts were not subjected to the same detailed analyses that those from the Hagen Site were. Had they been, it is our belief that the general results would have been the same. Indeed, we believe that our description of the Hagen Site stone assemblage would be and is replicated over and over again throughout the Salado core area.

Prefatory Remarks. More than a quarter of the stone artifacts recovered were basalt, but many different kinds of stone were used by the inhabitants of the Hagen Site:

basalt	100	schist and steatite	12	dacite	4
granite	50	felsite	8	diorite	4
sandstone	39	scoria	8	jasper	4
quartzite	31	quartzitic sandstone	7	azurite	1
porphyry	21	obsidian	6	epidote	1
quartz	19	chalcedony	5	gypsum	1
chert	17	flint	5	mudstone	1
gneiss	17	malachite	5	opal	1
				shale	1
					368

Most of these materials were readily available, some immediately adjacent to the village, and most no more than a few kilometers round-trip from Gila Pueblo.

Several types of stone came from considerably farther away. For example, most of the schist probably originated at the extensive outcrops which lie within a quarter of a mile to the south of Gila Pueblo. But the nearest occurrence of one variety, the purple talc schist from which the two shaft tools are carved, is 30 to 50 kilometers to the north. Obsidian is found 40 kilometers to the southeast and scoria, 70 kilometers east of the village. It often is impossible to determine the actual uses to which a specific artifact was put, but in the following descriptions and discussions an attempt is made to separate the objects into functional categories.

Cutting and Pounding Tools.

Mescal Knives. Mescal knives are thin, flat sheets of stone employed in the harvesting of agave and, perhaps, yucca leaves (Castetter and Underhill 1935:16; Castetter et al. 1938:28; Brown and Grebinger 1969:193-194, Figure 3). Some authors have identified similar artifacts as "hoes" and several suggested they were used for digging pits for houses and similar activities. The 30 specimens from the Hagen Site were too thin and fragile to have withstood rough withstood rough handling. They might have been helpful in light weeding or earth-loosening, but use-marks clearly indicated that they were utilized with a sawing motion. Drucker (1941:96, 169) describes the use of stone blades by Yuman-Piman peoples "for cutting or sawing" mescal leaves.

Table 7. Minerals Recovered from Gila Pueblo

	Room 98	Room 99	Room 100	Room 101	Room 102	Room 103	Room 104	Room 105	Room 106	Room 107	Room 108	Room 109	Room 110
Kaolin		1		1									
Potter's Clay		2											
Red Ochre		1		1	3	2	3	many			2		2
"Pink" Ochre					2								
Yellow Ochre					1		1			1			1
Juniper Ash							2				1		
Epidote													1
Azurite								many					1
Malachite	1	1		1	2	2	2	many	1	2			1
Chrysocolla					1	1		many	1	2			1
Turquoise Raw	1				2	1							
Disc Beads					3			2		1			1
Tabular Beads				1				1		2	1		6
Tesserae			1	1	2			1		1			6
Quartz Crystal	1	2	chips	3	2	1		3	2		2		4
Selenite Crystal				1									
Stalactite					1								
Mica													1
Chalcedony				1	1								
Jasper		4		3	1								
Petrified Wood												many	
Obsidian	1	6	many	11	4		2	many	1	5	2		2
Chert		1	chips	chips	3		1						
Tiger Chert Blade													1
Argilite Beads								many					
Copper Bell					1								

Table 8. Stone Artifacts Recovered from Gila Pueblo

	Room 98	Room 99	Room 100	Room 101	Room 102	Room 103	Room 104	Room 105	Room 106	Room 107	Room 108	Room 109	Room 110	Total
FLAKED STONE														
Projectile Points		5	1	5	2	2	2	6	1		3	1	4	32
Blade													1	1
Knife				1										1
Drill	1	1	1						1					4
Chopper						1								1
Scraper				1		1	1	7			2	1	2	15
GROUND STONE														
Manos	6	3		2	5	4	2	19		1	3	1	8	54
Metates	3							3					3	9
Paint Pallet				2		1		1	3				1	8
Paint Mortar								1						1
Stone Bowl						1								1
3/4 Grooved Axe	1	2			2	1		5	1	1	3		7	23
Double-bitted Axe									1					1
Shaft Straighteners		1		1		3	1	1	1	1	1		8	18
Spindle Whorl													1	1
Button	1													1
MISCELLANEOUS														
Large Sphere	1													1
Club-sized Ball					1									1
Hammerstones				1		2	4	7	1		1	1	3	21
Polishing Stones		2		1	2							1		7
Tablet				1										1
Lap Stone		1												1
Mescal Knives (ground and flaked)				1	3	1	1	2+9 frag.		1			5	14+

Most are porphyry:

porphyry	20
shale	5
sandstone	2
basalt	1
gneiss	1
quartzite	1
	30

Forms vary; all but a few of the mescal knives are broken; and often fragments of larger knives were reused, so generalizations necessarily are tentative. A sheet of stone was selected with a thickness of about 10 mm. Shapes ranged from ovals to rounded, elongated parallelograms and trapezoids and probably depended to a large extent upon the natural shape of the sheet. The majority of the edges were bifacially chipped to shape. Near the butt edge, on either side, a notch was bifacially chipped 15-30 mm in width and 5-10 mm in depth (Figure 24).

The hafted knife recovered from Red Rock House, a cliff dwelling located 65-70 kilometers north and a little east of Gila Pueblo, reveals how handles were attached. A wooden stem, slightly longer than the blade, was split longitudinally. The blade was clamped between the two pieces of stem by tightly wrapping the ends of the handle and securing the wrapping to the blade at the notches (Hough 1930:8, Plate 7). Hayden (1957: 144, 146; fn. 72; Plate 28f) suggests that in the "Hohokam-Salado area" the haft consisted solely of a simple cord or thong "wrapped about the tool lengthwise, through the notches." On page 64 of his Warrior Apaches, Baldwin (1965) illustrates a historic, hafted mescal knife.

There is evidence that at least one of the Hagen Site specimens had a split wooden haft. It was lying on the bench along the north end of Room 5. The knife is blackened, probably as a result of the fire which destroyed the room. On the face of the knife, near the butt, there is a relatively unblackened stripe 15-25 mm wide running between the hafting notches. This light swath almost certainly indicates the position and width of the haft which masked the upper portion of the knife during the fire and decomposed during the intervening years. One mescal knife from Gila Pueblo proper had its hafting preserved in the form of a hollow mold of adobe. The split handle was 17 mm in width and 407 mm in length. One end of the handle was split to receive the blade, resulting in a hatchet-shaped object.

Cutting edges have chipped serrations and tend to be slightly convex from end to end. A few are quite convex; a few are flat and straight; and one is concave. As the blade is used, the edge acquires bifacially ground polish and striations running parallel to the cutting edge. There is a tendency for it to wear more rapidly at one end than at the other. And the working edge, which originally was parallel to the butt, begins to diverge in an increasingly rakish fashion. After considerable use, one side may be only half as long as the other (Figure 24c).

Notched knives vary in size. The smallest whole one is 152 by 108? by 10 mm; the largest, 190 by 140 by 12 mm. Several broken specimens probably were even larger than the latter. About one out of every three is without notches,but similar to the notched variety in shape. Their dimensions, especially thickness and length, tend to be smaller.

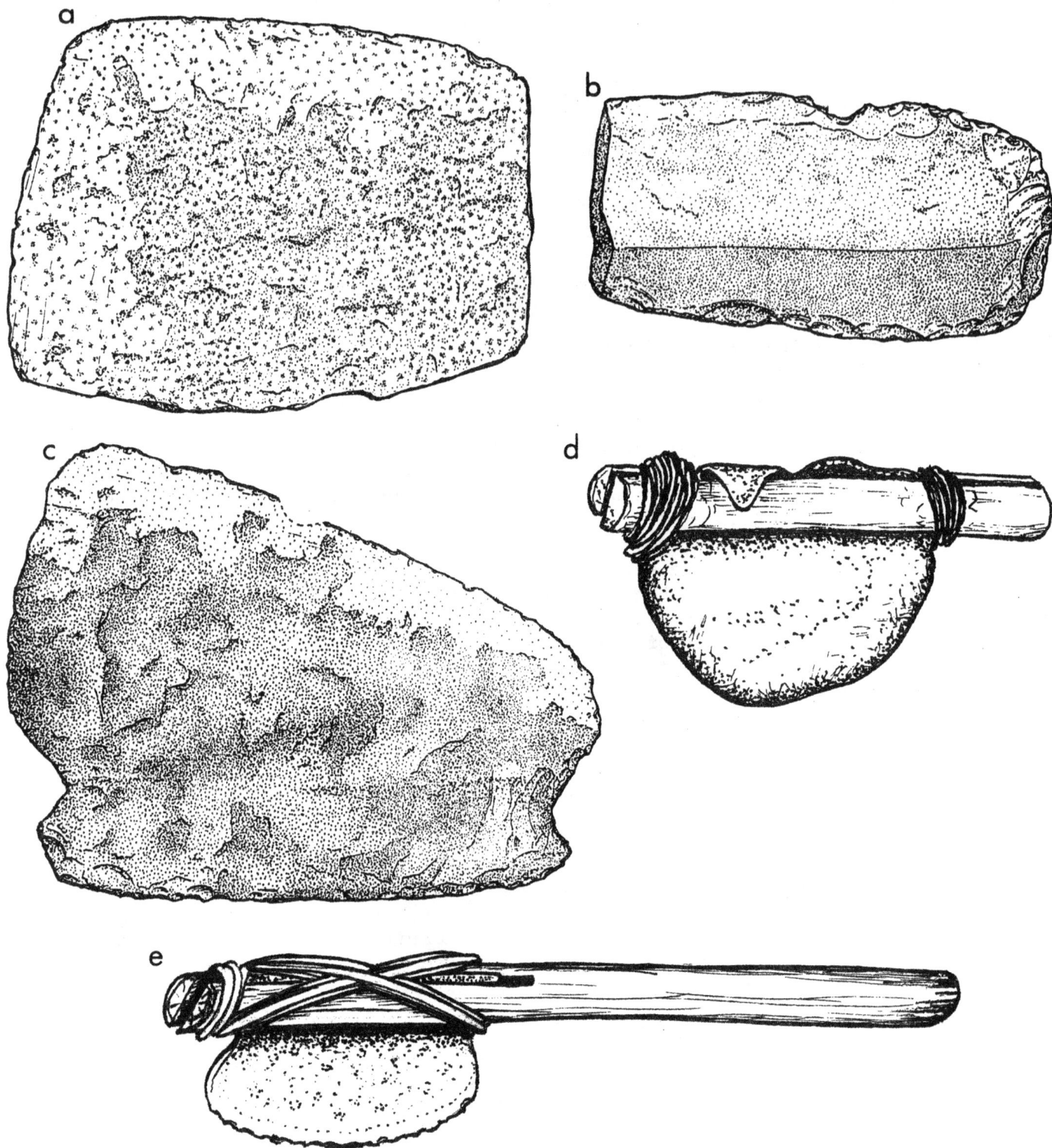

Figure 24. Mescal Knives.
a. Porphyry; Hagen Site, Room 2; 131 by 95 by 6mm; 84 gm.
b. Porphyry; Hagen Site, Surface; 117? by 60 by 12 mm; 108? gm.
c. Porphyry; Hagen Site, Room 5; 159 by 110 by 10 mm; 226 mg.
d. Early Historic Western Apache metal mescal knife bound with bailing wire. Collection, Arizona State Museum.
e. Circa 1440 hafting of the eared type of mescal knife reconstructed from an adobe mold at Gila Pueblo. The implement is hafted like a hatchet, but its serrated edge is used like a saw to remove agave leaves before the heart is roasted. The handle measured 40 cm.

Three of the 17 whole knives seem to constitute a slightly different variety (Figure 24b). They are somewhat shorter, only a little more than half as wide, and almost twice as thick as the other knives. One end on each is left unaltered; the remainder of the perimeter is bifacially chipped. A notch is chipped and ground into the approximate center of a longitudinal edge. On the opposite edge there is a second depression, considerably shallower than the first. The shallow notch is located 10 to 20 mm closer to the unaltered end than is the deep notch. The notches suggest that these three specimens were hafted.

Three knives come from the South Ruin: a fragment on the floor of Room S-1, a fragment in the fill of Room S-8, and a hatchet from the surface (Table 9). The other 27 were found at the North Ruin:

Surface - three fragments were on the surface.

Room 2 - six were in a pile on the east-central portion of the floor, near the south wall. Three are notched and three are notchless. Several feet to the north lay a hatchet. Elsewhere on the floor were an additional notched specimen and the nondescript fragment of a ninth mescal knife.

Room 3 - three were on the floor in a west-central location. One is a fragment; the other two are notched.

Room 5 - three notched mescal knives were stacked on the west end of the bench in front of a Tonto Polychrome jar.

Room 6 - two fragments were in the fill. Two fragments and two notched knives were on the floor; three of these were together against the west wall, about three feet from the southwest corner.

Room 7 - a notchless knife was on the floor.

Room 8 - a notchless knife and a hatchet were in the fill.

At Gila Pueblo proper, most of the mescal knives from the final Salado occupation were stored leaning against the south walls of habitation rooms. Mescal knives were a common occurrence in the Gila River drainage during late-prehistoric times. Hough (1930:8) emphasized "the many thin basalt blades found on the Blue and San Francisco Rivers." Haury (1945:134) says that mescal knives, slate palettes and three-quarter groove axes are "the most typical of the stone artifacts in the Gila-Salt region." The major difference between the mescal knives in our collection and those found elsewhere is the fact that most of the Hagen Site specimens were notched for hafting. Elsewhere, notching occurs much less frequently (Hough 1930:9). At Los Muertos, for example, "only about five per cent" of the thin, flat mescal knives are notched (Haury 1945:135). At the Hagen Site, between 70 and 75 percent are notched.

In addition to their use for cutting agave leaves, mescal knives would have been useful for many other tasks, such as the shelling of corn. During the summer of 1969, Jon excavated Room 17 in Unit Three of Pot Creek

Table 9. Hagen Site Stone Artifact Proveniences

PROVENIENCE

ARTIFACT	NORTH RUIN									SOUTH RUIN										UNK.	TOTALS
	Surface	Rm. 1	Rm. 2	Rm. 3	Rm. 5	Rm. 6	Rm. 7	Rm. 8	Total	Surface	Rm. S-1	Rm. S-2	Rm. S-3	Rm. S-4	Rm. S-5	Rm. S-6	Rm. S-8	Rm. S-9	Total		
CUTTING AND POUNDING TOOLS																					
Mescal Knives	3		9	3	3	6	1	2	27	1	1						1		3		30
Axes	10		11	2		3	1		17												17
Choppers			1	1		1		1	13	3	2					1			6		19
Hammerstones	12	3	1	1		2	1	2	19	15	3	3	1			2	1	1	26		45
Arrowheads		1				1			2												2
Knife		1								1									1		1
Scrapers	2	1		1		1		1	5	2	2		1						5	1	11
Scraper Planes	1		1						2	2									2		4
Shavers					1	1	1		2	1									1		3
Used Flakes	1	3	7	1		2	1	2	17	4	10	2	1		1	1	1	1	21		38
Flaking Anvils	2	1	3	3		2		1	11	3									3		14
Cores	22	4	1	1		1	1	1	31	7	9	3		1		2	2	2	25	1	57
Pottery Anvil							1		1												1

Table 9. Hagen Site Stone Artifact Proveniences, Continued

PROVENIENCE

ARTIFACT	NORTH RUIN									SOUTH RUIN										UNK.	TOTALS
	Surface	Rm. 1	Rm. 2	Rm. 3	Rm. 5	Rm. 6	Rm. 7	Rm. 8	Total	Surface	Rm. S-1	Rm. S-2	S-3	S-4	S-5	S-6	S-8	S-9	Total		
GRINDING AND RUBBING TOOLS																					
Metates	5	2			2	2			11	1[x]									1		12
Manos	10	5	7	2	4	13	4		45	2	1	2		1			1		7	1	53
Grinding Bases	3	2	3	2	3				13	3	1		1	1					6		19
Abraders	2	2		1		2			7	1									1		8
Shaft Tools	2								2												2
Pecking-Polishing Stones	4			1		1			6	2	1								3		9
Plumb Bob	1								1												1
FIREDOGS	2		1	5		1			9												9
LIDS	4						1		5	4									4		9
ORNAMENTAL AND RELIGIOUS OBJECTS																					
Plaque	1								1												1
Paint Pigments	2		1				1		4	2									2		6
Lightning Stone	1								1												1
Possible Fetishes	2					1			3	1									1		4

Table 9. Hagen Site Stone Artifact Proveniences, Continued

ARTIFACT	NORTH RUIN Surface	Rm. 1	Rm. 2	Rm. 3	Rm. 5	Rm. 6	Rm. 7	Rm. 8	Total	SOUTH RUIN Surface	Rm. S-1	S-2	S-3	S-4	S-5	S-6	S-8	S-9	Total	UNK.	TOTALS
UNCLASSIFIED OBJECTS	6	2	2	1	1	1			16	3	1						3		7	1	24
TOTALS	88	23	57	25	12	42	17	7	271	58	31	10	5	3	1	4	8	5	125	4	400*

x   Specimen actually was in the fill of the earth oven

.   Including a patty of grey hearth ash

*   The total of 400 stone tools is greater than the 368 pieces of worked stone because 26 tools are multi-purpose. For example, all but one of the pecked depressions used as flaking anvils are on the surfaces of other artifacts, especially manos.

Pueblo, which is located about 20 kilometers south of Taos in northern New Mexico. On the floor of the structure were bushels of corn that had been preserved when they were charred by the fire that destroyed the room. In one corner was a stack of unshelled corn. Immediately next to it was a mound of shelled kernels. With the kernels was a large, lanceolate-shaped knife of quartzite. Almost certainly the knife was used to shell corn. Its size is identical to that of the notchless mescal knives.

Axes. An ax is a chopping tool that is grooved for the attachment of a handle -- in contrast to a chopper, which is hand-held. All 17 Hagen Site axes had a three-quarter hafting groove (Figure 25). The smallest is 91 by 54 by 34 mm; the largest, 230 by 76 by 45 mm. They are pecked and ground from basalt or felsite cobbles. Maximum width and thickness normally occur just above the hafting groove. Most bits are lightly use-chipped and several are missing one or more large spalls (Figure 26a, b). But every bit is sharp and serviceable. Polls are not particularly battered. Hafting grooves vary from 21 to 45 mm in width, with a mean of 30 mm; depth varies from 4 to 10 mm. As would be expected, in general there is a direct correlation between ax length and the distance separating groove from poll. Grooves are deepest as they cross the outer edge and gradually decrease in depth as they cross the faces and approach the inner edge.

One ax is aberrant in that it has a raised shoulder, up to 10 mm in width, bordering the poll edge of the groove (Figure 26c). Another has a much narrower shoulder around the bit edge of the groove; it is created by a second groove which is considerably more shallow and narrow than the main hafting groove (Figure 26b). A second ax also has a narrow, shallow, secondary groove located just below the main groove. It is not as long as the major groove, covering only the outer portion of the left face. Another specimen has a second three-quarter groove located 10 to 15 mm above the major groove (Figure 26a). The secondary groove is fully as wide as the primary, but its depth is considerably shallower. It is especially curious in that it reverses the inner and outer edges. In order to have utilized the secondary groove for hafting, it would have been necessary to turn the ax upside down -- so that the original underside became the top and the top edge became the bottom. A single ax is double-bitted. Its hafting groove begins 43 mm from one bit and 52 mm from the other (Figure 25f).

All of the axes come from rooms in the North Ruin. Most were on the floors of their respective rooms:

Room 2	11
Room 3	2
Room 6	3
Room 7	1
	17

The 11 axes in Room 2 seem to be an abnormally high number. But it is not entirely unprecedented. Haury (1945:132, Plate 3a) reports nine in one room at Los Muertos -- a Hohokam site located about 110 kilometers west of Gila Pueblo and contemporary with it. And Moorehead (1906:97) found 22 in one room at another contemporaneous ruin near Phoenix.

Haury (1945:134) says that the three-quarter ax is one of the diagnostic "stone artifacts in the Gila-Salt region." At Los Muertos all 80 axes recovered were three-quarter groove. North of Gila Pueblo, during Pueblo IV

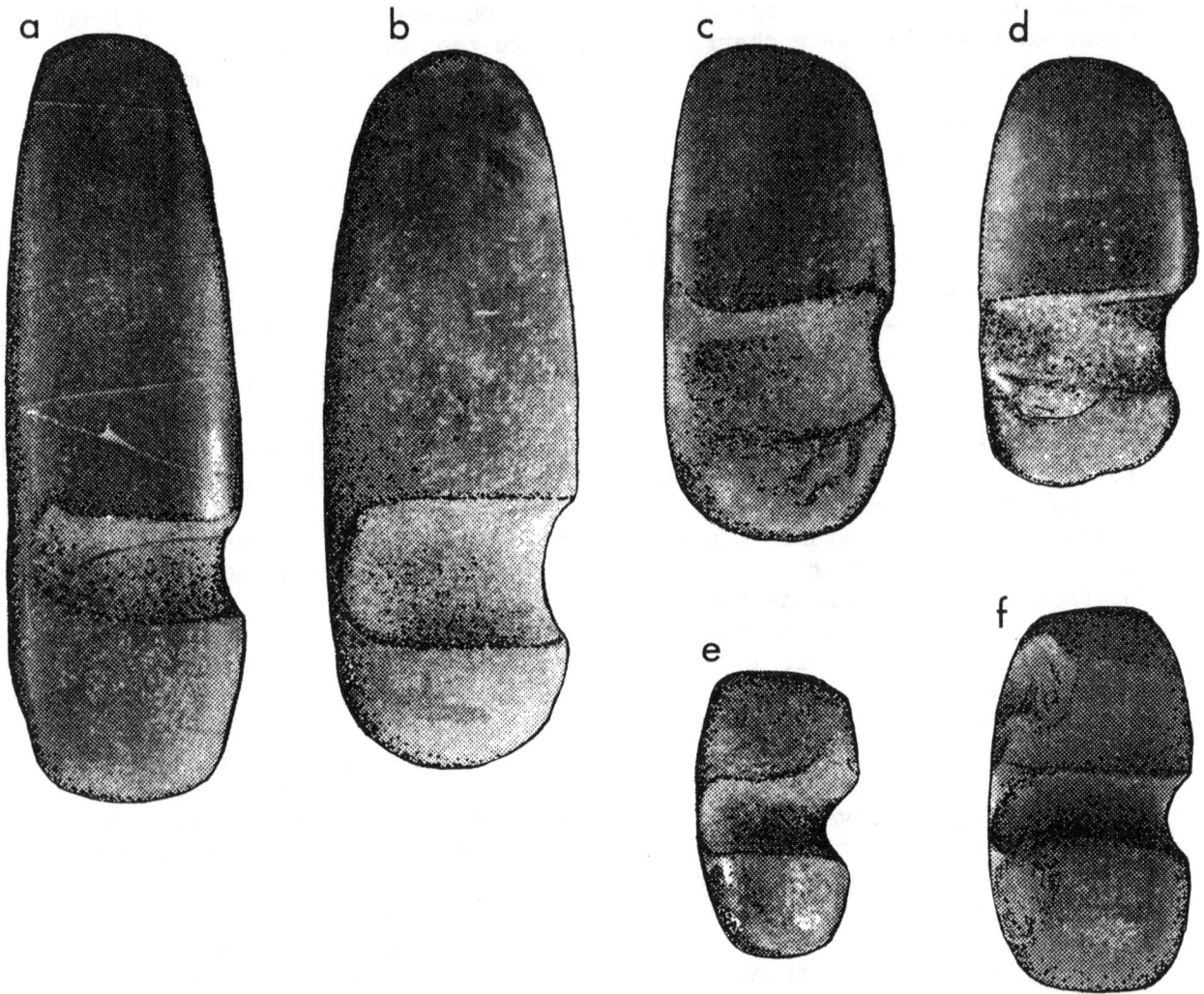

Figure 25. Axes.
a. Basalt; 230 by 76 by 45 mm; 1,416 gm; Hagen Site, Room 2; Southwest Archeological and Conservation Center catalog no. S1895/47.
b. Felsite, 212 by 81 by 53 mm; 1,385 gm; Hagen Site, Room 2; Southwest Archeological and Conservation Center catalog no. S1896/47.
c. Basalt; 146 by 75 by 52 mm; 527 gm; Hagen Site, Room 3; Southwest Archeological and Conservation Center catalog no. S2019/47.
d. Basalt; 128 by 69 by 40 mm.; 546 gm; Hagen Site, Room 2; Southwest Archeological and Conservation Center catalog no. S1894/47.
e. Basalt; 91 by 54 by 34 mm; 233 gm; Hagen Site, Room 2; Southwest Archeological and Conservation Center catalog no. S2018/47.
f. Basalt; 120 by 69 by 29 mm; 382 gm; Hagen Site, Room 3; Southwest Archeological and Conservation Center catalog no. S2020/47. Small, double-bitted axes of this type are now considered by many to be insignia of rank rather than tools.

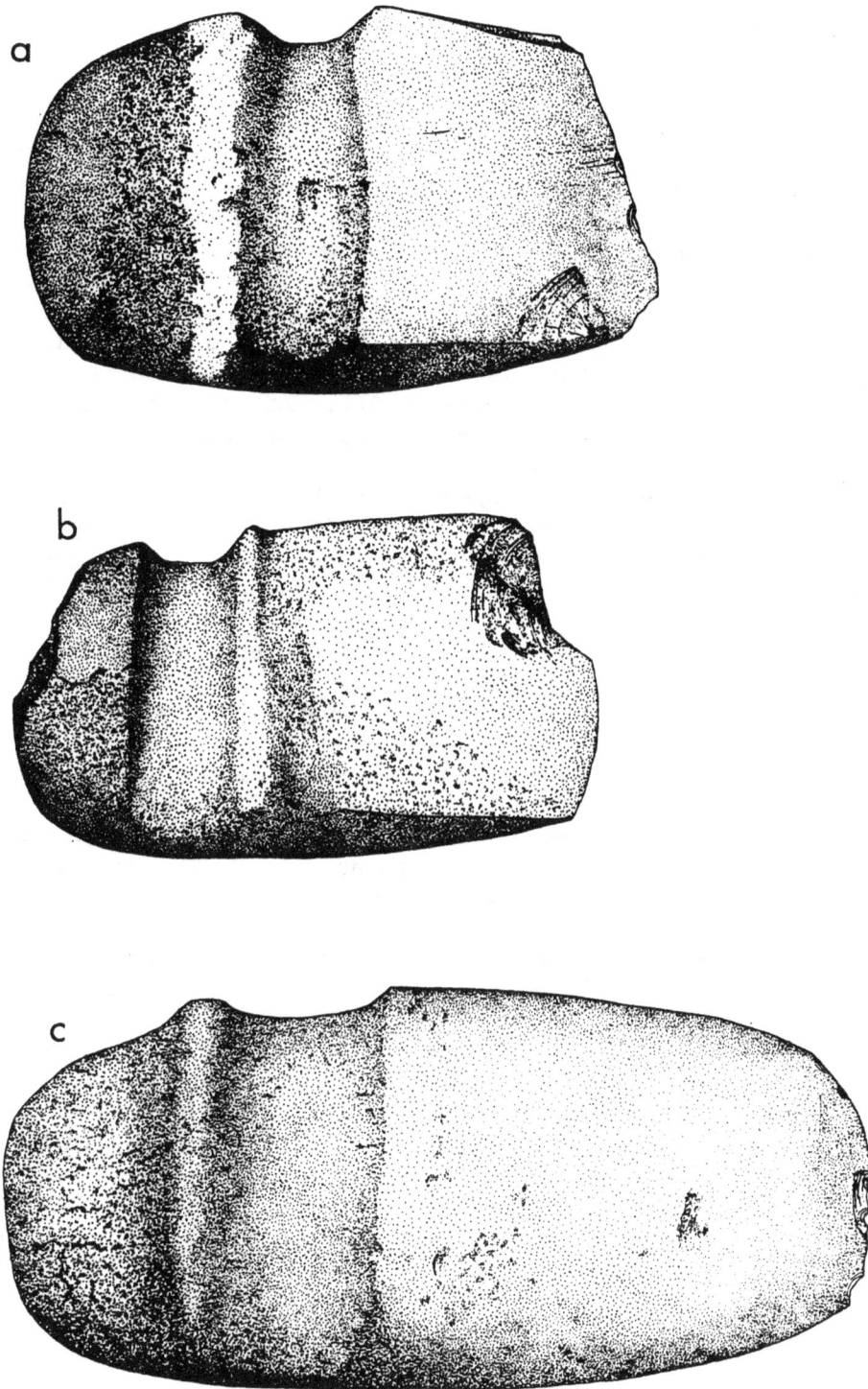

Figure 26. Aberrant Three-Quarter Grooves.
a. Basalt; 127 by 73 by 53 mm; 745 gm; Hagen Site, Room 3; Southwest Archeological and Conservation Center catalog no. S1877/47.
b. Basalt?; 117 by 64 by 46 mm; 529 mg; Hagen Site, Room 2; Southwest Archeological and Conservation Center catalog no. S1876/47.
c. Basalt; 168 by 77 by 54 mm; 1,045 gm; Hagen Site, Room 2; Southwest Archaeological and Conservation Center catalog no. S2021/47.

times, three-quarter-groove axes were plentiful at Awatovi (Woodbury 1954:27-36) and at Homolovi and Hawikuh (Reed 1950:131, 135). Whereas at Los Muertos all axes were three-quarter groove, north of Gila Pueblo hafting grooves were not exclusively three-quarter. In Pueblo IV contexts at Awatovi, for example, along with 22 three-quarter groove axes recovered were 16 full-groove axes (Woodbury 1954:27-37, Table 3). On the far eastern edge of the Pueblo area -- at Pecos and Gran Quivira -- three-quarter groove axes were extremely rare or nonexistent (Kidder 1932, Hayes et al. 1981:106).

Raised shoulders bordering the hafting groove are "rare in Gila axes, except for those dating from the late Pioneer and early Colonial Periods" (Haury 1945:131-132), which is almost a thousand years earlier than the occupation of the Hagen Site (Dean 1990). At Los Muertos none of the 80 three-quarter groove axes are shouldered. At Awatovi, one of the 22 axes is shouldered below the groove. In the Hagen Site assemblage, one of the 17 three-quarter groove axes is shouldered above the groove and another is shouldered below the groove. And one of the axes recovered by the students at Gila Pueblo is shouldered. Perhaps these shouldered specimens from Gila Pueblo and the Hagen Site were heirlooms salvaged from the Pioneer Period pithouse village located northeast of Gila Pueblo.

It is our belief that small, double-bitted axes well may have been badges of office or weapons of war or both, rather than utilitarian. Wherever they occur -- at Los Muertos, Awatovi, Besh-ba-gowah, and Gila Pueblo; for examples -- double-bitted axes tend to be smaller than companion single-bitted. In addition to being small in size, wherever they occur, they also tend to be relatively few in number. At Los Muertos 10 of the 80 axes are double-bitted; at Awatovi, one of 22; and at the Hagen Site, one of 17. Two double-bitted axes were recovered at Gila Pueblo proper: one was on the floor of Room 105 and the other was on the floor of Room 106. Both occurrences of the double-bitted axes at Gila Pueblo proper were associated with high status or foci of ceremonial artifacts or both. The one on the floor of Room 105 was in the possession of a high-status male at the time of his death.

Choppers. Choppers are hand-held axes. Because choppers are not hafted, their butts, which fit against the user's palm, are broad. In addition to not being hafted, choppers differ from axes in the way in which their working edge is produced. The bit of most axes is ground; that of choppers is flaked. Although most choppers have a bifacially-worked bit, seven of the 19 Hagen Site specimens have unifacial bits. More choppers are basalt than all of the other materials combined:

basalt	10
quartzite	4
quartz	2
granite	1
porphyry	1
quartzitic sandstone	1
	19

The smallest is 69 by 47 by 24 mm and weighs 96 gm. The largest is 165 by 151 by 52 mm and weighs 1,658 gm. Both are basalt. Mean measurements are 90 by 76 by 48 mm and 503 gm.

Many seem to have served more than one function. Some almost certainly were cores before they became choppers. Others look as though they were used as hammerstones. And one appears to be a hammerstone-flaking anvil, as well as a chopper. Most were surface finds. Six come from the South Ruin, including one in the fill and one on the floor of Room S-1 and one on the floor of Room S-6. At the North Ruin one was in the fill of Room 2, one in the fill of Room 3, and one on the floor of Room 6.

<u>Hammerstones</u>. Hammerstones are hand-held hammers. There are 45 in the Hagen Site collection:

basalt	24
quartzite	12
quartz	7
quartzitic sandstone	1
sandstone	1
	45

They range in size from the smallest; which is quartz, measures 65 by 42 by 36 mm, and weighs 109 gm -- to the largest; which also is quartz, measures 101 by 95 by 92 mm, and weighs 1,177 gm.

Hammerstones served many purposes. They were used to drive stakes, dress stone, roughen metates, and peck hafting grooves around stone axes. Because many of these tasks are accomplished most efficiently by sharp, angular edges and points; most of the Hagen Site hammerstones probably are reused cores. More than half of them are surface finds. And more than half of them come from the South Ruin, including three that were found in Room S-1 along with many cores and used flakes. In Room 6 a hammerstone was found pressed into the side of a posthole in the floor. Evidently the final use of the artifact was as a shim bracing the post in that hole.

<u>Arrowheads</u>. Two arrowheads were recovered. Both are small, triangular, chipped allover, side-notched, and come from the North Ruin. One is a thin, elongated specimen of chalcedony with a concave base (Figure 27b). It was found on the floor of Room 1. The other is compact, has an essentially straight base, is obsidian, and lay on the floor of Room 6 (Figure 27c). Similar small, triangular, side-notched arrowheads are a common occurrence in late-prehistoric contexts, especially throughout the Southwest, but also on the Plains and elsewhere.

Arrowheads are conspicuous by their low frequency at the Hagen Site. When Shiner (1961:6) excavated Room 97 at Gila Pueblo, he recovered six "projectile points." His six from a single rooms seems to be an abnormal abundance, just as a total of two arrowheads from the entire Hagen Site seems to be an abnormally small number.

<u>Knife</u>. There is one knife from the Hagen Site (Figure 28). It has a plano-convex plan. The plane edge is a thick butt; the remainder of the perimeter is bifacially chipped to a thin cutting edge. Both faces are chipped allover. The material may be Alibates flint. Neither the material

54

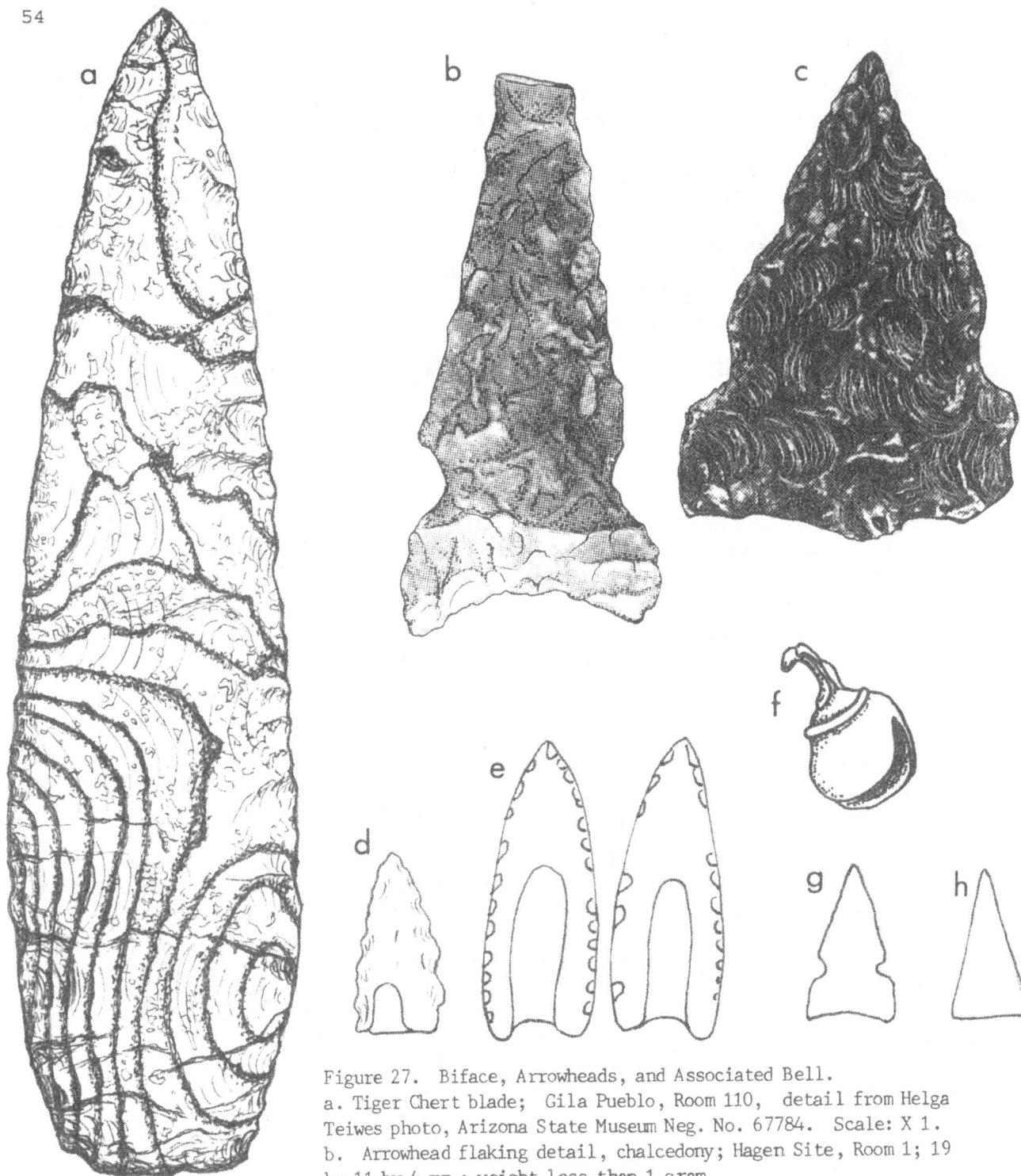

Figure 27. Biface, Arrowheads, and Associated Bell.
a. Tiger Chert blade; Gila Pueblo, Room 110, detail from Helga Teiwes photo, Arizona State Museum Neg. No. 67784. Scale: X 1.
b. Arrowhead flaking detail, chalcedony; Hagen Site, Room 1; 19 by 11 by 4 mm.; weight less than 1 gram.
c. Arrowhead flaking detail, obsidian; Hagen Site, Room 6; 17 by 13 by 4 mm.; weight less than 1 gram.
d. Fluted point, chert; Gila Pueblo, Room 101, subfloor. Scale: X 1.
e. Two views of fluted point found in medicine pouch of high status male; Gila Pueblo, Room 102, roof. Scale: X 1.
f. Copper bell found in medicine pouch with (e); Gila Pueblo, Room 102, roof. Scale X 1.
g. Profile of arrowhead typical of local manufacture, thick in cross section, most commonly obsidian like this example; Gila Pueblo, Room 100, fill. Scale: X 1.
h. Arrowhead typical of non-local manufacture associated with A.D. 1260 and 1440 raids, thin in cross-section, all chert; Gila Pueblo, Room 99, roof. Scale: X 1.

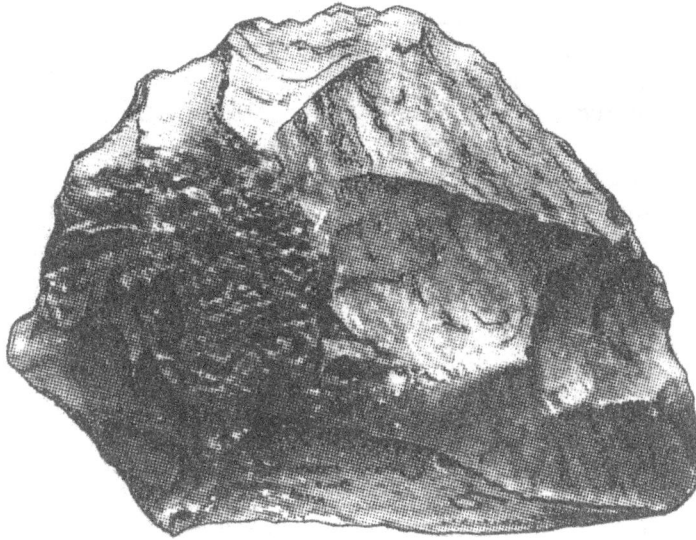

Figure 28. Knife.
    Flint; 35 by 14 mm.; 10 gm.; Hagen Site, South Ruin, surface; Western
Archeological and Conservation Center catalog no. S1880/47.

nor the form are typically Southwestern. Both have a Plains flavor. The
artifact is somewhat reminiscent of the core knives of Gran Quivira and the
Bristol bifaces of northeastern Texas and adjacent areas (Duffield
1963:43-45, Figure 13C-H; Hayes et al. 1981:110, Figure 134e-h). It was
found on the surface of the South Ruin.

    Lance Point. Although no large bifaces were recovered from excavations
at the Hagen Site, one was found in the ceremonial/redistribution Room 110 at
Gila Pueblo proper. We believe that it was a lance point, because it was
just 16 inches from the hand of the adult male, who lay unburied on the
floor. The artifact was still in use at the end of the Salado occupation,
perhaps as late as A.D. 1440. The blade of wood-grain tiger chert is 4 cm at
is widest and 19 cm in length (27a). It is similar to other wood-grain
blades, or fragments thereof, recovered from the Cutter Ruin, the Safford
area, and Point of Pines to the east; Kinishba to the northeast; Q Ranch
Pueblo to the north; and the Gipe Site to the northwest (John C. Whittaker,
personal communication 8/15/86). A biface from the Henderson Site near
Roswell also may belong with this assemblage. All of the well-provenienced
specimens appear to date from the 1300s or from the early 1400s. All appear
to be made from tiger chert, which is found in southwestern Wyoming and
northwestern Colorado (Ferg 1988:214-218).

    Scrapers. The traditional distinction made between knives and
scrapers -- knives have bifacial working edges, scrapers are unifacial -- is
not entirely arbitrary. It is based upon the characteristics of the two
edges. The prime requisite of a knife is that it cuts. And it cuts
precisely because it is bifacial. When scraping a hide or a yucca leaf,

the object is not to cut, so a unifacial working edge is chosen. An edge
beveled on only one side seldom makes a straight cut, because it has a
tendency to drift away from the bevel.

There are 11 scrapers in the Hagen Site collection:

basalt	3
chert	3
quartz	2
jasper	1
obsidian	1
quartzite	1
	11

They range in size from a tiny piece of quartz, 15 by 14 by 1 mm and weighing
1 gm, to the jasper scraper: 62 by 56 by 32 mm and 70 gm. Most measurements
are close to the means: 40 by 32 by 16 mm and 21 gm. Six are made on flakes
or spalls. Five are reused cores, including both the largest and the
smallest specimens. Based upon our small universe of 11 scrapers, scrapers
were relatively common at the South Ruin; this especially is true of flake
scrapers (Table 10).

Scraper Planes. A scraper plane is a core or spall with a flat basal
surface that terminates in a steeply-beveled, prepared edge (Figure 29a).
Use-polish and striations on the base lead back from the prepared edge and
indicate that scraper planes were used with a reciprocal motion. Haury
(1975:207-209, Figure 28, Table 14) believes that similar artifacts from

Table 10. Hagen Site Scraper Proveniences.

	Core Scrapers	Flake Scrapers	Totals
North Ruin	3	2	5
South Ruin	1	4	5
Provenience Unknown	1	0	1
Totals	5	6	11

Ventana Cave were used in working hides and preparing "certain plant foods."
Another possibility is that they were used in woodworking (Hayes et al.
1981:112).

The Hagen Site specimens are small The smallest is 54 by 47 by 20 mm
and weighs 54 gm.; the largest is 87 by 54 by 46 mm and weighs 237 gm. All
are basalt. Two come from the South Ruin. They were found together. With
them were a core and a scraper. The core, scraper, and two scraper planes
are blue-gray basalt; quite possibly all four artifacts were struck from the
same block of raw material. The other two scraper planes come from the North
Ruin; one was a surface fine, and the other was in Room 2.

Shavers. A shaver is a small artifact whose working edge is concave
(Figure 29b). Presumably it is used something like a drawknife in the
shaving and smoothing of shafts, although Cosner (1956:300) emphatically

57

Figure 29. Scraper Plane and Shaver.
a. Felsite?; 87 by 54 by 46 mm.; 237 gm.; Hagen Site, Room 2; Western Archeological
and Conservation Center catalog no. S1885/47.
b. Basalt; 59 by 51 by 17 mm.;   48 gm.; Hagen Site, South Ruin, surface; Western
Archeological and Conservation Center catalog no. S1910/47.

58

believes that this type of artifact was not used for shaving and scraping but rather "in cutting reed cane for arrowshafts." Irwin and Wormington (1970:29, Figure 2:28-29) suggest that Paleo-Indian "notches," which bear some resemblance to shavers, "are useful for scraping cylindrical objects and also for shredding vegetal fibers."

Two of the three Hagen Site specimens are made on basalt spalls about 50 mm in length and width and about 15 mm thick. One end of each is unifacially chipped into a working edge 25 to 30 mm wide and 5 mm deep. One working edge is fresh and sharp; the other, dulled from use. The sharp shaver comes from the floor of Room 7. The dull specimen was found on the surface of the South Ruin -- along with a scraper and a number of spalls, some of which are used flakes. The shaver, scraper, and used flakes all may have been struck from the same core. The third shaver is smaller than the other two, made of chert, comes from Room 6, and still has a sharp working edge.

Used Flakes. When a flake is used for cutting or scraping, there is a tendency for shallow, irregular chips to pop-off along the working edge. There is a total of 38 used flakes in the collection from the Hagen Site:

chert	12	quartzite	3	quartz	2	mudstone	1
basalt	9	jasper	2	chalcedony	1	sandstone	1
flint	3	obsidian	2	epidote	1	siltstone and	
						quartzitic sandstone	1
							38

Five of the used flakes have edges that are dulled and rounded-over -- like the "edge-abraided" flakes from Anasazi sites which Wheeler (1965) believes were used to cut and saw sandstone and which Wylie (1975) thinks were used to scrape pottery.

A seemingly disproportionate number of used flakes have South Ruin proveniences: 21 of 38. This especially is true of those with the rounded edges: four of the five are from the South Ruin. Several concentrations of used flakes occurred. At the North Ruin seven were found on the floor or Room 2. At the South Ruin many clustered in and about Room S-1. On or near the floor of that room were 10 used flakes, a hammerstone, four cores, a tool reject, a flake scraper, and many unused spalls. Most of these objects appear to have come from the same piece of basalt. Nearby, on the surface of the ground, were several other used flakes, a shaver, a scraper, and some unused spalls; all of the specimens in this cluster could have come from a single basalt core.

Flaking Anvils. Often referred to as a pitted stone or nut stone in previous literature, a flaking anvil is a stone with one or more small, shallow, conical, or concave depressions pecked into its surface (Figure 30). The depression is used as a seat in the bipolar flaking of cores and may be produced either intentionally or incidental to use or both (Honea 1965). Fourteen flaking anvils came from the Hagen Site: sandstone 96), basalt 93), granite (2), quartzite (2), and quartz (1). Depressions vary in size from 10 mm in diameter and little measureable depth to diameters of 25 to 30 mm and depths of 3 mm. All but one of the depressions are on reused or multi-purpose artifacts. And all are small enough to be held comfortably in one hand. Most are manos, cores, and hammerstones. Two chopper-hammerstones have these depressions. One depression is in the middle of the top of a the

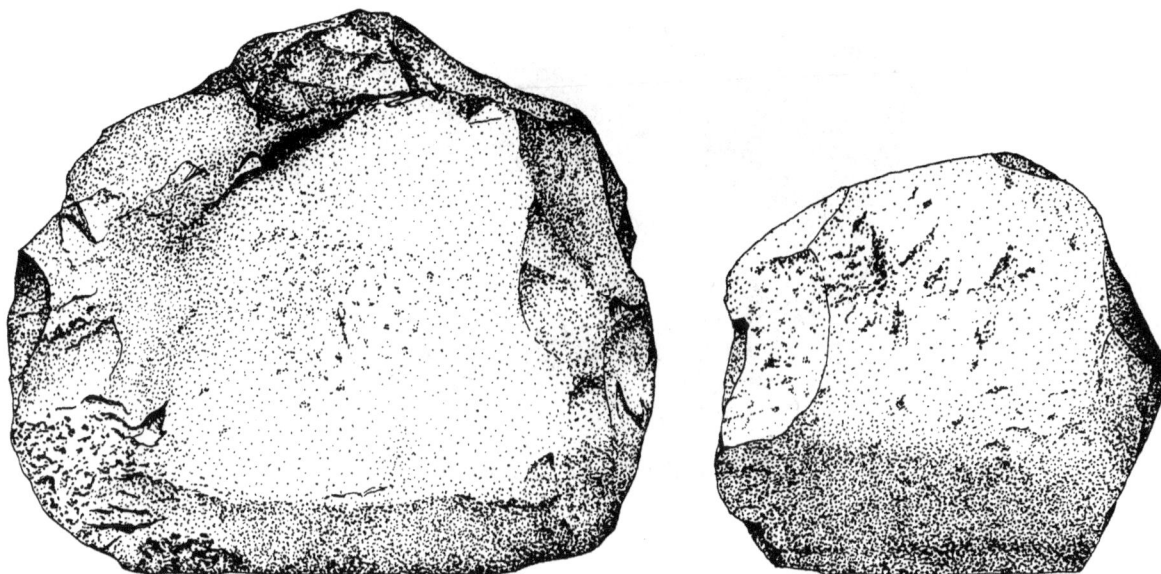

Figure 30. Flaking Anvils.
a. Sandstone; Hagen Site, Room 3; 62 by 58 by 46 mm.; 191 gm.
b. Basalt; Hagen Site, surface; 86 by 73 by 46 mm.; 3,812 gm.

handle of a pottery anvil, and another is in the center of the face of the same artifact (Figure 31). In the center of the floor of Room 3 were a grinding base and a one-hand mano (Figure 32b). In the center of the reverse surface of the grinding base is one anvil depression. And there are two depressions on the mano, one in the middle of the smaller and less-used of the two grinding faces, and one in the center of what probably is the leading edge.

Cores. A core is a block or cobble of stone from which flakes are struck. Fifty-seven were recovered at the Hagen Site; most are of fine-grained igneous materials:

basalt	23	quartzitic sandstone	4	sandstone	2
felsite	7	chalcedony	3	jasper	2
quartzite	7	chert	2	porphyry	1
quartz	4	obsidian	2		57

The smallest is 23 by 16 by 11 mm and weighs 2 gm. The largest is 108 by 92 by 90 mm and weighs 1,032 gm. About one in five have high points dulled or perimeters battered opposite striking platforms in such a manner as to indicate that they were worked by bi-polar percussion on flaking anvils. Many of these cores are multi-purpose tools: one is a used flake, two saw service as flaking anvils, five are scrapers, and seven were used for chopping or hammering or both. Cores were relatively abundant at the South Ruin, especially in Room S-1.

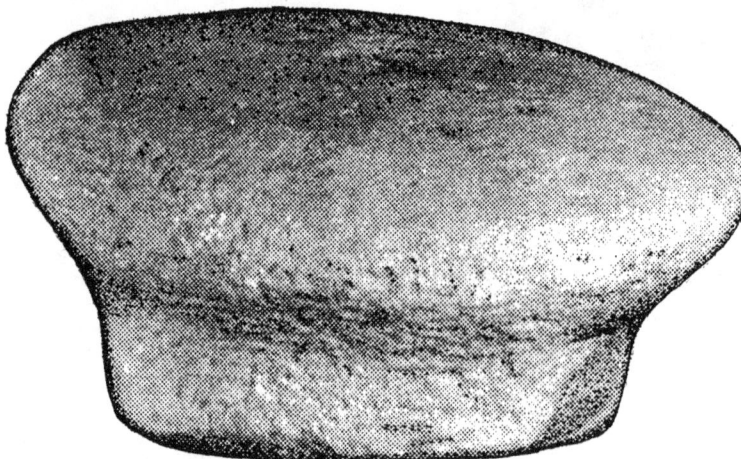

Figure 31. Pottery Anvil.
Sandstone; 103 by 97 by 55 mm.; Hagen Site, Room 7; Western Archeological and Conservation Center catalog no. S1911/47.

Pottery Anvil. The only pottery anvil recovered at the Hagen Site was lying on the floor of Room 6 (Figure 31). It has a mushroom shape, is carefully pecked and ground from a piece of sandstone, measures 103 by 91 by 55 mm., and weighs 580 gm. Maximum length and width are at the working surface, which is quite convex along both axes. In the center of both the face and the butt of the handle there is a flaking-anvil depression. Shape and dimensions are similar to those of a "grooved handstone" from Snaketown, a Hohokam site that lies 110-120 kilometers west-southwest of Gila Pueblo and was several hundred years earlier in time (Gladwin et al. 1937:Plate 45f). The size also is identical to that of pottery anvils used by modern Pimas (Russell 1908:126).

Grinding and Rubbing Tools.

Metates. A metate is a nether milling stone. Five whole and seven fragmentary specimens came from the Hagen Site. All are granite and all are trough metates (Figure 32). With the exception of the grinding area depressed into the major face, the boulders from which the metates are made appear to be little altered from their natural state. Most are lightly pecked, usually around the perimeter. One base was ground in order to flatten and steady it; another was spalled for the same reasons. Mean dimensions for the four whole specimens are 445 by 314 by 120 mm. One fragmentary metate has a length of at least 480 mm and a thickness of at least 190 mm. Another fragment has a width of at least 375 mm.
Seven of the eight metates for which it is possible to make absolute determinations have grinding depressions that are open at both ends. The other is closed at the proximal end. Grinding surfaces are concave along both axes. The longitudinal concavity tends to be quite pronounced, in most cases about 30 mm in depth. Width of the depressions on the four whole metates varies from 190 to 230 mm; depths, from 30 to 60 mm. Depression

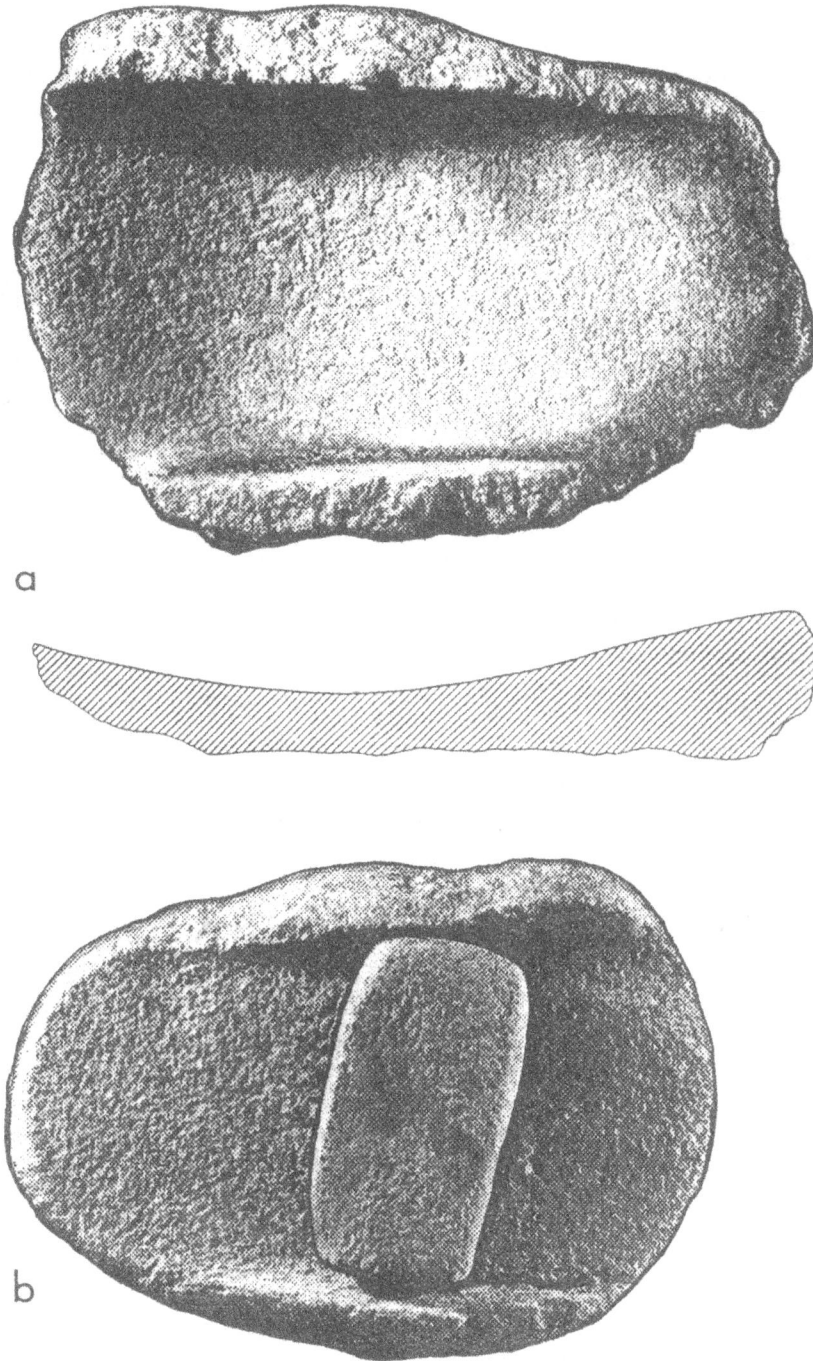

Figure 32. Trough Metates and Mano.
a. Metate; granite; 474 by 318 by 103 mm.; 14,325 gm.; Hagen Site, Room 6; Western Archeological and Conservation Center catalog no. S1970/47.
b. Mano; granite; 208 by 118 by 41 mm.; 2,028 gm.; Hagen Site, Room 5; Western Archeological and Conservation Center catalog no. S1969/47.
   Metate; granite; 465 by 325 by 144 mm.; Hagen Site, Room 5; Western Archeological Center catalog no. S1968/47.

depth in one fragmentary specimen is at least 122 mm. Depression walls are
not vertical. They slope inward from top to bottom. In several instances
the slant is gradual; but on one fragmentary specimen it is so exagerated
that the top of the grinding depression may have been as much as 120 mm wider
than the bottom.

In longitudinal section, the downward slope of the grinding depression
is gentle for the first 70 to 140 mm (Figure 32a). The length of the easy
pitch is directly related to the overall length of the depression. At the
end of the gentle slope the depression makes an abrupt descent to the level
of maximum depth, stays at that level for about 100 mm, and then gently
begins to rise as it approaches the distal end. On those specimens upon
whose surfaces the pecked roughening is not fresh, it can clearly be seen
that the outward grinding stroke ends about 350 mm from where it begins.
Shoulders bordering the sides of the grinding depressions seldom are even
approximately flat. Most are quite convex. Right shoulders tend to be
slightly wider than left shoulders. Most shoulders are 45 to 50 mm wide; the
widest is 105 mm.

The only metate found at the South Ruin is a fragment from the fill of
the earth oven. At the North Ruin:

1. Four fragments are surface finds, including the metate whose
    proximal end is closed.

2. One whole and one fragmentary metate were in the fill of Room 3.

3. A fragment was reused as a building stone in the common wall shared
    by Room 3 and Room 5.

4. At Room 5 a metate fragment was in the fill and a whole specimen
    was on the floor. With the whole metate were two manos -- one of
    which exactly fits the grinding depression (Figure 32b). The other
    mano is somewhat smaller. Room 5 had burned. On the floor was a
    10 to 15 mm layer of charred twigs and other roofing materials.
    The manos and the metate -- lying on its side -- were on top of the
    burned roofing material, indicating that they were on the roof when
    the room burned and suggesting that grinding activities took place
    on the roof.

At Gila Pueblo proper, most metates were located on roofs. One, located
on the roof of Room 98, gives us an intimate glimpse into the mechanics of
grinding. At the 1440 destruction of Gila Pueblo a young mother with an
infant and small child in her arms died on her knees, slumped over her
metate. To her right was a jar containing the charred remains of shelled
corn. On the metate were a mano and charred corn meal, which was in the
process of being turned from coarse meal into fine. Finished, finely-ground
meal, had fallen into a small, shallow bowl placed directly below the lower
lip of the metate.

Manos. A mano is the upper grinding stone used on a metate. Forty-one
whole and 12 fragmentary specimens came from the Hagen Site. Most are
granite 22) and sandstone (17). The remainder are basalt (4), diorite (4),
gneiss (4), dacite (1), and schist (1). There are two types of manos in the

collection: trough and one-hand. The basic difference between the two types is that the ends of the trough manos acquire a polished, convex cant as they rub against the walls of the grinding depression. The ends of the one-hand manos are not canted. There are a number of other noticeable differences -- including size, shape, and material of manufacture. Thirty-seven of the Hagen Site manos are trough and 13 are one-hand. Two others are broken trough specimens that were reused as one-hand manos. We were not able to identify the type of the remaining mano.

Trough Manos. Trough Manos are made of granite (21), sandstone (9), diorite (3), basalt (2), dacite (10, and gneiss (1). All were pecked to shape. But in many instances the alterations were minimal and the original, irregular shape of the natural cobble remains virtually unchanged. The smallest measures 147 by 108 by 33 mm. and weighs 808 gm. The largest is 244 by 140 by 100 mm; most of one corner is missing, so its present weight of 6,351 gm is less than its weight when last used. Mean measurements for 29 whole specimens are 194 by 104 by 56 mm. In no instance is there more than a single grinding surface on any major face and only rarely were both major faces on a single specimen used for grinding. Most grinding surfaces are convex along both axes, especially the longitudinal axis. A few surfaces are flat. As they moved back and forth in the grinding depression, mano ends were not parallel to the sides of the depression. As a consequence the grinding and polishing of the canted ends was not uniform from edge to edge. Rather, it was considerably more pronounced near the leading edge of the right end and near the trailing edge of the left end (Figure 33). This almost certainly indicates that manos primarily were held in and guided by the left hand.

About a third of the Hagen Site specimens have pecked finger grips. In some instances the grips are in only the leading or trailing edge; most often they are in both edges (Figure 34). Usually these grips are oblong, about 40 mm in length and 25-30 mm in width, and located in the center of the edge. But almost every conceivable variation occurs. The width of several is the same as the width of the edge on which they are situated. On one mano, not only has the entire width of both edges been used but so also has the entire length; in transverse section this mano is a truncated pyramid.

Excluding an unused mano blank from consideration, there appear to be two varieties of trough manos: regular (29) and crusher (8). Crushers are distinguished from ordinary manos primarily by virtue of being considerably thicker and heavier (Figure 34, Table 11). They also tend to be slightly longer and wider. They are made of the same materials as regular trough manos and their proveniences are the same. In every room in which a crusher variety was found, so also was at least one regular trough mano (Table 12). These facts should not be taken to indicate that the two varieties simply represent two stages of use: crushers being relatively newly-made and little-used and the regular variety being old, much-used, and well-worn. While the crushers appear to be new and little-used, so do some of the regular variety. Many of the regular variety never were much bigger than their present size. Elsewhere we have gone into greater detail documenting the fact that crushers are a separate variety of mano (Hayes et al. 1981:117).

Figure 33. Diagonal Bias of Trough Mano Ends.
   Mano; granite; 208 by 118 by 41 mm.; 2,028 gm.; Hagen Site, Room 5; Western Archeological and Conservation Center catalog no. S1969/47.

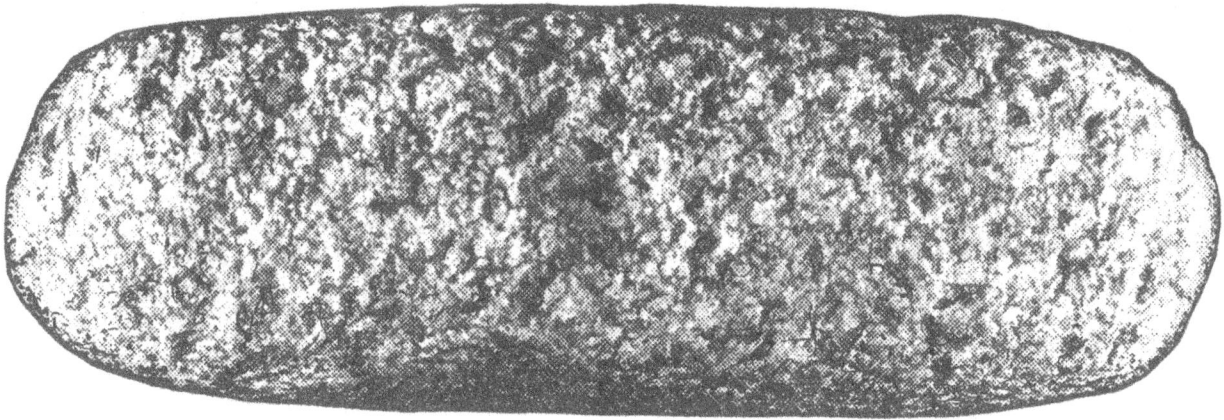

Figure 34. Crusher Variety of Trough Mano.
Granite; 281 by 118 by 91 mm.; 1,843 gm.; Hagen Site, North Ruin, surface; Western Archeological and Conservation Center catalog no. S1990/47.

Table 11. Hagen Site Trough Manos: Comparative Measurements of Regular Variety and Crusher Variety.

TROUGH MANOS

	Regular Variety (23 specimens)	Crusher Variety (6 specimens)
Mean Length	185 mm	226 mm
Length Range	146-253 mm	194-281 mm
Mean Width	100 mm	117 mm
Width Range	91-118 mm	102-140 mm
Mean Thickness	47 mm	92 mm
Thickness Range	32-73 mm	71-100 mm
Mean Weight	1,620 gm	4,488 gm
Weight Range	808-2,729 gm	3,173-6,351 gm

One-Hand Manos. Six of the one-hand manos recovered at the Hagen Site are sandstone, two are granite, two are basalt; one each are dacite, diorite, and schist. The smallest is 85 by 77 by 74 mm and weighs 418 gm.; the largest is 115 by 106 by 82 mm and weighs 1,460 gm. Mean measurements are 108 by 84 by 58 mm and 837 gm. The grinding surfaces of four whole manos are convex along both axes; three have flat faces, and the remaining two have concave faces. Both major faces of three specimens were used for grinding; but on two of these, the second face was used quite sparingly. Only a single one-hand mano has a finger grip. The perimeters of most are lightly battered.

Table 12. Hagen Site Mano Proveniences

PROVENIENCE

MANO TYPE	North Ruin							South Ruin					Unknown	TOTALS
	Surface	Rm. 1	Rm. 2	Rm. 3	Rm. 5	Rm. 6	Rm. 7	Surface	Rm. S-1	Rm. S-2	Rm. S-4	Rm. S-9		
Trough, regular variety	6	2	3		3	11	2					1	1	29
reused as one-hand						1								1
Trough, crusher variety	2	1			1	1	1	1	1					8
reused as one-hand							1							1
One-Hand	3	3	2	1				1		2	1			13
Unclassified	1													1
TOTALS	10	7	6	1	4	13	4	2	1	2	1	1	1	53

Discussion. A basic difference between Hagen Site trough manos and one-hand manos is that the latter lack the distinctive, polished, canted ends which characterize trough manos. At least some of the one-hand manos almost certainly were used on trough metates but were so short that their ends did not rub against the walls of the depression and did not become canted. One-hand manos may have been used primarily with grinding bases. A grinding base and one-hand mano found together on the floor of Room 3 in the North Ruin are illustrated in Figure 35. It also is likely that all three kinds of manos were used on a single metate. It is possible that corn grinding was at least a three-step process with crusher-variety trough manos used in the first step, regular-variety in the intermediate , and one-hand in the final. Or, perhaps, the lightly-battered perimeters of one-hand manos are the result of their having been used to crack kernels at the very beginning of the grinding process, in much the same manner that Cushing observed at Zuni in 1881 (Green 1990:203). Most trough manos are granite; a few are sandstone. Exactly the reverse is true of one-hand manos. Material of manufacture may be a correlate of size and shape: one-hand manos tend to be round and smaller; trough manos are more oblong and larger. The difference in materials may indicate slightly different functions and tends to substantiate the suggestion that one-hand manos were used with grinding bases.

Two of the six whole crusher-variety trough manos are too long to have been used with any of the four whole metates recovered. The longest crusher is 281 mm; the widest metate grinding depression is only 230 mm. Hayes and Lancaster (1975:154-156) do not consider crushers to be manos in the conventional sense of the term.

Most of the manos found in rooms were on the floors of those structures. As mentioned previously, at least two of the trough manos on the floor of Room 5 almost certainly were on the roof when it burned, suggesting that milling was done on the roof. Just as was the case with metates, manos were a relatively scarce occurrence at the South Ruin. This especially is true of the regular variety of trough manos. Only seven of the 53 manos recovered and one of the 29 regular-variety trough manos come from the South Ruin. There were more regular-variety trough manos in Room 6 than the combined total in all of the other excavated rooms at the North and South Ruins.

Grinding Bases. Nine grinding bases are gneiss, six are sandstone, and four are granite. Their form runs a wide gamut but most are small in size and portable. Six look like unusually small metates and were formed by flaking, pecking, and grinding (Figure 35b). The remainder simply are convenient-sized cobbles, unaltered from their original state (Figure 35a), or reused fragments of other artifacts. All have a grinding depression in their major face, usually in a central location and often covering all or most of the face. They seem to be too small to be efficient milling stones. Many still have varying amounts of pigment on them. Most probably were used for grinding paint and similar tasks.

The one-hand mano and grinding base on the right side of Figure 35 were found together on the floor of Room 3. In addition, a second grinding base was on the floor of Room 3. Other grinding bases recovered from the North Ruin include two from the surface; two from Room 1; three from Room 2, one of which definitely was on the floor; two on the floor of Room 5; and the reused fragment of one on the floor or Room 7. At the South Ruin three grinding

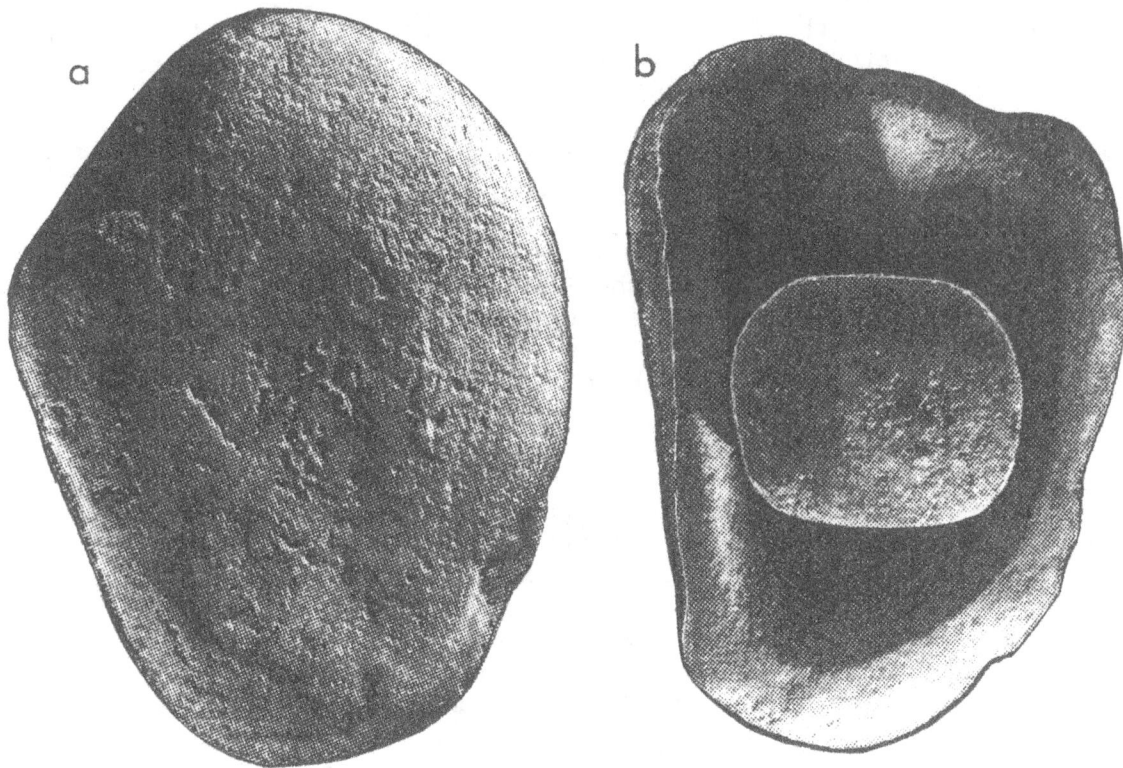

Figure 35. Grinding Bases and One-Hand Mano.
a. Grinding base; gneiss; 268 by 206 by 58 mm.; 4,860 gm.; Hagen Site, North Ruin, surface; Western Archeological and Conservation Center catalog no. S1976/47.
b. Mano; granite; 101 by 87 by 74 mm.; 1,108 gm.; Hagen Site, Room 3; Western Archeologial and Conservation Center catalog no. S1974/47.
   Grinding base; gneiss; 255 by 183 by 56 mm.; 4,155 gm.; Hagen Site, Room 3; Western Archeological and Conservation Center catalog no. S1975/47.

bases were found on the surface, one was in Room 3, and Room 1 and Room 4 each had one on its floor.

   Abraders. Eight pieces of scoria were recovered (Figure 36). All are small and conveniently can be held in one hand. Most are parallel-faced and all have at least one flat face. One was on the surface of the South Ruin. At the North Ruin two were on the surface; two in Room 2, including one on the floor; one in the fill of Room 3; and two on the floor of Room 6. In size and shape and even in such fine details as "small sand grains firmly embedded in the interstices" (Wedel 1936:83) - these artifacts closely

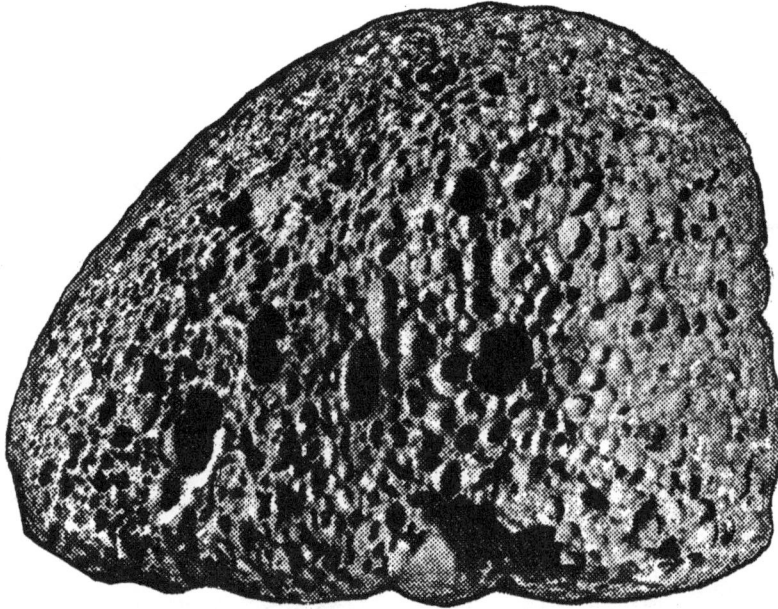

Figure 36. Abrader.
        Scoria; 90 by 65 by 48 mm., 160 gm.; Hagen Site, Room 6; Western Archeological
and Conservation Center catalog no. S2017/47.

resemble grainers used by historic and prehistoric Plains peoples (Wedel
1959:261, Figure 48; 86) Lehmer and Jones 1968:41, Plate 15j) and by Pueblos
"with a historical connection - Las Humanas, Pecos and Picuris" (Hayes et al.
1981:149). On the Plains, grainers served in the tanning of leather. Cut
from the cancellous tissue of the humerus of buffalo and other large animals,
grainers were used to sand hides to a uniform smoothness and thickness (Hodge
1910:592).

    Shaft Straighteners. A shaft tool is a grooved implement used in the
manufacture and reconditioning of arrow shafts and similar wooden
implements. Two were recovered from Room 2. They are carved and ground from
steatite and have a rounded-rectangle shape, slightly longer than they are
wide. Their grooves are at right angle to the long axis, are highly
polished, and have longitudinal striations. They were used for wrenching and
straightening.
    Both specimens are relatively small. The smaller of the two is 71 by 50
by 32 mm (Figure 37a). It has a battered appearance and is only roughly
finished. Most of the base is missing, but the break is not fresh. One end
of that surface remains intact. Across it there is a groove 8 mm wide and 3
mm deep. Opposite that surface, on the main face, there are two grooves.
These grooves are 12 mm wide and 6 mm deep. The ridge between the two
grooves is segmented by seven evenly-spaced notches which run from edge to
edge at right angle to the long axis. The second shaft tool is slightly
larger than the first and much more carefully finished (Figure 37b). All
surfaces, and especially the base, have been ground flat. Its three grooves
vary in width from 12 to 14 mm and in depth from 8 to 14 mm.

Figure 37. Shaft Straightners.
a. Schist; 71 by 50 by 32? mm.; 160 gm.; Hagen Site, Room 6; Western Archeological and Conservation Center catalog no. S1908/47.
b. Schist; 74 by 66 by 27 mm.; 229 gm.; Hagen Site, Room 2; Western Archeological and Conservation Center catalog no. S1909/47.

Pecking-Polishing Stones. At the Hagen Site we recovered nine small
river cobbles that resemble pottery polishing stones, except for the fact
that their perimeters, especially pointed ends, are battered (Figure 38).
Use-striations on the faces of some indicate that they were rubbed back and
forth with a transversally reciprocal motion. Most are quartzite; the others
are a fine-grain quartzitic sandstone. Seven come from various locations at
the North Ruin. The other two were collected from the surface of the South
Ruin.

Firedogs. Firedogs are blocks of stone whose size and shape lend them
to use around hearths to support cooking vessels. Most of the nine recovered
at the Hagen Site are roughly pecked to shape. At least one is a reused
fragment of a larger artifact. Plans tend to be round; sections,
plano-convex (Figure 39). Five are granite, two dacite, one basalt, and one
sandstone. Sizes range from 138 by 109 by 105 mm to 192 by 142 by 112 mm.
The granite specimens are the smallest. All of the firedogs come from the
North Ruin. Five were on the floor of Room 3. The others were in Room 1
(20, Room 2 (1), and Room 6 (1). Each of those rooms had a hearth. One of
the Room 3 firedogs was in a hearth. Next door, in Room 5, the fireplace had
been plugged and there were no firedogs.

Lids. A lid is a round cover for vessels, cists, or other receptacles
(Figure 40). We recovered nine at the Hagen Site: sandstone (3), schist (3),
basalt (1), gneiss (1), and granite (1). Plans are round or approximately
so. Sections are parallel-faced or, occasionally, plano-convex. They were
shaped by spalling but the shaping was minimal. Little attention was paid to
finishing; there is occasional pecking of faces or perimeters. All have a
thickness of between 25 and 45 mm. All but one are between 100 and 135 mm in
diameter. The exception is considerably larger; it has a length of 235 mm
and width of 185 mm. Lids seem to be overrepresented at the South Ruin; four
of the nine came from there.

Pipe. In Room 111 at Gila Pueblo, Alan Ferg recovered a conical pipe
carved from a piece of vesicular basalt (Ferg et al. 1993:6). He describes
it as being 44 mm in length, biconically drilled, and similar to a vesicular
basalt pipe from Las Colonias (Euler and Gregory 1988:312) and to two pipes
from the Kuykendall Site (Mills and Mills 1969:138, Figure 58c).

Bowl. A shallow, round, vesicular basalt bowl was recovered from Room
103 at Gila Pueblo. It sat next to the Tonto Polychrome human effigy vessel
which is illustrated in our Figure 23. This stone bowl compares well with
similar artifacts reported from Arizona W:10:37, Arizona W:10:56, and Arizona
W:10:65 in the Point of Pines area by Alan Olson (1959:157-160, 263, 333).
It contains traces of hematite. A mano from this room also is stained with
hematite. But the mano is too large to have been used within the bowl.

Ornamental and Religious Objects. In addition to the plaque, paint, and
possible fetishes discussed below; a small chip of low-grade turquoise was
found on the surface of the South Ruin. It does not appear to have been
worked or used.

Plaque. A piece of white opal was in the fill of the centerpost of the
early floor in Room 2 (Figure 41). One end is missing. If the artifact were

Figure 38. Pecking-Polishing Stones.
a. Quartzite; 39 by 38 by 20 mm.; 46 gm.; Hagen Site, South Ruin, surface; Western Archeological and Conservation Center catalog no. S1916/47.
b. Sandstone; 64 by 55 by 29 mm.; 132 gm.; Hagen Site, Room 6-1 Western Archeological and Conservation Center catalog no. S1917/47.
c. Sandstone; 116 by 73 by 24 mm.; 293 gm.; Hagen Site, Room 6; Western Archeological and Conservation Center catalog no. S1915/47.

symmetrical, the complete specimen measured about 77 by 42 by 6 mm. It is parallel-faced in section and probably had a rounded-rectangle plan. Both faces and all edges except the broken one are ground and polished. Opalized quartz occurs in a vein at Blue Tank, about six and a half kilometers south of Gila Pueblo.

Paint Pigments. Five pieces of malachite were recovered at the Hagen Site. At least two of these had been ground, presumably in order to remove pigment. Four are small chips. The fifth is a relatively large nodule, one entire face of which is ground smooth and convex along both axes. It was on the floor of Room 7. One each were on the floors of Room 2 and Room 5. The other two come from the surface of the South Ruin. One additional source of paint is a lump of ash. One face is ground flat. It looks as though fine ash was moistened and formed into a wad which later was ground to remove pigment. It was in the fill of Room 2.

Figure 39. Firedog.
     Granite; 142 by 139 by 111 mm.; 3,256 gm.; Hagen Site, Room 3; Western
Archeological and Conservation Center catalog no. S2013/47.

     A similar wad of ash, which had been enclosed in plainweave cloth, was
found in a bowl in Room 103 at Gila Pueblo. We wonder if it might not be
residue left from the leaching of lye during the production of hominy. A
Tonto Polychrome vase stored in Room 102 was completely filled with ash from
what appeared to be juniper twigs and needles. Whether it was for culinary
purposes or for paint was not possible to determine. Potters clay, creamy
white kaolin, and pink ochre -- a red ochre which contains some kaolin and
which could have been used in its unaltered state for the production of
Salado Polychromes -- were recovered from Gila Pueblo proper; all of these
occur abundantly at Blue Tank.
     Although no pieces of hematite were found at the Hagen Site, at least
eight stone tools were stained with red pigment, indicating that hematite was
ground upon them. Most of these were grinding bases. Both grinding bases
illustrated in Figure 35, for example, are stained with hematite. The
artifact on the left is stained on the face illustrated; the artifact on the
right is stained on the reverse face. Other artifacts upon which hematite
was ground are an ax, a chopper, a mano, and a used flake. The ax and one of
the grinding bases also appear to have black ground upon them. A core has
yellow pigment ground in the cavity provided by a large flake scar. Most of
these artifacts upon which pigment was ground come from the North Ruin and
most were found on the floors of rooms.
     Lightning Stone. Sometimes called firestones, lightning stones are
"white quartz pebbles of large size . . . . The use to which they are put is
as follows: At one time during the rain ceremonies the drum is beaten to

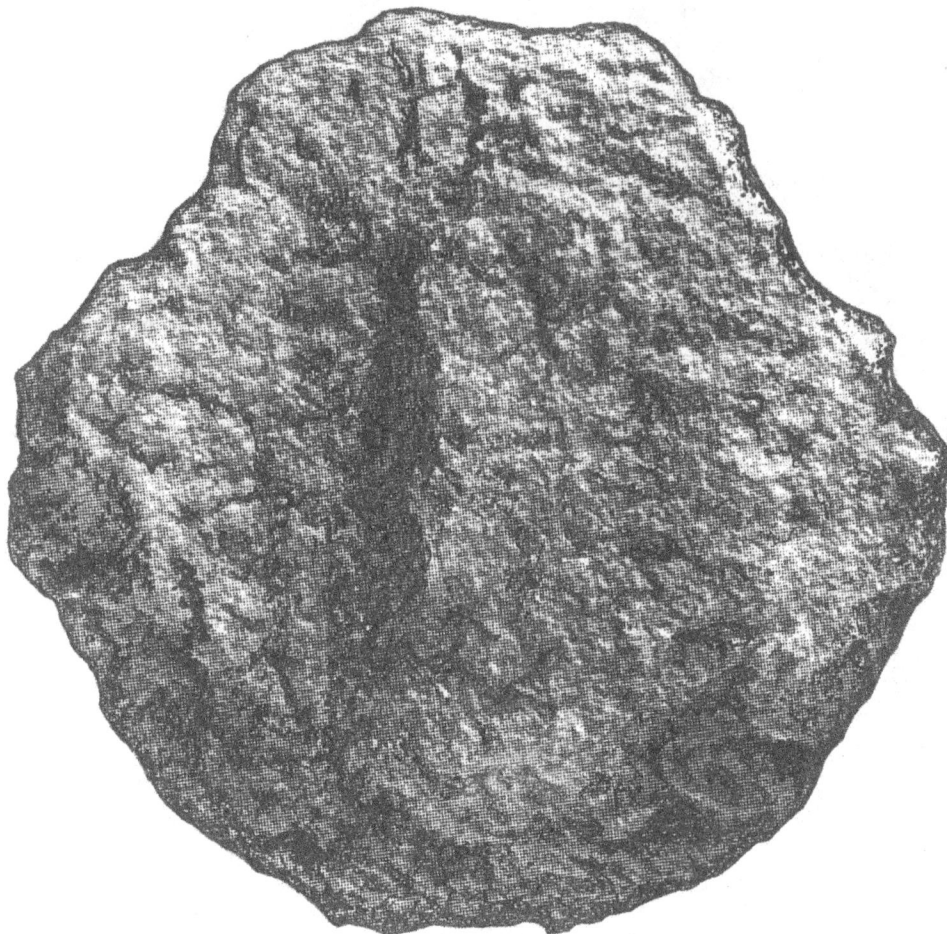

Figure 40. Lid.
        Schist; 125 by 122 by 27 mm.; 502 gm.; Hagen Site, North Ruin, surface; Western
Archeological and Conservation Center catalog no. S1912/47.

represent the thunder and the white quartz pieces are rubbed together. The
rubbing produces an incandescent glow which resembles lightning" (Jeancon
1923:68, Plate 59b). In the past only quartz artifacts have been identified
as lightning stones. From the Las Humanas excavation at Gran Quivira came
several quartzite cobbles whose sides and ends have uncommonly flat and
vertical, beaten perimeters (Hayes et al. 1981:132, Figure 176). We believe
those quartzite specimens also may be lightning stones. On the floor of Room
2 at the Hagen Site was an oval quartzite cobble (Figure 42). One side and
one end of this specimen are beaten flat; the other end was beaten so hard
that much of it is missing.

        Possible Fetishes. Four objects from the Hagan Site which are of
unusual materials, have unusual shapes, have been altered in unusual manners,
or various combinations of these may be fetishes (Figure 43). All are small

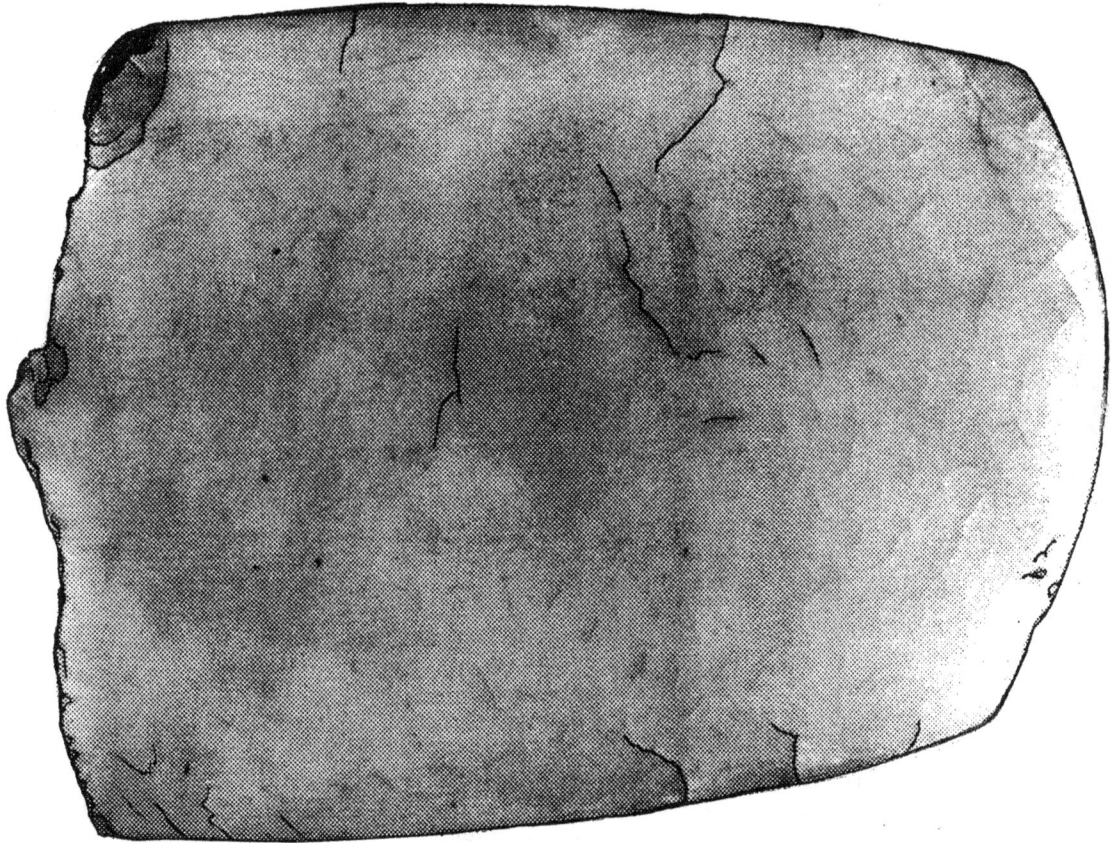

Figure 41. Plaque.
Opal; (57) by 42? by 6mm.; (25) gm.; Hagen Site, Room 2; Western Archeological and Conservation Center catalog no. S1901/47.

and light in weight. One, a slightly polished pebble of milky quartz, was surface find at the South Ruin. The other three were on or near the floor of Room 2:

1. a fragment of a sandstone concretion which may have served as a receptacle,

2. a piece of botryoidal chalcedony, and

3. a lump of gypsum whose rounded-rectangle plan and biconvex sections probably were achieved by flaking.

A fifth object, from Room 98 at Gila Pueblo proper, is a real stranger! It is fine-grained greenstone: an unaltered sphere the size of a bowling ball. It was lying on the floor, immediately adjacent to the north wall. Carol and Frank Crosswhite tell us that similar green stones still are

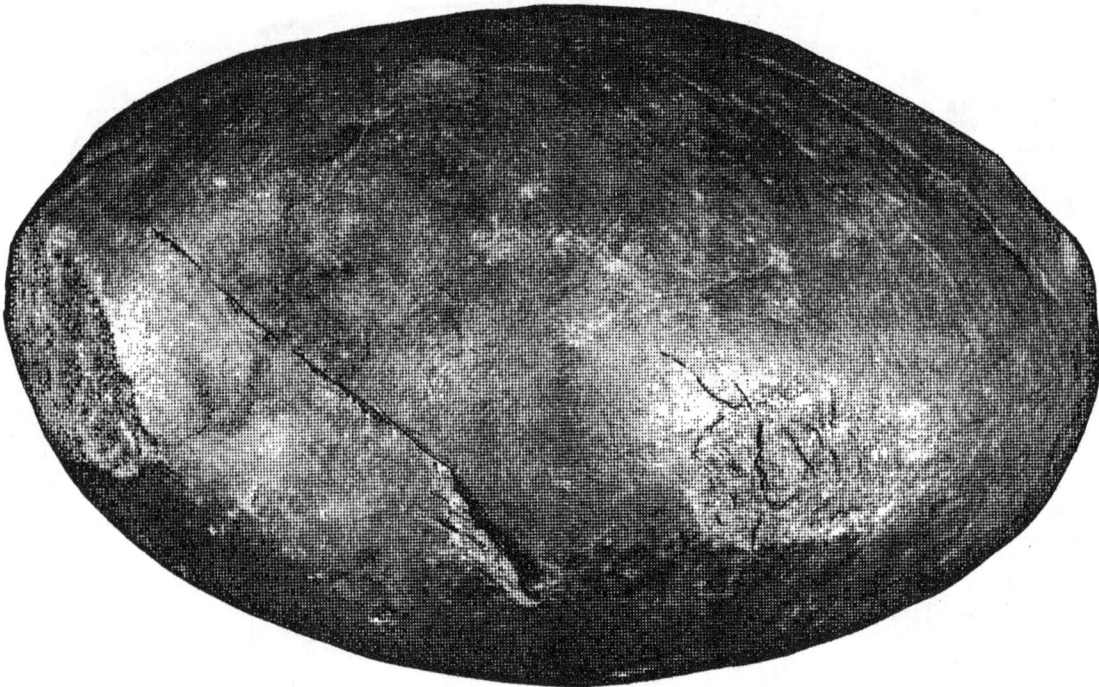

Figure 42. Lightening Stone.
    Quartzite; 128 by 90 by 66 mm.; (1,017) gm.; Hagen Site, Room 2; Western Archeological and Conservation Center catalog no. S1944/47.

venerated by present-day Pimas. We wonder if this manuport may not symbolize the Southwestern equivalent of the Aztec's Chalchihuitlique, Lady Precious Green, the patroness of springs and streams and lakes.

    It also looks as though there may have been a hunting shrine somewhere on the surface of the Hagen Site. Anton "Rocky" Miller has given us photographs of three animal bones, each of which has a projectile point embedded in it: 1) a deer sternum (Figure 44a), 2) a deer vertebra (Figure 44b), and 3) a piece of cancellous tissue from an unidentified large mammal (Figure 44c). These artifacts were salvaged by the bulldozer operator who cleared the Hagen Site and, in turn, passed them on to Rocky.

Plumb Bob. A single plumb bob was recovered from the surface of the Hagen Site. It was retrieved by Rocky Miller while the area was being bladed. It is a piece of diorite which measures: 126 by 40 by 26 mm (Figure 45). Its suspension groove was pecked and ground around the body of the plumb bob, about a third of the way down the body from the top. This plumb bob is virtually the same size as those from Casas Grandes (Di Peso 1974:2:518-519; 696, fn. 30; 7:237) but smaller than those from Snaketown (Haury 1976:Figure 14.32a-b).

Unclassified Objects. We were unable to identify 24 artifacts. Most are fragmentary or little-altered by manufacture or use and are slabs of schist

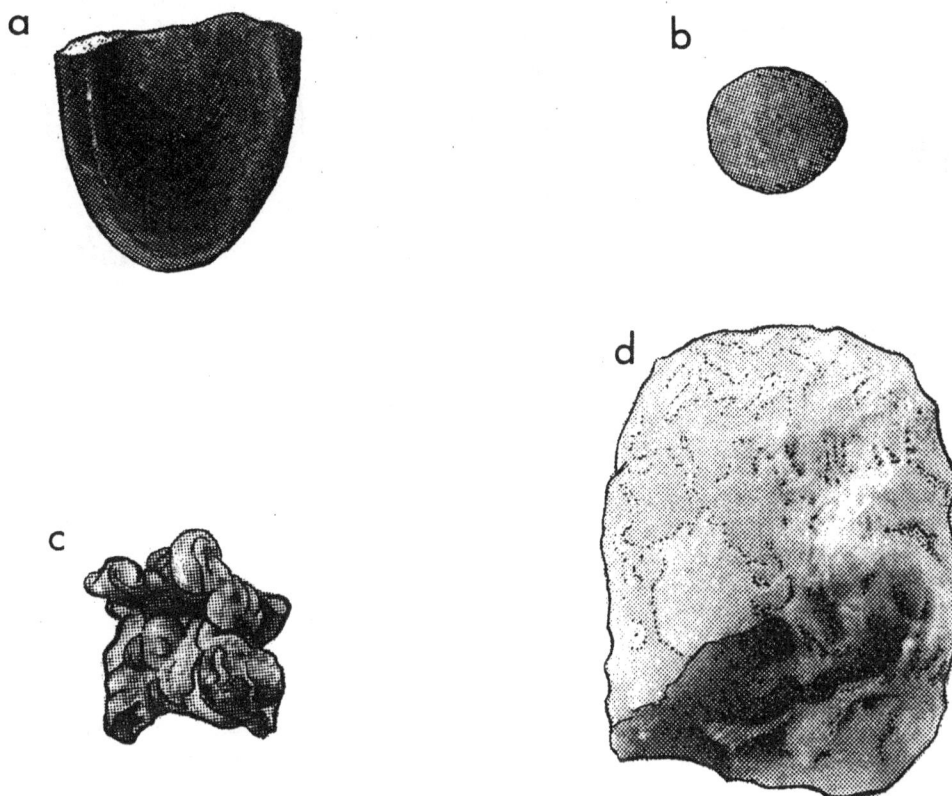

Figure 43. Possible Fetishes.
a. Sandstone; (36) by 34? by 21? mm.; (17) gm.; Hagen Site, Room 2; Western Archaeological and Conservation Center catalog no. S1898/47.
b. Quartz; 21 by 19 by 15 mm.; 7 gm.; Hagen Site, South Ruin, surface: Western Archeological and Conservation Center catalog no. S1899/47.
c. Chalcedony; 30 by 20 by 16 mm.; 11 gm.; Hagen Site, Room 6; Western Archeological and Conservation Center catalog no. S1900/47.
d. Gypsum; (66) by 58 by 42 mm.; (135) gm.; Hagen Site, Room 2; Western Archeological and Conservation Center catalog no. S1897/47.

or granite, spalled to shape, and sometimes pecked or ground. Several may be doors and one, perhaps, may be a hatch cover. The majority probably are grinding tools.

Concluding Remarks. As may be seen in Table 3, most of the artifacts which occurred with much greater relative and actual frequency at the North Ruin than at the South, are objects that take skill and time to manufacture by pecking and grinding: mescal knives; three-quarter groove axes; metates;

Figure 44. Possible Hunter Shrine Artifacts.
Scale: X 0.8.
a. Deer sternum with projectile point; Hagen Site, surface.
b. Deer vertebra with projectile point; Hagen Site, surface.
c. Unidentified large mammal cancellous tissue with projectile point; Hagen Site,
surface.

manos, especially the regular-variety of trough manos; and firedogs. Objects
which were relatively more common at the South Ruin tend to be simple and
related to flaking: hammerstones, scrapers, used flakes, and cores. Perhaps
this simply reflects the fact that most of the artifacts at the North Ruin
come from rooms that burned, while none of the South Ruin proveniences
burned. When houses at the South Ruin ceased to be inhabited, valuable stone
tools were removed. At the North Ruin, artifacts were left in place in the
rooms.

One other thought occurs to us. Admittedly we have a very small amount
of data from which to generalize, but an examination of Table 9 suggests to
us that perhaps Room 2 at the North Ruin may have served as something other
than simply as a living room:

1. Two-thirds of all North Ruin ornamental and religious objects
were there.

2. Both of the shaft tools at the Hagen Site were there.

3. Nearly three-quarters of the axes at the Hagen Site were
there.

4. One in three of all the mescal knives at the Hagen Site were
there.

5. Lots of used flakes were there.

6. But there were few or no arrowheads, choppers, flaking anvils,
hammerstones, knives, metates, or scrapers.

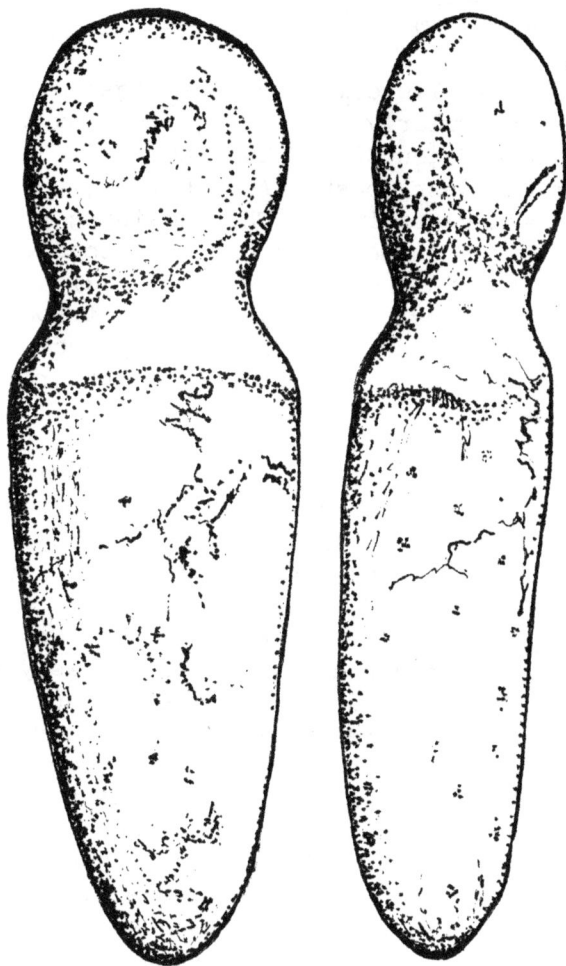

Figure 45. Plumb Bob.
Front and side views; diorite;
Hagen Site, surface; 126 by 40
by 26 mm.

SHELL

HAGEN SITE

One whole and six fragmentary mollusk shells came from the Hagen Site. The relative scarcity of shell is not particularly surprising, in view of the distance between their sources and the Hagen Site. Two shells, Clinocardium, must have come from the West Coast. Another, Glycymeris, is from the Gulf of California. One is unclassified. The remaining three -- Conus, Trachycardium, and Andara -- came either from the West Coast; the Gulf of California; or, in one instance, the Gulf of Mexico (Table 13). All were found at the North Ruin: two on the surface, one on the floor of Room 1, two in Room 2, and two in Room 3. Four shells are too fragmentary and nondescript to warrant further description or discussion. Of the remaining three, one is a tinkler and the other two were painted.

Tinkler. The Conus shell was manufactured into a tinkler by grinding-off the spire at the shoulder (Figure 46a). A perforation for suspension was created by filing a transverse groove through the body wall near the narrow, anterior end. It was resting on the bottom of the central posthole in Room 3.

Painted. The two fragments of Clinocardium shell are from the edge opposite the beak. Their convex outer surface is covered with a thick, pasty coat of azurite paint. Some of the azurite lips-over a short distance into the convex inner surface. One fragment also has red hematite paint covering the corrugations along the inner edge. The two pieces were found together in the windrow of dirt churned by a bulldozer that was clearing the site preparatory to land development activities. The whole specimens from which these fragments came probably closely resembled two whole shells illustrated in Figure 53h and Figure 53i. One of these later two was on the floor of Gila Pueblo's Room 97; the other comes from the Roosevelt Lake area. At the large, contemporary Salado pueblo of Besh-Ba-Gowah, two kilometers north of Gila Pueblo, "some of the shells were painted" (Vickery 1939:32). Between A.D. 900 and A.D. 1100 the Hohokam began painting "on the convex sides of Cardium shells, generally in the form of designs rather than an all-over wash" (Gladwin et al. 1937:146).

GILA PUEBLO PROPER

The shell recovered from Gila Pueblo is summarized in Table 14. The most significant fact emerging from the study of this collection is that the disaster in A.D. 1340 served to preserve the most beautiful shell from the entire occupation. The slat altar which separated Rooms 110 and 105 was associated with Conus shell tinklers, three circular pendants ground from Glycymeris maculata, and a richly carved Oliva shell. Before the altar in Room 110 was a rare, handsome trumpet cut from a Cabbage Murex, Hexaplex brassica. Glycymeris shell bracelets and Conus shell tinklers were fairly common throughout the wreckage.

At this time period, two of the shell species which could be identified were the same as those which were export specialties of the trading center of

Table 13. Hagen Site Mollusk Shells

Latin Name	Common Name	Source	North Ruin Provenience	Totals
Gastropoda				
Conus sp.	Cone Shell	May belong either to a single West Coast species or to one of thirteen from the Gulf Coast	Room 3, at bottom of centerpost hole	1
Pelecypoda				
Andara sp. or Arca sp.	Ark Shell	One species is found from San Diego south; five species occur in the Gulf of California	Room 2, fill near floor	1
Trachycardium?	Cockle	There is one species on the West Coast and two in the northern portion of the Gulf of Mexico	Room 3	1
Clinocardium, cf. C. nuttalli?	Nuttall's? Cockle	Nuttall's Cockle is found from San Diego north to the Bering Sea	Surface	2
Glycymeris gigantea	Dog Cockle	Gulf of California	Room 2	1
Unclassified	Unclassified	Unclassified	Room 1, floor	$\frac{1}{7}$

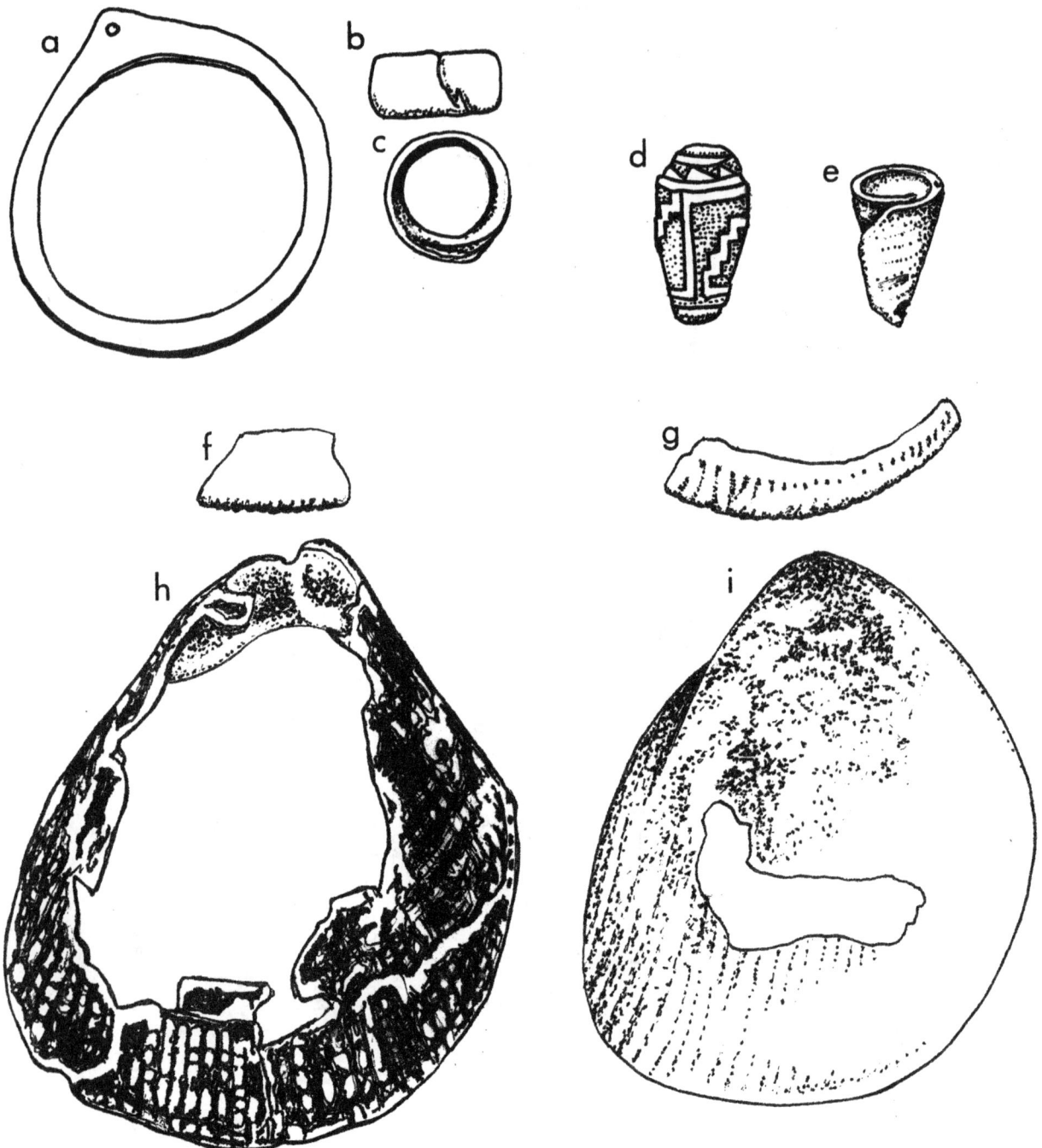

Figure 46. Shell artifacts.

a. Glycymeris maculata pendant; Gila Pueblo, ca. 1340, from slat altar between Rooms 105 and 110. Scale: X 1.

b. Tube Worm bead; Gila Pueblo, ca. 1440. Scale: X 1.

c. Oliva sp. ring; Gila Pueblo, ca. 1440. Scale: X 1.

d. Carved Oliva shell; Gila Pueblo ca. 1340, from slat altar between Rooms 110. Scale: X1.

e. Conus shell tinkler, spire ground off and notched for suspension; Hagen Site, Room 3. Scale: X 1.

f. Painted Shell, Clinocardium, cf. nuttalli?, (Nuttall's? Cockle); Hagen Site, surface; 39 by 20 by 6 mm.; 4 gm.

g. Painted Shell, Clinocardium, cf. nuttalli?, (Nuttall's? Cockle); Hagen Site, surface; 78 by 21 by 6 mm.; 7 gm.

h. Azurite painted shell, Clinocardium, cf. nuttalli? (Nuttall's Cockle); Roosevelt Lake, 145 by 118 by 47 mm.; 108 gm.

i Painted Shell, Clinocardium, cf. nuttalli?, (Nuttall's Cockle); Gila Pueblo, Shiner's Room 97; 134 by 108 by 52 mm.; 131 gm.

Table 14. Gila Pueblo Shell

	Room 98	Room 99	Room 100	Room 101	Room 102	Room 103	Room 104	Room 105	Room 106	Room 107	Room 108	Room 109	Room 110	Room 111
MARINE SHELL														
CALIFORNIAN PROVINCE														
Gastropods														
Haliotis sp.														1
PANAMIC PROVINCE														
Gastropods														
Turritella														
leucostoma							1							
Hexaplex brassica														
Trumpet													1	
Melongena patula														
Trumpet									1					
Nassarius iodes														
Beads	1		1	many										
Oliva sp.				1										
Carved												1		
Rings			2											
Olivella dama	2													
Conus sp.	1	6	2	2	1			5					3	
Tinklers										1				
Conus perplexis		1												
Pelecypods														
Glycymeris gigantea				1										
Bracelet frags.		1	1	4	2	1	3		3				2	
Glycymeris maculata														
Pendants						3		1	1				8	
Pinctada														
mazatlanica														
Pendant								1						
Laevicardium elatum	3	4	4	6	6	3	1	1	3	9	many	1		
Beads	4	2	3	10				1			3		6-7000	
cf. Dosinia														
ponderosa, Beads													1	many
FRESH WATER SHELL														
Pelecypods														
cf. Quadrula sp							1							

Paquime at Casas Grandes, Chihuahua. The Conus shells from this period most closely match the profile of Conus ximenes. Conus ximenes and Conus perplexus, although easily identified by differences in the soft parts, are very difficult to distinguish by shell alone, especially when they occur as archeological specimens. Di Peso (1974:Vol. 8; 163-173, 1971) found that Conus ximenes was an important trade item from Casas Grandes through the Mimbres area and northward. The Gila Pueblo shells date ca. A.D. 1340, when Casas Grandes still was active in the trading of shells. The incised shell from the slat altar resembles a roller seal (Figure 46e). It best matches Oliva spicata -- a species traded exclusively by the folks at Casas Grandes (Di Peso 1974:Vol. 8, 169-171). Glycymeris gigantea, which measures 180 mm, was present at this period as bracelets. These specimens must have been dredged from a depth of from 7-13 meters in the Gulf of California (Keen 1971:55). Beach specimens tend to be in such poor condition as to render them unfit for the manufacture of bracelets. These bracelets were an important trade item, which we suppose were fabricated elsewhere and brought to the Salado as finished products. Glycymeris maculata is a very small Glycymeris; it measures only 35 mm in its largest dimension. All specimens were made into circular pendants, which were too small to use as bracelets. Brody (1977:50, Fig. 17) illustrates this type of pendant being used as earrings on several figures on a Mimbres Black-on-white bowl.

The shells in use at the end of the Salado occupation of Gila Pueblo present a very different picture. Glycymeris giganta bracelets and Glycymeris maculata pendants were less numerous. Many specimens obviously were dead shells scavenged from beaches. There was a wider variety of species, but no indication of trade specializations. Particularly conspicuous was a large amount of Laevicardium elatum, which was used as the raw material for the fine shell beads manufactured at Gila Pueblo.

Among this wide variety of shell species was a Melongena patula trumpet. Both the Murex trumpet from the previous period and this specimen were rather small. The spire was ground-off of both shells; otherwise, they were unaltered. Sound is produced on these trumpets by placing the lower lip against the shell and blowing across the aperture. They produce an impressive sound indoors. But outdoors the sound quickly dissipates. The shell effigy ceramic trumpet recovered at Arizona W:10:37 at Point of Pines illustrated by Olson in 1959 (205-207, Fig. 41) produces a really impressive blast much sharper in pitch and louder in volume than what can be produced by these small shells. Since these small shell trumpets were not suitable for signalling, we suggest that they had some traditional use, perhaps connected with the Ehecatl manifestation of Quetzalcoatl.

FAUNA

Only a few faunal remains came from the Hagen Site (Table 15). At the South Ruin three pieces of unworked bone were on the floor of Room S-1: two from a blacktailed jackrabbit and one from a whitetail deer. At the North Ruin a small fragment of unidentified and probably unworked bone was on the floor of Room 1. Also at the North Ruin were fragments of five awls split and ground from artiodactyl metapodials: four in Room 2 and one in Room 3. Three are mule deer; we were not able to identify the others.

Table 16 is a compilation of the worked bone recovered from Gila Pueblo, and Table 17 documents Gila Pueblo's useable meat. Edible meat at Gila

Table 17. Gila Pueblo Useable Meat.

Species	Individuals	Pounds of Meat Per Individual	Useable Meat	Percentage of Total Meat
Mule Deer	13	100.00	1300.00	44.08
Whitetailed Deer	10	70.00	700.00	23.37
Unidentified Deer	3	85.00	255.00	8.65
Blacktailed Jackrabbit	92	3.00	276.00	9.40
Dog	18	12.50	237.00	8.05
Probable Dog	3	12.50	37.50	1.27
Rabbit	50	1.75	87.50	2.97
				97.79

Pueblo was calculated using values established by White (1953:397-398), adjusted for the size of local subspecies. Deer constituted 76.10 percent; hare and rabbit, 12.37 percent; and dog, 9.32 percent. No other species yielded meat totaling as much as one percent. The percentage of meat produced from dogs is extraordinary for a site in the Southwest. On the Plains, dogs were valued as beasts of burden. In Mesoamerica, however, they were more important as food. The Gila Pueblo Salados appear to have leaned toward the southern pattern.

At the time of the final attack upon Gila Pueblo, evidence of the skins of three dogs were found on the rooftops in the form of paw bones and distal tail vertebrae. Since it is too hot at the altitude of Gila Pueblo for turkey breeding, it is possible that dogs were sometimes sacrificed as substitutes for turkeys. Precedent for sacrificial use of dogs comes from Gran Quivira in central New Mexico, where a medium-sized Indian dog had been struck at least four times on the head, its chest opened, and then skinned. Some of the claws and the distal tail vertebrae were removed with the skin. Presumably this is a Southwestern form of the Mesoamerican heart sacrifice. The dog lay on its left side, with its head to the north, in a pit beneath Kiva M. It was covered with matting and accompanied by a sacrificed female turkey (McKusick 1981:61).

Table 15. Hagen Site Faunal Materials

Latin Name	Common Name	Element	Provenience	Comments
Lepus californicus	Blacktailed jackrabbit	Right zygomatic process, mandible	Room S-1, floor	Unworked
Odocoileus virginianus	Whitetail Deer	Right 3-4 metatarsals	Room S-1, floor	Unworked
Unidentified	Unidentified	Unidentified	Room 1, floor	
Artiodactyla	Unknown Artiodactyl	Unidentified	Room 2, fill	Awl fragment, artiodactyl
Odocoileus hemionus	Mule Deer	Right 3-4 metatarsals	Room 2, fill	Awl fragment
Odocoileus hemionus	Mule Deer	Right 3-4 metatarsals	Room 2, floor, southwest corner	Awl fragment
Artiodactyla	Unknown Artiodactyl	Metapodial	Room 2, floor, northwest corner	Awl fragment, artiodactyl
Odocoileus hemionus	Mule Deer	Right 3-4 metatarsals	Room 3, fill	Awl fragment

Table 16. Gila Pueblo Faunal Materials

General: * = Worked, p = pup

	Room 98	Room 99	Room 100	Room 101	Room 102	Room 103	Room 104	Room 105	Room 106	Room 107	Room 108	Room 109	Room 110	Room 111	Total MFC
PISCES															
Fish			1												2
AMPHIBIA															
Bufo Spade Footed Toad											1			1	2
Hyla Tree Toad				1											1
REPTILIA															
Kinosternon sonoriense Sonoran Mud Turtle					2										2
AVES															
Cathartes aura Turkey Vulture								1*							1*
Buteo jamaicensis Red-tailed Hawk								1							1
Lophortyx gambellii Gambel's Quail	3			2	2									1	8
MAMMALIA															
Sylvilagus sp. Rabbit	3	3	3	17	1	1	2	6	1		3	2	6	6	50
Lepus californicus Blacktailed Jackrabbit	15	10	5	15	4	1	3	15	1	3	6		11	5	92
Ammospermophilus harrisii Harris' Antelope Squirrel			1											1	2

Table 16. Gila Pueblo Faunal Materials, continued

General: * = Worked, p = pup

	Room 98	Room 99	Room 100	Room 101	Room 102	Room 103	Room 104	Room 105	Room 106	Room 107	Room 108	Room 109	Room 110	Room 111	Total MFC
Spermophilus variegatus Rock Squirrel		1	1											2	4
Thomomys bottae Botta's Pocket Gopher	1	3		7		1				1	1				15
Peromyscus sp. White-footed Mouse				9							1			1	10
Neotoma albigula White-throated Wood Rat	1		1		1					1					4
Canis sp. Dog/Coyote				1p						1	1				3
Canis latrans Coyote														1*	1*
Canis familiaris Dog	2	1,2p		2,1p	2,1p		1,1p			2		1	2		18
Procyon lotor Raccoon			1												1
Lynx rufus Bobcat		1													1
Cervus elephas Elk													1		1
Odocoileus sp. Deer	1	3*		2*		5*		3*				1*			3,14*
Odocoileus hemionus Mule Deer	1,1*	2*		4,4*		1,3*		1		2	1*		3,6*	2,1*	13,18*
Odocoileus virginianus White-tailed Deer		4*		4*			1,3*	1,6*	1*		1,2*			4	1,8*
Bos/Bison Cf. Bison				1											1

Table 16. Gila Pueblo Faunal Materials, Continued.
Worked Bone Detail

	Room 98	Room 99	Room 100	Room 101	Room 102	Room 103	Room 104	Room 105	Room 106	Room 107	Room 108	Room 109	Room 110	Room 111	Total
BONE TUBES															
Cathartes aura, ulna. Turkey Vulture								1							1
BONE AWLS															
Canis latrans, ulna. Coyote														1	1
Odocoleus sp. Deer															
metapodial	3	3		2	3			2				1			14
metacarpal					1										1
metatarsal					1										1
O. hemionus Mule Deer															
antler					1										1
ulna													1		1
tibia	1														1
metapodial		2		2											4
metacarpal													2	1	3
metatarsal				2							1		3		6
O. virginianus Whitetail Deer															
tibia					1										1
metapodial														2	2
metacarpal	2	1	1					1			1			2	8
metatarsal	3	3		4	1		3	3	1		1			4	23
HAIR PINS															
O. virginianus Whitetail Deer tibia			1				1								2
	9	9	2	10	8	0	4	7	1	0	3	1	6	10	70

90

In terms of the ecology of the area today, it is not unexpected to find both whitetail deer and mule deer represented. The Hagen Site is situated in a portion of the Pinal Mountain foothills which is relatively open and grass covered and in which one would expect to find mule deer. Nearby are dense, brushy areas favored by whitetail. Near Kellner Canyon, for example, where McKusick lives and only a distance of three kilometers west of Gila Pueblo, whitetail deer are seen on the brushy south side of the canyon and mule deer are seen on the grassy north side even today.

According to the late Carmen Blalack and other old timers, the water table in the canyons draining into Pinal Wash used to lie only a couple of feet below the present surface. All this changed forever in 1929 when miners at the Old Dominion broke through into an underground river and dropped the bottom out of the water table. Until that time the washes in Kellner, Ice House, and Six-Shooter Canyons ran the year around and had fish and turtles in abundance.

All of the fish, amphibians, reptiles, mammals -- except bison and elk -- and birds -- except the small Indian domestic turkey -- recovered during the excavations of the Hagen Site and of Gila Pueblo proper could have been native to the area. The most important factor in the mammalian remains is the predominance of hares over rabbits, which indicates to us that the environment was being asked to provide more than it actually could on a sustained basis.

The bison and elk samples from Gila Pueblo proper occurred in lenses of trash relating to the reoccupation of Room 111. These lenses were deposited midway between the roofs of the burned Salado occupation and the present surface, indicating a reoccupation date in the 1600s. The fact that elk and bison remains were present suggests that those who reoccupied the site may have had the use of a horse to transport meat of such large animals over the relatively long distance from the mountains to the north and the plains to the east.

The small Indian domestic turkey presumably was imported for sacrificial or ceremonial purposes. This breed of turkey was especially dedicated to the worship of Tlaloc. The acceptable sacrifice was the head and blood. It is interesting in this regard that the Acoma people still associate the symbol of the turkey with the practice of human sacrifice. Small Indian domestics were a specialty product of the Tompiro Pueblos in central New Mexico. During this time period they were traded from there into sites such as the University Indian Ruin and the Reeve Ruin in southeastern Arizona and also were raised at Casas Grandes in Chihuahua (McKusick 1986:10-11, Figures 16 and 17).

VEGETAL MATERIALS

HAGEN SITE

All of the vegetal material recovered at the Hagen Site came from the North Ruin. A few small pieces of ponderosa pine and juniper posts and roof timbers found in Room 2 and Room 6 were mentioned in earlier the Architecture section. A lump of hearth ash was discussed as paint under Stone. In addition to these, charred plant specimens were in Room 5 and Room 6. They include both yucca and corn. Yucca leaf, leaf base, and fiber all are present. Some of the fibers appear to be twisted into cordage (Figure 47).

Hugh Cutler, who analyzed the vegetal materials, told us that the corn is what he would expect to find in the general vicinity of the Hagen Site. Ears are both eight-row and ten-row, kernels are small to medium in size, and at least some of the corn probably is flint. With the exception of some corn kernels in the fill of Room 6, all of the vegetal materials were on the floors of Room 5 and Room 6. The corn in the fill almost certainly was on or near the roof at the time the structure burned. Some of the other plant remains probably fell from the roofs to floors when the rooms burned. Corn kernels were in a bowl on the floor of Room 6. The twisted yucca fiber was in a Gila Polychrome bowl on the floor of Room 5. Also on the floor of Room 5 was a small, smudged-redware bowl containing unidentified plant material.

GILA PUEBLO PROPER

Although Gladwin found datable ponderosa pine beams, all of the framing materials which we recovered from the south end of Gila Pueblo were juniper. Roofing and a cradleboard were made of reeds. Twined matting was made from what appears to be Rhus trilobata: squawberry. Plain-weave, plaited matting appeared to be made from yucca. A fiber apron was made from yucca or agave. A fragment of coiled basketry was preserved by a thick impasto of red, iron-oxide paint. A fragment of charred, four-rod, split-stitched, coiled basketry also was recovered. No identification of plant species could be made. The cradleboard from Room 110 was made from parallel, vertical reeds. Large amounts of cotton seed and ash were present. Plain-weave, cotton cloth samples averaged 20 threads per inch.

Cultivated food remains included corn, cotton seed, tepary beans, sieva beans, common beans, and winter squash. Black walnuts were the only gathered food we identified. Today, seeds provided by Gary Nabhan of Native Seed Search have been grown on irrigated plots with the same degree of success for each variety as is evidenced by the Gila Pueblo sample. Cotton germinates better and produces a more reliable crop than does corn. Tepary beans can produce five crops during a growing season, and will sow themselves. Sieva beans still do better than common beans. Winter squash still do well, if sufficient irrigation water is available. None of these crops will produce today when watered only by rain.

Figure 47. Yucca Cordage.
  Yucca fiber; Hagen Site
Room 5; 30 by 24 by 4 mm.;
weight less than 1 gram.

BURIALS

We recovered one extramural adult inhumation at the Hagen Site and eight subfloor infant burials at Gila Pueblo, proper. In addition, we are including details here regarding four infant burials that Shiner (1961) recovered from Gila Pueblo.

SUBFLOOR CHILDREN

Intramural interments of infants and small children are labeled by number on Figure 48. They are discussed below by room number.

Room 97.

Burial 1. "Burial I was an infant placed without offerings in a narrow, shallow grave. The deterioration was so advanced that only a few small bones were recovered. The head was to the west and the body had been at least partly flexed" (Shiner 1961:7).

Burial 2 and Burial 3.

Burial II was found in the deeper portion of a double grave. The infant body, in a flexed position, had been placed with the head to the south. Bones were severely decayed, and the only offering was the cloth-wrapped copper bell. Before Burial III was interred, Burial II was covered with a layer of fist-sized rocks. The former was in the same condition as Burial II and had no artifacts with it (Shiner 1961:7).

Burial 4. "Burial IV, a small child, lay with the head to the west. It was semi-flexed and in poor condition. At the head was a well-worn mano. A plainware jar and a crude hand-molded dish were placed at the feet" (Shiner 1961:7).

Room 99.

Burial 7. This interment, located along the west wall of the room and in front of the sealed doorway to Room 100, provided neither grave goods nor recoverable bones. The burial pit measured: 71 cm north-south, 26 cm wide at the north end, and 31 cm wide at the south end.

Room 101.

Burial 8. The infant was buried along the east wall. No recoverable bones remained. Non-perishable grave goods consisted of a small pottery disc -- the size of a game counter -- and a small, red, corrugated bowl. This Salado Red bowl is a miniature example of the predominant mortuary offering recovered by pot hunters on the San Carlos Apache Reservation east of Gila Pueblo. This is a pottery type usually found at earlier time levels, and may indicate this is one of the first burials made in this section of the pueblo.

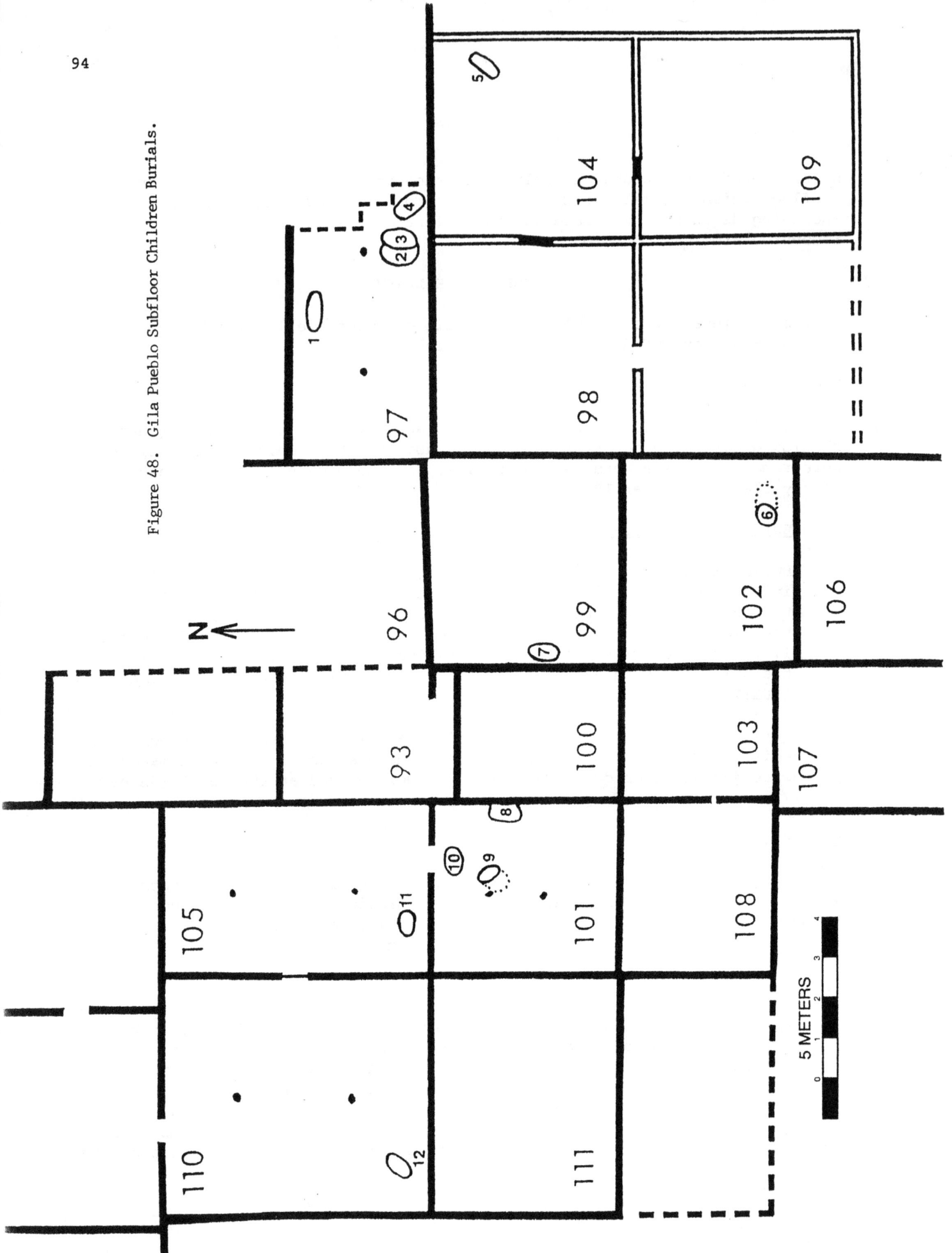

Figure 48. Gila Pueblo Subfloor Children Burials.

Burial 9. The main shaft of this small grave was vertical in direction and elliptical in outline, with its axis running from northwest to southeast. A cavity was dug into the southwest wall on the level of the floor of the main shaft. The infant lay on its left side, with its head to the west-northwest. Seventy-one pieces of bone, representing major elements of a young infant, were recovered. The vertical shaft was floored with the deliberately broken halves of a long, rounded-rectangular stone tablet. If the tablet was once painted, no traces of paint were visible at the time of excavation. Above this tablet, the shaft appeared to have been largely filled with a bundle of perishable goods into which had been tucked a handsome knife of petrified wood.

Burial 10. No recoverable bone remained from this interment, located in front of the doorway between Room 101 and 105. The only non-perishable offering was a small Tonto Plain bowl.

Room 102.

Burial 6. Three flat stones closed the top of the shaft leading to a subfloor burial in the southeast corner of the room. The shaft was 28 cm from east to west and 25 cm from north to south. The shaft was 26 cm deep. The burial cavity, itself, was dug for a distance of 48 cm into the west wall of the shaft. A premature infant was interred on its right side, with its head to the west. No offerings were found.

Room 104.

Burial 5. An infant was buried beneath the floor, in the northeast corner. Although the pit was fairly large, the infant must have been very young, as only two small scraps of bone persisted. Presumably the head was to the southwest end, but orientation could not definitely be established.

Room 105.

Burial 1. This interment was quite elaborate. The burial pit measured: 26 cm deep, 46 cm east-west, 30 cm north-south. The pit was completely lined -- sides and bottom -- with small cobbles of Schultz granite. The granite is an exotic, coming from a location west of Miami. It deliberately had been worked into rough, golf-ball-sized spheres about 5 cm in diameter. The infant was tiny and premature, so small that it was entirely enclosed between the deliberately broken halves of a San Carlos Red-on-brown bowl. Over the infant was a mass of very fine argillite beads measuring 2 mm in diameter. It appears to us that these beads were once a necklace composed of two long or three short strands. The beads are so fine in size that their bulk measures only about 70 ml in volume. The color of the argillite matches the brilliant stone that comes from the area around Prescott -- rather than the darker, brownish argillite that comes from the area around Gila Pueblo. South of this burial was a circular pit of less formal construction, which may have served to contain offerings made at a later time.

Room 110.

Burial 12. The interment was about 2 cm above the floor of the pit, suggesting that the infant was wrapped or lay in a cradleboard. The head was oriented to the north-northeast. Bones were very poorly preserved. There was a small hole in the floor of the pit, which was irregular in depth. No offerings were found in the hole, or elsewhere in the pit. The hole may have been left by the removal of a rock during the excavation of the pit.

Ethnographic Parallels. In order to try to rationalize why some infants had offerings and why others did not and why a child was buried beneath the floor of Room 97, we spoke with a Hopi friend who was born in 1903. We asked this man if the grave goods were in any way meaningful to him. He replied that, indeed, they were! He said that infants who had bowls buried with them had lived long enough for their naming ceremony to have taken place, at which time bowls customarily are given. The infants without such bowls had been stillborn or had died very soon after birth. The child, he said, had been named but had not yet gone through its first initiation. He indicated that in the early 1900's this initiation took place between the ages of five and seven, depending upon the interest of the child in matters spiritual. It was very unusual for a child to be initiated as early as age five. Early initiations only took place as the result of a mystical vision or experience considered valid within the established religious structure. One function of this first initiation was to give the child to the spirits. Before this initiation, an infant or child who died was returned to the earth beneath the household into which it was born. After the initiation, it belonged to the spirits and was buried in the same cemetery as older tribal members. When questioned about differences in status implied by presence or absence of offerings, he was completely blank. This was an incomprehensible idea to him. He found the grave goods meaningful only as an indication of successful completion of rites of passage. Hopi-Tewa-Apache story teller Michael Lacapa indicates that differences in burial goods reflect hereditary family responsibilities, which vary from family to family.

Whether or not grave goods denote status in a modern Hopi context, where egalitarianism is a cultural ideal, it appears that the inclusion in the burials of presumably stillborn infants of a copper bell, a rare knife of petrified wood, and a beautiful necklace of argillite beads are noteworthy. All of these items were trade goods, making them even more precious than offerings of pottery, which could have been made locally. The San Carlos Red-on-brown bowl which sheltered the argillite-covered fetus is also an item of trade. William Underwood told us that San Carlos Red-on-brown was the preferred mortuary vessel throughout the Globe area in late Salado interments. It is possible that the fetus buried in Room 105 possessed hereditary status, and as a result was buried more formally than was usual for the child of average status who had not yet received its naming bowl.

EXTRAMURAL ADULT

The only burial encountered at the Hagen Site was the inhumed bones of a female who had died somewhere in her late teens or early twentys. She stood about 156 cm tall. Her bones show no evidence of pathologies; her cause of death is undetermined. Her burial pit was small and shallow. It was about 30 cm longer than she was and perhaps twice her breadth. The floor of the grave sloped downward 15-20 cm from head to foot. She lay in a fully extended, supine position with arms extended at her sides. Orientation was east-west, with her head to the west. Just to the outside of the upper portion of her right leg lay a Gila Polychrome bowl. M. Y. El-Najjar examined her remains and told us that she "is of the Southwest Physical Type described by Seltzer (1944). She is very much like females from the Salt River" Valley. He has only seen one other Salado burial but has read the work of others on the subject, which leads him to conclude that she fits better among the Salado than the Hohokam.

DISCUSSION

Adult Salado burials are supine, fully extended, arms in a normal position along the sides. Most are accompanied by offerings. The single pottery vessel interred with the Hagen Site burial may not be an accurate indicator of the amount of grave goods which accompanied Salado women. For example, Burial A at Tonto Cliff Dwellings' Lower Ruin also was accompanied by a single pottery vessel. In addition to the piece of pottery there were three mats, a cotton blanket, a cotton cloth smeared with a vegetal substance and rolled into a bundle, a bundle of cotton yarn, a mass of yucca fiber, two baskets, a leather rattle, a gourd container, a spindle stick, 25 wooden-tipped arrow tied together by a rag, a bow, a cradleboard, and various pieces and parts of corn, bean, squash, gourd, and cotton plants. Burial A was interred in a dry cave and its perishable grave goods desiccated and survived. If Burial A had been inhumed at the Hagen Site, most of the furnishings would have rotted and disappeared; only the single bowl would have been present at the time of excavation.

An interesting aspect of the subfloor infant burials at Gila Pueblo is the manner in which they were laid to rest. Whereas the normal position for Salado adults is on their backs in an anatomically correct position, the infants in Room 97 were flexed in the fetal position. We wonder if there is not a rational, correlating pattern of flexed burials/immature individuals/no naming-bowl offerings on the one hand and extended burials/more mature individuals/naming-bowl offerings on the other. Perhaps those immature individuals who had not yet received a name and formal place in Salado society were being returned to the earth in the same fashion in which they had arrived: in a flexed, fetal position.

With the possible exception of avoiding north, the orientation of Salado burials has no apparent pattern. The young-adult female at the Hagen Site lay with her head to the west. At Tonto Cliff Dwellings, the five reported burials were oriented east, west, south, southeast, and southwest (Steen et al. 1962:26, 65-66). At Besh-ba-gowah, where Vickery (1939:21) uncovered more than 350 burials, she discerned "no definite orientation though a majority have the heads to the east or southeast." The subfloor burials at Gila Pueblo seem to fit no obvious pattern: two had their heads to the west; two, to the south; one probably to the southwest; two to the north or south; two, to the east or west; one, to the north-northeast; and one, to the west-northwest.

We do not have mean reconstructed height for human remains from Grasshopper Pueblo, but the reconstructed stature for a high-status, male burial there was 166.9 cm or 65.7 inches (Griffin 1967:51). Mean male stature for our local Salado populations is 165 cm for males and 160 cm for females (Table 18). Comparable male means have been calculated for the Pueblo peoples at Hopi: 163.8 cm, at Zuni: 163.5 cm, and at Taos: 164.1 cm (Scott 1981:133).

Gavan's (1940:10-12) comments on the skeletal remains from the original excavation at Besh-ba-gowah confirm that the population was short -- not over five and a half feet in height. Most interesting to us is his comparison of facial characteristics of remains from Besh-ba-gowah, Kinishba, Tuzigoot,

Table 18. Salado Stature.

Reconstructed Statures For Salado Populations In The General Vicinity Of Gila Pueblo -- GP: Gila Pueblo, BBG: Besh-ba-gowah, PP: Pinal Pueblo, MB: Miami Burials.

MALES

Site	Height in cm	Height in inches
GP	169.09	66.57
MB	167.50	65.95
MB	167.08	65.78
GP	167.00	65.75
PP	166.81	65.67
MB	164.72	64.85
BBG	156.03	61.43
Range	156.03-169.09	61.43-66.57
Median	166.81	65.67
Mean	164.60	64.80

FEMALES

Site	Height in cm	Height in inches
MB	162.71	64.06
MB	161.11	63.43
PP	160.68	63.25
PP	160.27	63.10
PP	158.14	62.23
MB	157.92	62.18
MB	156.27	61.53
Range	156.27-162.71	61.53-64.06
Median	160.27	63.10
Mean	159.59	62.83

Swarts Ruin, Pecos, Puye, and Old Zuni. He found more similarity among the samples from Besh-ba-gowah, Pecos, Puye, and Old Zuni. As the only group which appears in both lists, Zuni is the common denominator in comparisons of stature and morphology.

The apparent large size of some skeletal remains from Gila Pueblo led us to wonder if the inhabitants of the ceremonial/redistribution complex were taller than other Salados in the neighborhood. This was tested by an examination of samples from Besh-ba-gowah, Pinal Pueblo, and from Salado burials unearthed in the town of Miami during a ditching project. Whole bones which could be used to reconstruct stature were rare, due to the destruction of skeletal remains by soil conditions. Stature reconstructions were based upon Trotter and Gleser's racial tables for estimating stature from length of limb bones (Anderson 1969:127). The tables were tested by calculating stature on all long bones of an adult female from Pinal Pueblo. She had been buried in a trench just large enough to accommodate the body; which, in turn, provided an accurate value for live stature. As would be expected, the tables for persons of Mongoloid-type most closely matched the known stature of the control. The results of the comparison of reconstructed statures for these sites indicate that a man from the ceremonial/redistribution complex at Gila Pueblo was the tallest, and a man from Besh-ba-gowah was by far the shortest -- with the other two ranging in-between. Our sample is quite small. Generalizing from it, the most conspicuous feature is that all the local Salado populations were very well nourished. Youths were slender and gracile. Adults of middle age displayed muscle and tendon attachments indicating the spread and increased weight that tend to accompany middle age. The profusion of gatherable wild foods in the area and the availability of both mule deer and whitetail deer undoubtedly contributed to the sturdy bones of this population.

Another factor that may have contributed to high nutrition was the availability of large quantities of cottonseed with which they could supplement their diet. Some have expressed doubt that cottonseed was used for food, but cottonseed was found as a component of 18 percent of Antelope House coprolites, 25 percent of Inscription House coprolites, and 30 percent of Glen Canyon coprolites (Fry and Hall 1986:177, 185). Of 16 samples of Antelope House coprolites containing cottonseed, four samples were composed of more than 20 percent cottonseed; the highest sample contained 27.7 percent cottonseed. Cottonseed is the third most common cultigen component in Antelope House coprolites, exceeded only by corn and squash. Our aged Hopi informant told us that cottonseed was rendered for oil to lubricate piki stones. The Pima parch cottonseed to eat like popcorn (Castetter and Bell 1942:198), and so do the Hopi (Beaglehole 1937).

No coprolites were recovered from Gila Pueblo, but large quantities of carbonized seeds and plant remains were. Corn was greatest in bulk, with cottonseed in almost equal quantity. Tepary beans were third in bulk. Squash rinds and stems were much less common, as were sieva beans and common beans. The emphasis upon corn and cottonseed and the relatively minor use of squash and beans are parallel at Antelope House and at Gila Pueblo. The specialization in the production of soft goods also is parallel.

CLOTHING, PERSONAL ADORNMENT, AND STATUS

At the time of the third destructive fire -- The Third Fire, which terminated the Salado occupation of Gila Pueblo -- the weather was warm and, in all probability, very little clothing was being worn. Nevertheless, some individuals were conspicuously adorned. The fire was widespread and the heat intense. The only human remains which persisted were those which were protected by wall and roof fall. Probably some of the covered bodies were consumed by ravens and vultures, leaving even less evidence to be excavated. The result was bits and pieces of burned bone scattered throughout the rubble with occasional intact sections of dismembered bodies protected by large overlying boulders that had fallen from the walls, or groupings where the bodies of women covered those of one or two infants or children. These bones were in-place and better represented, but were gnawed by rodents, nevertheless. Areas of bones protected from the fire by bulky muscles were the best preserved. If any substantial amount of clothing had been present in these piles of bodies, some should have been carbonized; but no indications of cloth, cordage, or hide were found.

Fragments of Glycymeris shell bracelets and Conus shell tinklers were recovered throughout the fill of the central complex but could not definitely be associated with any specific garments, items of adornment, or skeletal assemblages. We suspect that men wore loin cloths, pouches, leggings, hair pins, earrings, and necklaces; whereas women wore aprons, stomachers, and Glycymeris shell bracelets. Both undoubtedly wore footless stockings and blankets or shawls over the shoulders in cold weather.

Leggings. The remains of the largest male found at Gila Pueblo lay on the northern portion of the second story roof above Room 105. He appeared to have been clad in leggings. Five Conus shell tinklers were found beside the unburned bones of the right leg -- one each at the hip, thigh, knee, calf, and ankle. The tinklers were not close enough together to have produced a sound against each other, but instead may have served as fasteners such as are found on brush chaps. Presumably the leggings were two separate units, suspended at each hip from a belt. Certainly the density of catclaw thickets in the Pinal Mountain foothills would make such garments highly desirable for hunters, traders, and other travelers.

The Conus shell placement lateral to the leg bones of this individual is strongly reminiscent of the lines of Conus shells lateral to each leg in the Burial of an Early American Magician (McGregor 1943:272, 273, 283). McGregor suggested that the man in the very high status burial may have been wearing leggings. Hopi informants agreed at the time of excavation that the Magician was a shaman whose ceremonial function was to increase the strength and resources of the group. In line with these duties, he also may have served as a war leader (McGregor 1943:295, 296).

More recently, Jonathen E. Reyman has suggested that the Magician was a Pochteca trader or a local employee of such a trader (Riley and Hendrick 1978:256). The Magician died nearly 300 years before the man with the leggings at Gila Pueblo. Contemporaneous with the Magician is the Mimbres bowl: Rabbit Hunt with Net (Brody 1977:Figure 115). The painted decoration on the bowl depicts three men hunting rabbits. One hunter wears leggings (Figure 49b). As early as these two examples of leggings are, there is

Figure 49. Leggings in the Late-Prehistoric Southwest.
a. Mimbres Black-on-white bowl design showing a woman wearing leg coverings as well as an apron overlaid with a stomacher (Bradfield 1929: Plate 79, No. 364).
b. Mimbres Black-on-white bowl design showing man with leggings (Brody 1977:Figure 115).
c. Tabira' Polychrome jar design showing man with leggings; Gran Quivira, Mound 7, Room 172, upper fill (Hayes and et al 1981: Figure 114e).

certainly contemporaneous documentation of leg coverings in the Codex Mendoza -- which pictures Aztec war regalia dating from A.D. 1440-1469 (Ross 1978:105). On the eastern periphery of the Southwest culture area, at Gran Quivira, a Tabira Polychrome jar decoration records a bear hunting scene (Hayes et al. 1981:Figure 114e). One of the hunters wears obvious leg coverings (Figure 49c). Tabira Polychrome was produced between A.D. 1650 and 1672. Plains Indians wore leggings into the historic period.

Gila Pueblo was on a major trade route to the south (Wood 1985:Figure 20), so the trader model might be relevant. William Underwood excavated approximately 1,000 burials in the general vicinity of Gila Pueblo, the vast majority of which were Salado interments. Of these, only two could be considered high-status. Located at Pinal Pueblo on the hill across Six

Shooter Canyon from Besh-ba-gowah, one grave was over two meters in depth -- oriented east-west, with steps leading down into the west end. The body had been covered with two mats -- one over the upper torso; the other, over the lower. The large skeleton of a male, less than 18 years of age at the time of death, was lying on its back with head to the west. Grave goods included 19 or 20 bowls and jars; a bow decorated with thickly-applied azurite and hematite paint; arrows crested in the same blue and red paints; and a number of blue-painted, slightly-flattened sticks or wands similar to those designated #10 in the diagram of the burial of the Magician (McGregor 1943:272-273). The paint on these sticks is a thick impasto which is identical to the thick red and blue paint on basket and shell specimens recovered from the excavations at Gila Pueblo and the Hagen Site. The adhesive which bound this still-brilliant paint is a very durable plastic, perhaps lac.

Although Underwood's high status burial is not nearly as elaborate as is the burial of the "Magician," and is widely separated from it in time, the presence in Six Shooter Canyon of both blue-painted sticks or wands and leggings may indicate some enduring significance. Azurite blue face paint is considered a sign of war, and may elicit a rage reaction from San Carlos Apaches of Yavapai ancestry even today. The femur of the Gila Pueblo man with leggings had a healed lesion resulting from a serious knee injury at some time before his death, which may indicate a more than usually active role in the community.

Red Apron. The only garment which survived the Third Fire relatively intact is a woman's apron. On the floor of the northeast quadrant of Room 110, the ceremonial room, an adult female was formally laid-out on her back with her head to the west and her feet to the east, just as she would have been in a grave. To her left was a child of about six years of age. To her right was an infant in a cradleboard. The childrens' heads were even with the woman's shoulders. The apron worn by this woman was made of coarse fiber, probably yucca. Each tassel was individually made of an S-spun yarn, Z-twisted back upon itself to form a two-ply unit about 15 cm in length. Construction of the apron was similar to Specimen No. 41 from Montezuma Castle (Kent 1954:60-61).

The apron was dyed a vivid scarlet with an organic material. The red was more brilliant than any cactus fruit, berry, bark, or lichen dye in collections with which it was compared, but was a good match for the color produced by cochineal. The cactus on the grounds of Gila Pueblo were thickly infested with cochineal insects until both cactus and insects were exterminated by Eastern Arizona College in the late 1970's. Cochineal insects are still present near a late Salado site in Kellner Canyon about 5 kilometers south of Gila Pueblo. Although cochineal is not known from the prehistoric Southwest, it was a major item of trade among Incas and Aztecs (Vietmeyer 1987:42-43). There is no reason why it could not have been produced at Gila Pueblo. The Gila Cliff Dwellings fiber collection includes a red-dyed tassel of 15 strands which may be part of an apron similar to the burned fragments found at Gila Pueblo (Anderson et al.1986:214-215).

Shell Bead Stomacher. Even more impressive than the apron itself is a stomacher of fine Clinocardium shell beads which was worn over it, draped in a graceful curve across the front with pendant loops at each side dropping from fastenings of what appear to be whale ear bones. From the bulk of calcined shell that protected a portion of the apron from the fire, we estimate that the number of beads in the stomacher was enormous, probably as many as six or seven thousand! Two thousand five hundred and seventy-six beads were sound enough to to recover and restring. A Mimbres woman on a bowl at Cameron Creek Village in southwestern New Mexico is wearing a stomacher of identical form over a much longer apron or skirt (Figure 49a) (Bradfield 1929:Plate 79:364). J. J. Brody (1978:16-17, 19, 21) points out that Mimbres bowls with life-form designs occur as mortuary offerings. He believes that figures with part or all of the face painted black represent deceased persons. Following his reasoning, the person pictured wearing the stomacher may represent a high status lady ready for burial, just like the lady laid out with her children in the ceremonial room at Gila Pueblo. The Mimbres lady and the Salado lady are separated in time by almost 300 years, but the stomachers that each wore were the same size. This may indicate that the stomacher is a standardized insignia of status which persisted over a long period of time, because of its socio-politico-religious significance.

Pouches. A second badly burned skeleton, found in the southwest corner of the ceremonial room, was an old adult male. Found among the skeletal remains were two triangular arrowheads: one of obsidian, the other of chert. Neither of these points is notched. They are the atypical type associated with the attackers and the same type found in the chest cavity of the high status man in Room 105. The chest of the man in the ceremonial room rested upon a large storage jar; his knees and lower legs were on the floor. His right forearm rested on the floor. No clothing remained. In his right hand he held a staff at least 40 cm in length and topped by a large blade of tiger chert. On his right hip were the charred remains of a plain-weave cotton pouch containing six carbonized kernels of corn, a spherical red quartzite concretion, a quartz crystal, and a flake scraper of gray-banded chert.

Evidence of a similar pouch was found with the torso of a younger man who died on the roof above the wall separating Room 99 and Room 102. This pouch contained a chalcedony "desert rose," an obsidian nodule, a quartz crystal, a copper bell, and a Clovis point that is similar in size and shape to the one Emil Haury (1975:v, 179-180) found at Ventana Cave. The torso of this man lay prone on the roof over a stone ball about 6 cm in diameter. Both Pueblo and Apache peoples encase stone balls of this size in rawhide to attach them to a wooden handle in a free-swinging manner. A wrist thong is passed through a hole in the opposite end of the handle to form a very effective club or mace.

A Tonto Polychrome male-human-effigy jar was recovered from Room 103 (Figure 23a). The personage depicted has pierced ears. He is wearing a patterned blanket over his shoulders, is dressed in a loincloth and footless stockings, and has a pouch on his right hip. On the pouch is a bold six-pointed, white star decoration. We wonder if this star may not be a precursor to the Aztec's Ce Acatl and the Pueblo people's Morning Star, a sort of patron saint of warriors (Day 1992:56; Parsons 1923:166). We next discuss hair pins, but we have one final observation to make regarding pouches: the only persons who appeared to be armed at Gila Pueblo wore pouches or hair pins.

Hair Pins. The remains of a large, older male were found lying on his right side, with his head to the south, on the floor or Room 105. From the orientation of the triangular, white, chert arrowhead within his chest

cavity it was apparent that he had been shot in the back with an arrow. His
attackers had killed him by smashing his head with a metate. He apparently
had been looking up when the blow came, as his neck broke and his face was
oriented toward his back. A double-bitted ax -- which well may have been a
weapon, rather than a tool -- lay to his right, level with his shoulder. Two
bone hair pins were in-place at the top of his head. One was a small section
of metapodial shaft. This pin is elliptical in section, sharply-pointed at
one end and squared at the other as though it had served as a device for
attaching a feather or fiber ornament. The other bone pin is an impressively
large ornamental pin made from the shaft of a deer tibia (Figure 50a). The
attachment hole reminds us of the Santa Cruz Phase Hohokam hair pin that
Haury (1976:Figure 15.4) found at Snaketown. Berlant (Brody et al.
1983:Figure 6) illustrates a Mimbres bowl depicting a man in a bat costume
with two hair ornaments (Figure 50c). One of those is an excellent
representation of the larger type of Gila Pueblo hair pin. The other may
represent the smaller pin, to which perishable decorations were attached.
The pins were not only similar in form, but also were worn in the same
position and placement.

One of the many people killed on the roof was a male who lay on the
southwest corner of Room 100, with his head to the east and his legs
extending across the southeast corner of the collapsed roof or Room 101.
Apparently he was killed on the second-story roof of Room 101 and his body
slipped partially onto the roof of Room 100 when it collapsed. The man wore
a large hair pin similar to the one in Room 105 (Figure 50b). In addition,
he wore a necklace or bracelet of dog whelks. Also on the roof of Room 101
was a straight hair pin cut from the metapodial of a whitetail deer, probably
the second of the two pins which apparently constitute a set. Room 101 was
the residential unit of which Room 105 was the storeroom. Beneath the floor
of Room 105 was the vault containing the highest status infant burial. These
remains may represent two or three generations of a family who carried high
inherited status.

The large pins both were cut from the tibae of whitetail deer and had
circular hollows drilled in their heads, which originally may have held sets
which were lost or destroyed in the fire. The Mimbres bowl design had a
similarly-ornamented head from which was suspended a feather tassel. Both
large pins were very black and glossy due to the carbonization of the oil
with which they were impregnated. They are strongly reminiscent of a large,
oil-impregnated, mammal-bone hair pin which was recovered from the
high-status burial of a very tall man excavated at Grasshopper Pueblo, which
was sent to McKusick for species identification. All three pins were so
thoroughly penetrated by oil that they must have been worn constantly for a
long period of years. The hair pin from Grasshopper Pueblo had a socket in
the end for the insertion of an ornament similar to the one shown on a Tabira
Black-on-white sherd recovered from Mound 7 at Gran Quivira (Figure 50d).
Classic Tabira Black-on-white dates to the first three-quarters of the
seventeenth century (Hayes et al. 1981:75, Figure 118).

Graduated-Shell Necklace. The fragmentary skeleton of a woman lay on the
floor of the northern half of Room 111; her head was near the eastern wall.
In the general vicinity of her neck was a mass of very thick, graduated-shell
beads which we assume are the remains of a necklace. The shell is so thick
that Dosinia ponderosa; a large, heavy-walled bivalve which may be collected

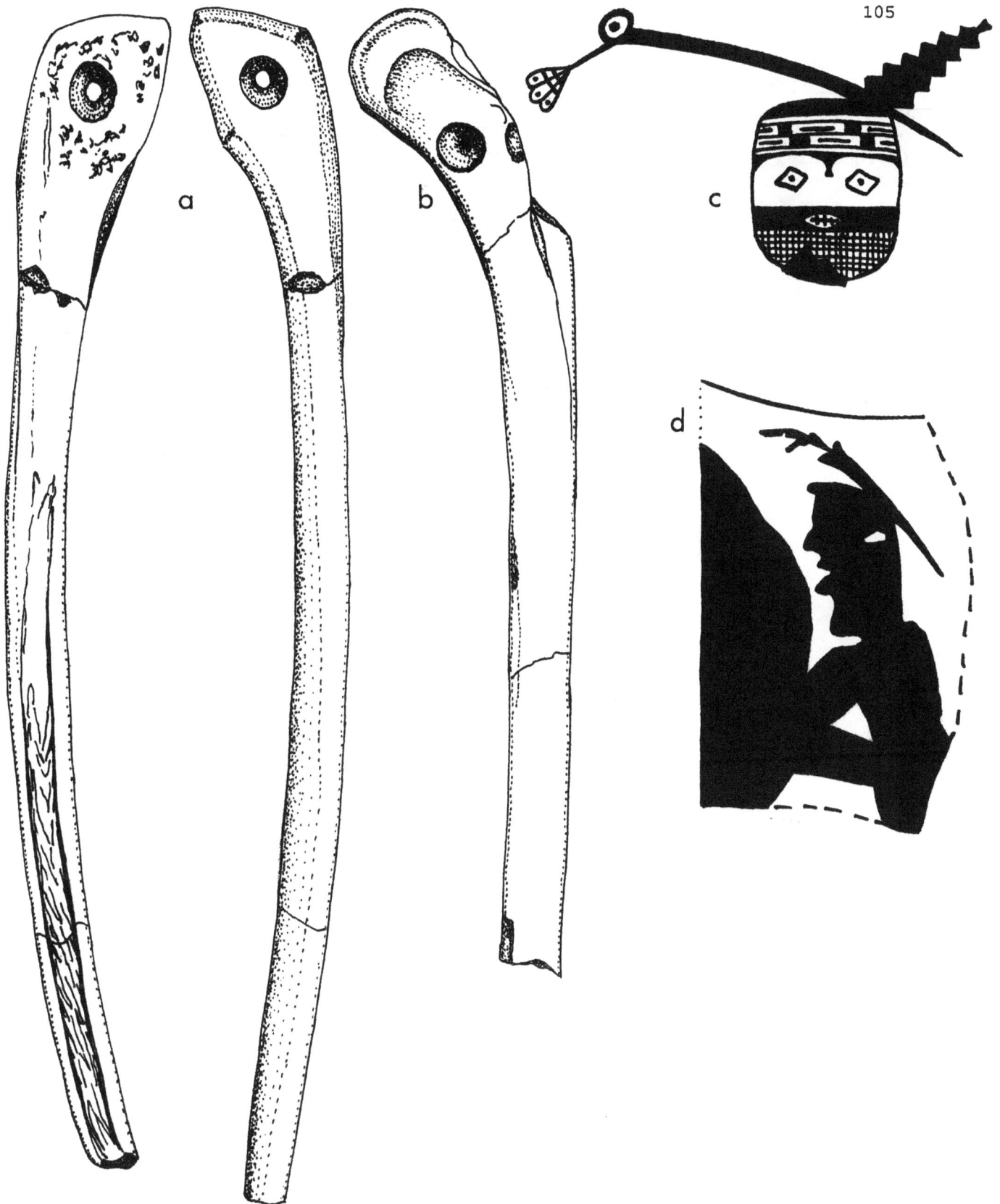

Figure 50. Hair Pins in the Late-Prehistoric Southwest.
a. Gila Pueblo, Room 105: two views of a hair pin made from the tibia of a white-tailed deer. Scale: X 1.
b. Gila Pueblo, Roof of Room 101; hair pin made from the tibia of a white-tailed deer. Scale: X 1.
c. Mimbres Polychrome bowl depiction of man in bat costume (Brody et al 1983: Figure 6).
d. Tabira' Black-on-white sherd; Gran Quivira, Mound 7 (Hayes et al, 1981: Figure 118).

on the mud flats of the Gulf of California; is the most probable source of raw material (Keen 1971:16). This necklace is a good match for one from a cremation displayed at the Sharlot Hall Museum in Prescott, Arizona. Unfortunately, the Sharlot Hall necklace was procured by a hired pot hunter; there is no record of whether it came from a Hohokam, Prescott Culture, or Yavapai cremation.

The association of this handsome necklace with the remains of a woman was unexpected. However, a woman depicted on a Mimbres Black-on-white bowl from the Treasure Hill Site is wearing a necklace (Brody 1977:189, Fig. 148). The necklace from Room 111 may be an insignia of office, similar to the stomacher from Room 110.

THE SALADO AS SEEN FROM GILA PUEBLO

SALADO DEVELOPMENTAL PERIOD: THE PINTO PHASE ENDING WITH THE FIRST FIRE

Based upon conversations that we had with Harold Gladwin over 20 years ago -- which, in turn, were based upon the pottery types we recovered -- it appears that the Salado developmental period at Gila Pueblo began no later than about A.D. 1225. The redistribution complex centered about Ceremonial Room 110 is not typical of residential or storage rooms known from previous excavations. It is unique in the site and may even be unique within the Salado culture. Associated painted pottery includes Pinto Polychrome bowls and small, bulbous-necked jars which appear to be transitional to Gila Polychrome. This period of occupation appears equivalent to the late Roosevelt Phase and the early Gila Phase and was terminated about A.D. 1260 by The First Fire.

The First Fire was caused by attackers who were not local to the area. We base this assertion on the presence of an arrowhead type which is not found in burials or associated with occupational deposits at Gila Pueblo or the neighboring Salado sites. The portal outside Room 100 would have given relatively easy access to the roof and may even have been set on fire by the defenders of the pueblo. There is no evidence of a floor or of ladder holes in Room 100 at this time period, and apparently there was no hatch leading to the roof. No fire pit was found in this surface, so no smoke hole was necessary. Thus it appears that the exterior door leading to Room 100 was no danger to the security to the pueblo.

All the rooms which existed at this time were burned in The First Fire, and there is evidence of conflict in Room 110. In spite of the damage, however, the pueblo remained as a working unit. The rubble from the fire was cleaned-up, and the room plan remained unaltered. However, portales were not rebuilt, and the knee-high balustrades which surmounted the exterior walls probably were added during this reconstruction.

SALADO FLORESCENT PERIOD: THE GILA PHASE ENDING WITH THE SECOND FIRE

The loss of personnel brought about by the attack or raid at the time The First Fire seems to have stimulated the most prosperous period in the entire history of the southern portion of Gila Pueblo. The hearth in Room 103 was cleaned-out following The First Fire but was never used again. Room 103 remained a storage room for more than 80 years. After A.D. 1325, new residential units were built which had increasingly large numbers of rooms. Room size also increased. Family living space expanded. In our conversations with Harold Gladwin, he said that Room 99 is an excellent example of residential rooms found in the main body of the pueblo. He also told us that the adjacent room Room 102 is a good example of a storeroom. The rectangular hearth of Room 99, with its basalt firedogs, is suitable for the support of the small Gila Polychrome bowls which were popular during the early portion of the Gila Phase. Doorways were above-floor and had a modified T-shape; often with only one side of the T, or with the two sides of the T having different heights.

The Florescent Period is coterminus with the occurrence of well-developed Gila Polychrome pottery. All painted effigy jars were Gila

108

Polychrome. Gila Polychrome bowls were beginning to be made in larger sizes and, by the end of the period, hearths were being rounded to fit them. Shell work reached its zenith, exemplified by a carved univalve which could have been rolled like a cylindrical seal to produce a design.

The Florescent Period was brought to a close by an earthquake, an attack of the Pueblo, and The Second Fire. John Hohman has suggested a model for the destruction of Gila Pueblo as the result of conflict with the inhabitants of Besh-ba-gowah; a larger, neighboring pueblo. Pinal Creek fronts the east face of Gila Pueblo. Until 1929, when the shaft of the Old Dominion Mine breached the local water table, Pinal Creek ran the year around. Folks still alive today used to fish in it. Gila Pueblo lies upstream from Besh-ba-gowah, at a location where the creek bottom widens considerably and the surrounding ground is relatively flat. Almost certainly the place where Gila Pueblo was built was chosen because of this anomaly of the creek and almost certainly both the people at Gila Pueblo and those at Besh-ba-gowah led water from this creek to their fields. The production of corn requires ample supplies of water at the time of silking, lest the kernels fail to set in the cob. In years when monsoon rains were late in coming or less than adequate, the folks at Gila Pueblo may have used available irrigation water before it ever reached Besh-ba-gowah. Water has ever been a touchy subject in the Southwest.

In various public lectures Irene Vickery stated her strong conviction that the entire site of Besh-ba-gowah had been destroyed by fire several times. She also found evidence of an earthquake, with telephone-pole-sized pine roof beams "twisted and broken like toothpicks." The canyons south of Globe are underlain by a fault system which is quite active. Gila Pueblo may have fallen victim to one local quake, and Besh-ba-gowah may have suffered similar damage at a later time. The earthquake which occurred at about A.D. 1340 brought the walls of Gila Pueblo down farther in just a few minutes than they had collapsed in all the hundreds of years since the site had been abandoned. The attack following the earthquake came so swiftly that it must have originated in the immediate area. Besh-ba-gowah had the proximity and the manpower and the motive to have brought about the decimation of the populous of Gila Pueblo, which occurred at the time of The Second Fire.

HIATUS

Following The Second Fire, Gila Pueblo was abandoned for a period of about five years. We base this temporal estimation of the relative amount of plaster washed down from still-standing walls, as compared to the amount of plaster washed from the unstabilized walls of Room 110 following our Eastern Arizona College excavation. Gladwin's excavations did not penetrate as deeply as this hiatus period, so Haury's two tree-ring date clusters at A.D. 1345 and A.D. 1385 fall after this hiatus. The most probable date for the reoccupation and reconstruction of Gila Pueblo is A.D. 1345, which places The Second Fire about five years earlier: ca. A.D. 1340.

SALADO REFUGEE PERIOD: THE TONTO PHASE ENDING WITH THE THIRD FIRE

The Refugee Period is so-named because the original living units were broken up into small dwellings, and the new singe rooms added to the pueblo were randomly constructed without the overall planning which was apparent in the previous two periods. There also was greater variety in pottery designs. The pottery in Room 107, the most recently built room in this section of the pueblo, included designs which were identical to those found at Besh-ba-gowah. Polychrome bowls were large and broad, with recurved rims bearing simple designs above the life line.

The site may have been resettled first by inhabitants of some of the small, local, hilltop sites who drew together for mutual protection. The Besh-ba-gowah pottery designs may indicate social intercourse with or expansion from that site. We have no terminal date for the occupation of Besh-ba-gowah. Vickery's finding that the entire pueblo burned suggests violence; but whether this occurred before or after The Third Fire, which closed the curtain on the Salado occupation of Gila Pueblo, is not known. A lack of very late Tonto Polychrome at Besh-ba-gowah suggests that Pinal Pueblo and Gila Pueblo lasted longer.

By the early 1400's, the Gila Pueblo Salados were suffering from various pressures. A large population was overstressing their environment. The preponderance of jackrabbits in proportion to cottontails indicates that the area was denuded of woody vegetation. A water well excavation in Kellner Canyon indicated that Salado artifacts lay on a six-foot-deep layer of black soil in the canyon bottom. This was covered with nearly a foot of adobe which had washed over it, topped by a thin layer of topsoil just beneath the present ground surface. It is easy to appreciate the problem that sheet erosion caused by deforestation would have posed for the Salado farmers. Coupled with this was disruption from raiding.

At least a portion of the North Ruin at the Hagen Site was consumed by fire about A.D. 1400. This was at or about the time of the destruction of Gila Pueblo and perhaps was caused by the same attack. The attack at Gila Pueblo occurred when the roof was covered with vessels containing large quantities of both shelled and unshelled corn. Forty years of experience in the growing of corn in nearby Kellner Canyon have demonstrated to us that it is absolutely necessary to harvest and dry all corn before the fall equinoctial rains. Fail to do so, and mold is the result. Early in the season, when the corn is in full tassel, full ears are produced. Later in the season there is little pollen left, and the ears are poorly filled. From all appearances, full cobs were harvested as they matured and dried whole. Mature kernels from sparsely filled cobs at the end of the season probably were saved as shelled corn, in order to reduce the space needed for storage. The partially-filled cobs of green corn still on the stalk at the end of the growing season could have been cooked fresh or fermented into beverage.

Casas Grandes in Chihuahua fell during a spring equinoctial festival (DiPeso 1974:Vol. 2, p. 405; Vol. 8, pp. 273-274). We think this to be the case, because: 1) the mescal ovens in the local brewing complex were full, indicating a festival; and 2) a very young macaw was found in the rubble of the breeding complex, which was destroyed at the fall of Casas Grandes. Macaw chicks emerge from the shell in mid-March. It is possible that Gila

Pueblo fell at a similar festival commemorating the fall equinox. We know that the fall harvest had been completed just prior to the fall of the pueblo.

The scene at the time of the attack was one of a busy, peaceful community. Women were grinding corn on the roof; surrounded by children playing with miniature pottery, fired-clay dogs, and four real puppies. Almost every jar and bowl which was small enough to move was on the roof. A great many were filled with corn, both shelled and unshelled. A number of the bowls were nested, most often in sets of five, as though they were wares being offered for trade. Because we see no evidence of resistance, the attackers may have been among the inhabitants as guests or customers or both. Carbonized remains of food set-out in bowls included gruel and a rabbit and quail stew, with the meat still on the bones. There also was evidence of a soup, whose main ingredient was rodents which either had been ground upon a metate or whose bones had otherwise been rendered small enough to swallow with ease. One woman was at a metate with a jar of shelled corn to her right. Ground meal lay in a bowl in front of the metate. She fell across her grinding stone, her body covering those of two children. The body of a puppy lay nearby. The bodies of several other women covered those of small children. Children six and seven years of age died holding toddlers and infants in their arms. Men fell singly and in small groups. The attackers invaded the ceremonial room and killed all left alive there. Even Room 105, the most remote and isolated area in all of the southern portion of the pueblo, was entered. Three people died in front of the doorway, and 11 people who had taken refuge there were slaughtered. We recovered the remains of 70 Salado people from the floors and roofs of 13 of the rooms destroyed in this attack (Figures 51-53, Table 19). The population was composed of infants, small children, and adults. There were remains of only a single person between the ages of 12 and 21. It appears that the motive for the attack was the capture of slaves. Arrowheads associated with the attack were identical to those which marked The First Fire destruction. William Underwood said that precisely this same projectile point type is characteristic of the Armer Complex, a Classic Period Hohokam site located on the northern side of Roosevelt Lake. Underwood (personal communication) suggested a model in which Armer Complex slavers carried off vigorous youths, young women, and strong children; driving them south along the trade route which leads to Mexico from this area. The pueblo was destroyed. But by this time, the Tonto Basin platform mound sites had passed from power; and Besh-ba-gowah recently had been abandoned. At first this model seemed overly fanciful to us. Upon a careful reexamination of the skeletal materials recovered, it seems to us that slaving presents a plausible explanation for the absence of a significant portion of the able-bodied population from the record. In any event, the task of burying so many dead was insuperable. Not long after this disaster the pueblo was burned, perhaps by surviving neighbors. This was The Third Fire.

FINAL DAYS OF GILA PUEBLO: ENDING WITH THE FOURTH FIRE

We have an archaeomagnetic date of A.D. 1430 for Room S-9 at the Hagen Site. That tells us that a generation after The Third Fire there were Salado people living at or near Gila Pueblo. The north wall of the ground floor of Room 111 at Gila Pueblo was little damaged by The Third Fire; the collapsed roof

Figure 51. Gila Pueblo Unburied Remains on Ground Floor.

KEY

A = Adult
B = Infant to 24 months
C = Child
F = Female
L = Large
M = Male
O = Old
S = Small
V = Very
Y = Young

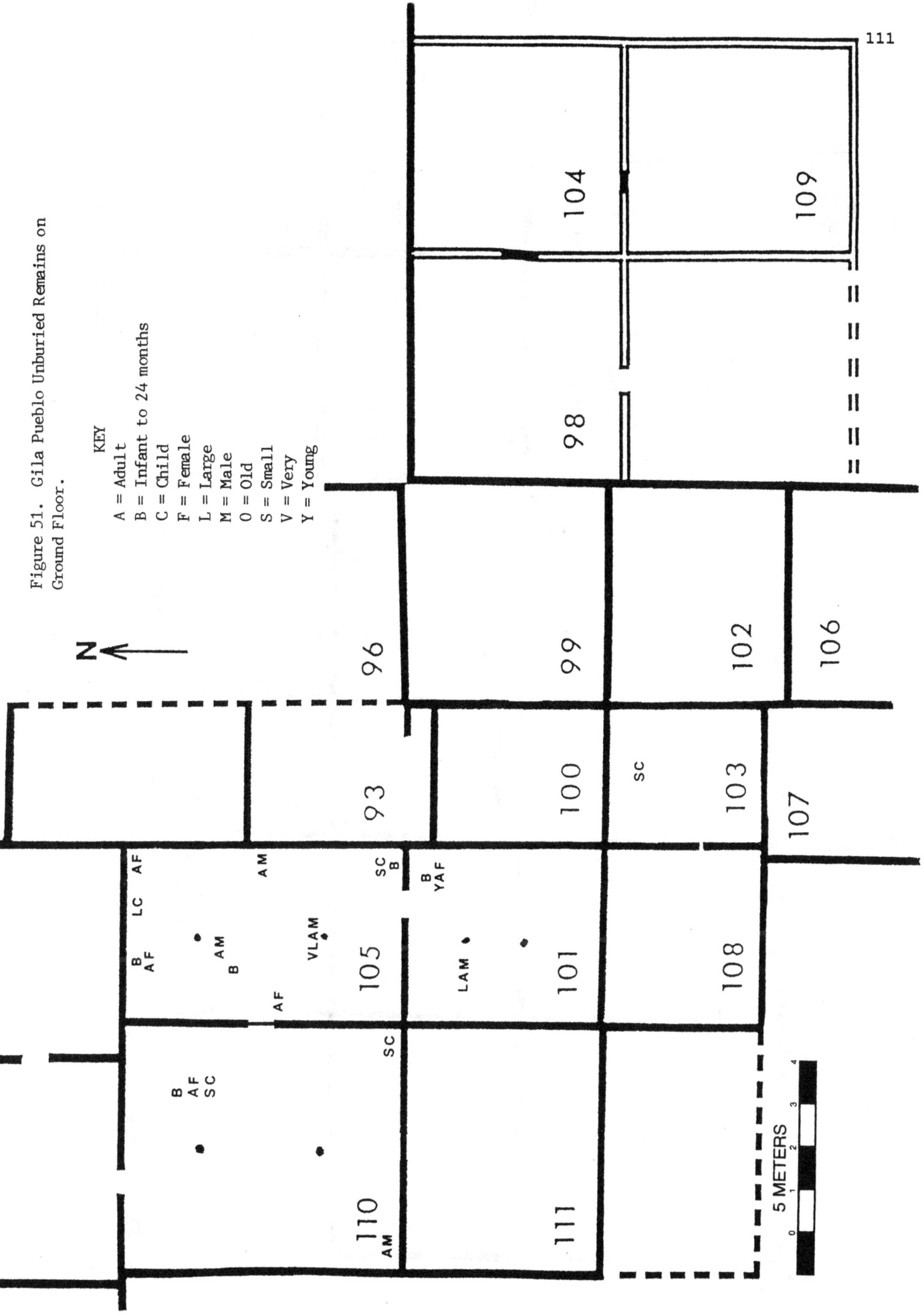

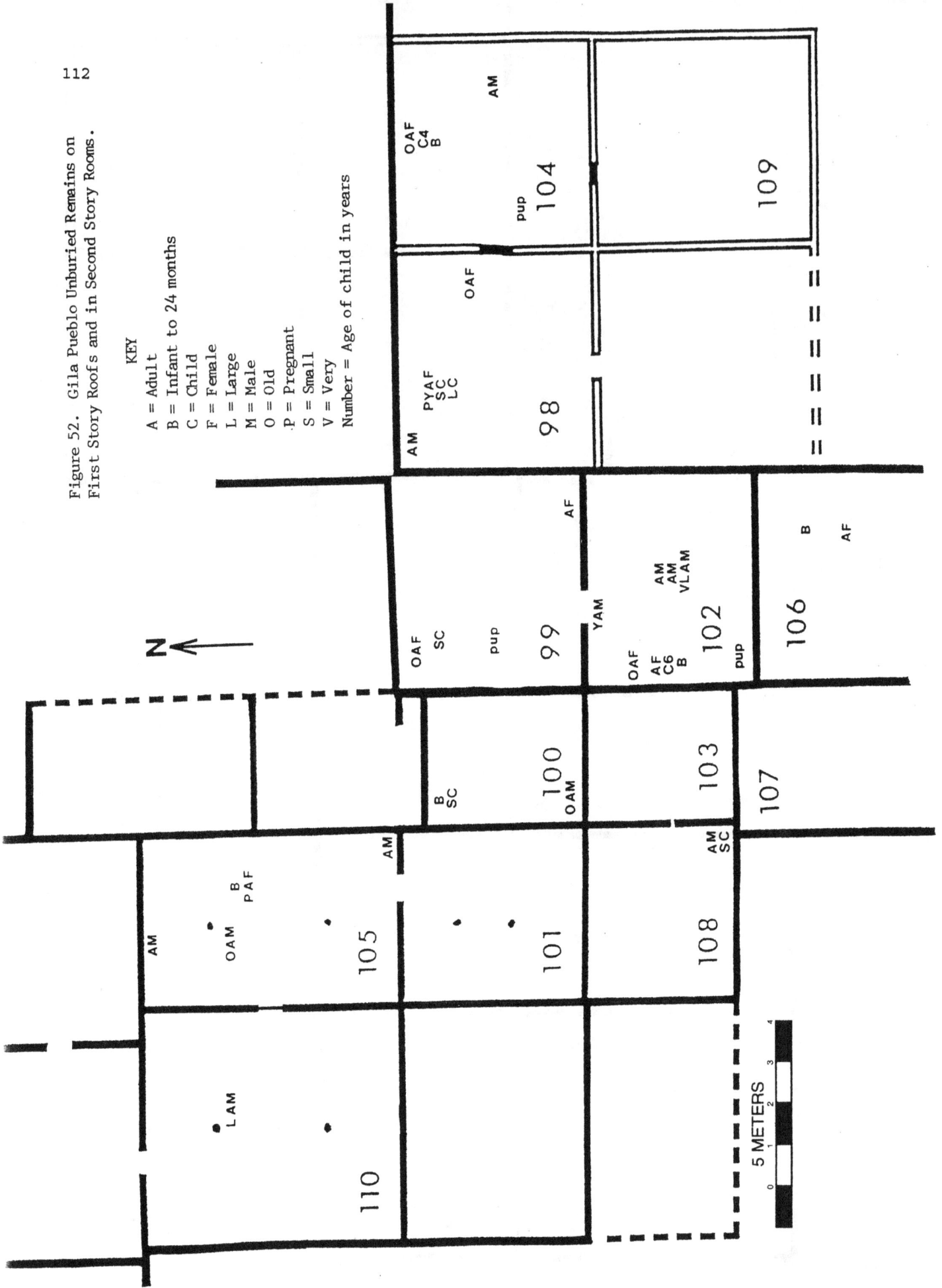

Figure 52. Gila Pueblo Unburied Remains on First Story Roofs and in Second Story Rooms.

KEY

A = Adult
B = Infant to 24 months
C = Child
F = Female
L = Large
M = Male
O = Old
P = Pregnant
S = Small
V = Very
Number = Age of child in years

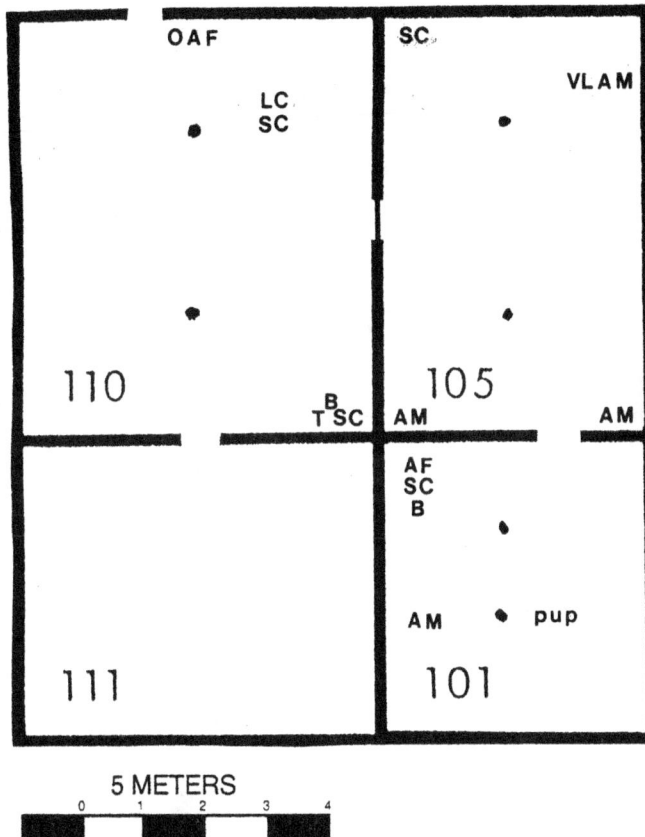

Figure 53. Gila Pueblo Unburied Remains on Second Story Roofs.

KEY

A = Adult
B = Infant to 24 months
C = Child
F = Female
L = Large
M = Male
O = Old
S = Small
T = Adolescent
V = Very

protected it. At least a hundred years after The Third Fire, someone else camped in Room 111. The Third Fire burned a quantity of cotton bolls stored in the second story of Room 101 and the northern portion of Room 111. The fire was so hot that the plaster on the north wall of Room 111 had been fired like pottery in a kiln. It was quite sound, although cracked and blackened. Two areas of plaster looked like birds. One resembled a duck; the other, a turkey. The folks who had camped in the room also saw the resemblances, and completed the pictures by adding an eye to each bird.

The reoccupation of Room 111 resulted in two lenses of trash: one in Room 110 and one in Room 101 containing, in addition to local species, the bones of elk and bison. These lenses are located midway between the collapsed roofs of the Salado occupation and the present surface. We estimate the date of this camp lies somewhere in the 1600s, since a horse would have been an appropriate mode of transport for meat from such large animals.

Later yet, someone dug a rectangular shaft down to the floor of Room 111, cremated therein the body of a large adult male wearing a necklace composed of 335 brass beads, and refilled the shaft. Alan Ferg (personal communication 1993), who has carried-on an extensive study of these beads, dates them as post 1890. This cremation is Fire Four.

Emil Haury suggested to us that the remains might represent a Yavapai cremation. There is abundant local tradition, much of which is recorded and on file at the Globe Historical Society Museum, of early Yavapai in the area. Native Americans of Yavapai ancestry living on the nearby San Carlos Apache Reservation today are quite firm in their assertion that the Mountain Spirits are Yavapai dieties, not Apache. It is their belief that the

Table 19. Gila Pueblo Unburied Human Remains

	Room 98	Room 99	Room 100	Room 101	Room 102	Room 103	Room 104	Room 105	Room 106	Room 107	Room 108	Room 109	Room 110	Room 111	Total
In Utero	1							1							2
Infant, birth to 24 months			1	2	1		1	4	1				2		12
Small Child, 2 to 7 years	1	1	1	1	1	1	1	2			1		4		14
Large Child, 8 to 10 years	1							1					1		3
11 to 21 years													1		1
Young Adult, 21 to 25 years															
Male					1										1
Female	1*			1											2
Adult, 26 to 39 years															
Male	1			2	3		1	8			1		2		18
Female		1		1	1			4*	1				1	1	10
Old Adult, 40+ years															
Male			1					1							2
Female	1	1			1		1	1					1		6
Total	6	3	3	7	8	1	4	21	2	0	2	0	12	1	70

Total adult males......22
Total adult females....17

* Pregnant female.

Mountain Spirits have lived on Mount Graham or Mount Turnbull or both for a
very long time, and certainly long before the Apaches came upon the scene.
The Indians who jumped from the precipice at Apache Leap between Superior and
Miami were Yavapais. Older residents in the area remember that a band of
Yavapais lived in Wheatfields, down Pinal Creek from Globe; until they moved
away, in order to take jobs connected with the construction of Roosevelt Dam.

Gifford (1930-1932:232) describes a Yavapai cremation as follows: "The
dead were cremated, usually within the dwelling, which was pulled down over
the corpse, or on a pile of brush outside if the dwelling were a cave.
Personal belongings were consumed in the flames. The camp was shifted. If
the person died in a cave, all food stored therein was abandoned."

CONCLUSIONS

The archaeological record at Gila Pueblo consists of four occupation
periods. Earliest, and not documented in this monograph, was a Hohokam pit
house village which extended down the ridge north-northwest from the restored
pueblo. This village may have dated in the A.D. 800s or A.D. 900s. Second
was the Salado occupation extending from perhaps A.D. 1225 to about A.D.
1440. Third was the camp in the remains of Room 111 of the bison and elk
hunters. Fourth was the apparent Yavapai cremation in this same room
postdating 1890.

The record of the Salado occupation consists of three vignettes provided
by disastrous fires. Each of these fires brought a period of occupation to a
sudden end. But each also preserved many details of life in-place, which
otherwise would have been lost to us and to posterity.

Ceremonial/Redistribution Complex. The 13 rooms at the southern end of Gila
Pueblo excavated during the early 1970's included a portion of a
ceremonial/redistribution complex. This addition to the pueblo was first
constructed sometime between about A.D. 1225 and an attack with fire which
has been dated at about A.D. 1260 by archaeomagnetism and radioactive
carbon. The complex was built upon a relatively clean surface and at ground
level. Only a few black-on-white sherds were recovered from beneath the
lowest floor.

Ceremonial Room 110 was surrounded, at least on the south and east, by a
double row of rooms. At its beginning there were raised doorways in the
north, south, and west walls. The east wall had a rectangular floor level
aperture which, for the entire duration of the use of the room, was filled by
a wooden construction. There was a second story covering Rooms 101, 105,
110, and 111. The only access to Room 105, other than through the wooden
construction, was through Room 101. The single cooking hearth found was in
Room 103. We assume that all but Rooms 103 and 110 were used for storage
during this period. Around A.D. 1260 the pueblo was attacked and burned, but
the survivors reroofed and continued using the rooms in the same pattern as
before.

About A.D. 1340 the pueblo was badly damaged by an earthquake, and
immediately attacked and burned. The inhabitants seem to have been wiped-out
at this time. The floors were covered with a foot and a half of rubble
interspersed with unburied bodies. Mud plaster washed from the walls,
covering the wreckage and giving the appearance of sterile soil. Test pits
indicate that this is the level to which Gladwin dug.

After a hiatus of at least five years, the pueblo was reoccupied, apparently by two separate groups. A large adult male had taken shelter from the earthquake in the west doorway of Room 110. His lower legs were caught in the rubble, and he died in the fire. His skeleton was plastered-over, and the ground floor rooms west of Room 110 permanently were separated from the complex. The bottoms of the doorways of the rooms east and south of Room 105 were raised at this time to correspond with the new floor level. These doorways and the door to Room 111 were blocked during a period of general remodeling -- which tree rings tell us took place about A.D. 1385. Rooms 101, 103, and 108 were fitted with the lipped, round hearths that characterized late rooms. Room 110 now had a large, shallow hearth which probably only saw service as a source of illumination. During the latest Salado occupation of the pueblo, the ground level of Room 105 contained three raised granary bases and other storage vessels. The second story of Room 105 was a work room for the production of ground pigments. The room above 110 was a work room for production of arrow shafts and probably also was used for the dressing of hides. The rooms above 101 and 111 contained unspun cotton. The ground level Room 101 appeared to be the headquarters of a high status person and contained, among other things, an 18-inch selenite crystal.

Controlled Access To Stored Food And Raw Materials. The attack-with-fire which ended the Salado occupation of the main portion of Gila Pueblo came at about A.D. 1440. At this time the ceremonial/redistribution complex served several purposes. It provided a setting for ceremonial and other integrative activities of the community. It served as a locus for communal food storage. Occupying by far the most space, however, were several commercial activities. It appears to us that among the goods which the folks at Gila Pueblo were exporting were: 1) cotton cloth, 2) fine Clinocardium shell beads; 3) turquoise disc beads, tabular beads, and mosaics; 4) ground pigments; and nests of five polychrome bowls. The complex served to safeguard valuable raw materials such as unspun cotton and Clinocardium shells. It served as a place for the manufacture and storage of ground pigments such as azurite, malachite, red and yellow ochres, specularite, and white pigment that appears to have been made from gypsum. It also seems to have been used for the storage of finished turquoise jewelry. All effigy vessels; bird, human, and quadruped; found within the rooms were from this complex. These appear to have been items of status rather than trade.

Personal Adornment. Among the 70 unburied dead excavated from the wreckage of the ca. A.D. 1400 level of these 13 rooms were six persons with elaborate personal adornment. Five of the six were found within or on the roof of the ceremonial/redistribution complex. Of these 70 persons, whose remains littered the late level of the excavated area, the only ones who had any sign of a weapon were the two men with the pouches on their belts and the older male with the hair pins who died in Room 105. And, to us, the beautiful blade of tiger chert appears more ceremonial than utilitarian. It may be that weapons were signs of rank, rather than customary equipment for the inhabitants of the pueblo.

High Status Infant Burials. After a major rebuilding of the pueblo, which has been tree-ring dated at A.D. 1385, subfloor burials appear for the first time. Of three burials beneath the floor of Room 101, two included a small bowl. The third was more elaborate. The burial pit was shaped like a boot, with the infant placed in the side cavity and offerings in the main shaft. The bottom of the shaft was floored with the two halves of a rounded-rectangular stone tablet that had been broken deliberately. Above the broken tablet was a flaked knife of petrified wood.

Just inside Room 105 was another elaborate subfloor burial of a very premature infant. The interment was made in a vault that was lined with a layer of cobbles about the size of golf balls. The tiny fetus, only about six inches in length, was covered with a long strand of argelite beads and enclosed between to halves of a San Carlos Red-on-brown bowl. Just south of this burial was a circular pit of less formal construction, which may have held perishable offerings buried at a later time.

Status Summary. In summary, the presence of older adults and younger adults with elaborate personal adornment and the burials of infants and fetuses with offerings within a ceremonial/redistribution complex suggest to us that hereditary high status was present at Gila Pueblo during the later portion of Salado occupation. The men with leggings, however, have no younger counterparts. They may exemplify achieved status in the role of hunt or war leaders.

Breakdown of Central Control. Gila Pueblo and its sister pueblo Besh-ba-gowah were not isolated settlements located somewhere far back in the Southwestern hinterlands. They were cosmopolitan trade centers sitting smack in the cultural mainstream at their point in time. In all respects, they were typical products of their era.

The social system of the Gila Pueblo Salado is indicated by the dual division of village layout. Dual division of communities in the New World apparently began with the Olmecs about 1,200 B.C. Three major sites in the Gulf Coast lowlands; San Lorenzo, La Venta, and Laguna de los Cerros; display this settlement form (Miller and Taube 1993:15). Creel and McKusick (1994:Figure 4) describe a dual division of the Galaz Site in the Mimbres Valley, which is closer to Gila Pueblo and Besh-ba-gowah in both time and space. And closer still, Kinishba and Grasshopper -- with arroyos running through the center of their pueblos -- very strongly resemble what is seen at Taos Pueblo today, where the Pueblo River physically separates the two halves of the village. In our estimation, Morris (1986:544-545) has it exactly correct: the dual division he sees at Antelope House is ancestral to both modern Western Pueblo and Rio Grande Pueblo.

Presumably, the cardinal directions are based on the movements of the sun: north-south on the solstices and east-west on the diurnal path of the sun and on the equinoxes. Whereas some contemporaneous communities -- such as Kinishba and Grasshopper, for example -- are divided by watercourses; Besh-ba-gowah is divided on a north-south axis and Gila Pueblo, on an east-west. These variations may indicate community specialization in ceremonial observances of the solstices at Besh-ba-gowah and of the equinoxes at Gila Pueblo. In any case, the final destruction of Gila Pueblo appears to have occurred during a celebration at about the time of the fall equinox.

Situated as it is on a main trade route along the San Pedro River, the Gila Pueblo neighborhood received goods from the Casas Grandes area to the south in the form of specialty shells, copper bells, and scarlet macaws.

Possibly more important were ideas of Mesoamerican origin evidenced by basket-form vessels and human-effigy vessels. Remains of birds of sacrifice suggest the veneration of local manifestations of Mesoamerican supernaturals. These include the Old Fire God, Xiuhtecutli; the Rain God, Tlaloc; the Sun; the Wind God/Ehecatl and the Morning Star/Ce Acatl manifestations of Quetzalcoatl; the Corn Mother and the Water Goddess manifestations of the Great Mother; and the Sorcerer and Xipe Toltec manifestations of Tezcatlipoca.

John Hohmann's 1992 doctoral dissertation is the most comprehensive examination of Salado mortuary practices ever undertaken. It is unique in the insights into Salado social organization which it has produced. Equally unique is the archaeological record provided by three catastrophic fires at Gila Pueblo; which starkly provide family groupings of persons with their tools and weapons in their hands, their food cooking on their hearths, and their customary attire upon their bodies. The conclusions derived from these complementary masses of data agree in large measure.

The Gila Pueblo data indicate a social organization involving the following elements:

1. A major pueblo with one large outlier community, the Hagen Site, and a series of several smaller outliers.

2. Dual division of the pueblo, which is evident at Gila Pueblo when first built and is present in the Southwest at least as early as A.D. 1100.

3. Hereditary high status involving two sets of males and females, which is also identifiable in the Southwest at least as early as A.D. 1100. This status is unrelated to the accumulation of material goods, but involves the control of raw materials and trade goods as well as ceremonial functions.

4. An office held by a large, mature male; perhaps a hunt or war chief; which may involve achieved status.

In addition to serving as a focus for religious activity, the ceremonial/redistribution complex served several other functions. Its storerooms were a repository for food, precious raw materials, and finished trade goods. Small rooms with hearths served as dwellings and larger ones as places of group-manufacturing activity.

Five main exports can be identified:

1. Ground pigments -- including red, yellow, and black iron oxides and blue and green copper oxides.

2. Turquoise disc and tabular beads and turquoise mosaic.

3. Nests of five polychrome bowls.

4. Fine shell beads.

5. Cotton cloth.

Many authors have produced models of the prehistoric life cycle. At Gila Pueblo we now have concrete evidence of the Salado life history and family composition. The infant began its life on a reed cradleboard by its mother's side. As a toddler it was cared for by another child, six or seven years of age, or by an aged female. The typical family consisted of the mother and father, children spaced at three to four year intervals, and perhaps a grandparent. The aged and infirm could look forward to good care and light tasks suited to their abilities.

Within this basic framework of trade-network position, Mesoamerican-based world view, village organization, and both hereditary and achieved leadership; there appear changes through time which are parallel to contemporaneous developments in other, much larger, communities.

The beginning of raiding in the local area can be documented at A.D. 1260 at Gila Pueblo. The social system appears to have continued unaltered by this attack, and the pueblo achieves its highest fluorescence during the following 80 years. When the pueblo was destroyed about A.D. 1340, all ceremonial artifacts were concentrated on or in front of the permanent slat altar which separated Rooms 110 and 105. Presumably, there was a single focus of central control at this time.

When the pueblo was rebuilt in 1345 -- only five years later -- the ceremonial room was divided into two mirror-image halves, with two separate sets of looms and the addition of a sipapu in the middle of each half. One focus of central control obviously had given way to two agencies of control. The northern half of the room was more formal in appearance, and presumably was the remnant of the old regime. The southern half of the room was less well organized. It became better organized in the renovation of 1385, but never equalled the precision of the northern section.

By the fall of Gila Pueblo in about 1440, there were five foci of ceremonial objects in the southern end of the pueblo alone, plus a "rectangular kiva which had a platform at one end" (McGregor 1965:423) which was excavated by Gladwin. Presumably, ceremonial paraphernalia were distributed among various lineages in the pueblo -- each of which had to cooperate in providing their portion of a ceremony, in order to make contact with the supernatural possible and effective.

While these thing were happening south of Globe, even more drastic events were transpiring in the southern part of Arizona. Teague (1993:435-454) outlines the oral history account of an actual war in which one platform-mound community after another was decimated. According to tradition, warriors from south of Benson or Baboquevari arose to strike Casa Grande, Lower Santan, Upper Santan, Sweetwater, Casa Blanca, Los Muertos and, last of all, Pueblo Grande. Flood and drought data indicate that this occurred at about A.D. 1358.

This breakdown of Hohokam central control was foreshadowed by attacks on the outlying settlements, like Gila Pueblo. It also coincides with the breakdown of social control at Gila Pueblo, which we see no evidence of in 1340. It is evident in 1345, just five years later, and only 13 years before the final destruction of the Hohokam social system. With trade to the Hohokam region disrupted, it is no wonder that post-1440 contact with Casas Grandes in Chihuahua is so conspicuous.

SUGGESTIONS FOR FUTURE RESEARCH

During the course of analyzing the artifacts recovered from our excavations, all sorts of nagging and intriguing suggestions for future research considerations began to present themselves. For example, whether or not several of the categories of stone tools abundant at the Hagen Site are especially diagnostic of that site in particular or the Salado Culture in general is not possible to determine at this time. Published comparable data from other Southwestern sites are insufficient. Examples of some of the specifics that we suggest be considered in future analyses are:

1. Mescal Knives. The Salado were not the only desert dwellers who made use of mescal knives. Nor were they the only people who notched their knives. But a characteristic of late Salado sites may be that most knives are notched, whereas elsewhere only an occasional knife is notched. At the contemporary late Hohokam site of Los Muertos, only about one mescal knife in 20 was notched. At the Hagen Site most of the mescal knives were notched, and at the Tonto Cliff Dwellings all three whole specimens were notched.

2. Firedogs. The use of firedogs by late-prehistoric inhabitants of the Southwest was not limited to the Salado. But few are reported in the literature from contemporary southern Arizona sites. The large, hemispherical Hagen Site specimens are quite distinctive. In subsequent analyses, if they occur elsewhere, they will be readily recognizable. recognizable.

3. Trough Manos. Trough manos from the Hagen Site were characterized by diagonal polish near the leading edge on the right side and near the trailing edge on the left side. This probably is diagnostic not of the Hagen Site or the Salado Culture in particular, but of trough manos in general.

Another artifact category that may or may not be distinctively Salado are the large Clinocardium shells that were given a thick coat of paint, usually blue, on their exterior surface.

THE SALADO TODAY

What became of the Salado -- the people of Gila Pueblo and Besh-ba-gowah and the Tonto Cliff Dwellings? It is our belief that the Western Pueblo peoples of yesterday are the Western Pueblo peoples of today. We are not the authors of this thought. It goes back at least to the fertile mind of Frank Hamilton Cushing. He was only a very few months into his epic four and a half years sojurn at Zuni when he realized that what he was seeing at Zuni was the result of the mingling of Anasazi and Mogollon ancestral cultures and when he began visiting and making notes on ancestral Zunian ruins in the White Mountains and in the Verde Valley (Green 1990:99; 100; 119; 146; 154; 175; 372, fn.31; 387, fn. 38).

What especially is exciting to us is the fact that we believe that we can see certain of yesterday's Salado traits and characteristics and patterns being perpetuated by today's Hopis and Zunis and Acomas and, even more fascinating, by the Navajo of today: such things as the Hopi corn symbol, the Hopi's tradition of burying naming bowls with infants, and the Navajo's tradition of incorporating intentional mistakes and spirit exits in various items of manufacture. We discussed the naming bowls continuum earlier, in conjunction with our description of Gila Pueblo subfloor infant burials. Elsewhere, we have described the Salado corn symbol in detail (Young 1967:31-32, Table 3). Basically, it is as Florence Hawley Ellis described it in 1928 (p. 53): a black dot in a white square (Figure 54). It is our thesis that the traditional Navajo practices of incorporating intentional mistakes and leaving spirit exits in various items of manufacture have their origins in antecedent Salado practices.

Broken Life Lines. Elsewhere Young (1967:20-28, 1982:35-45) has documented the inclusion of life-lines in the decorational motif of Salado polychrome ceramics. Life lines are heavy, thick, black lines that occur at various locations on Salado polychrome vessels: at or near the rims; at various locations above, at, or below the shoulders of jars; and at various locations between the rim and center of bowls (Figure 55). Not all Salado polychrome life lines are broken, but many are. We see a direct continuation from the prehistoric Western Pueblo Salado through the historic Western Pueblo -- see, especially, Fewke's many 1898 Sityatki illustrations -- to the contemporary Navajo practice of leaving a spirit exit in the decoration of such items as ceramics, rattle sticks, sandpaintings, and woven articles (Ellis 1928:58; Franciscan Fathers 1929:287, 294, 367, 375; Hill 1937:16, 21; Kluckhohn and Leighton 1962:201, 306; Tschopik 1941:48).

Intentional Imperfections. Young (1967:49-52, 1982:54-55) has documented elsewhere the Salado practice of incorporating intentional imperfections in the decoration of their polychrome ceramics. In the examination of a collection of 521 whole Salado polychrome vessels Young made a quarter of a century ago, he noticed that as the course of repeated design elements and motifs were followed in the decoration a given piece of pottery -- in almost half of the vessels in the sample one or several of the motifs, rather than being exact replicas of their fellows, were slightly different. For example, a single negative white rectangle with a black dot in its center would appear in one half of a dual-balanced design, but not in the other half (Figure 56c). In other contexts the same white rectangular

122

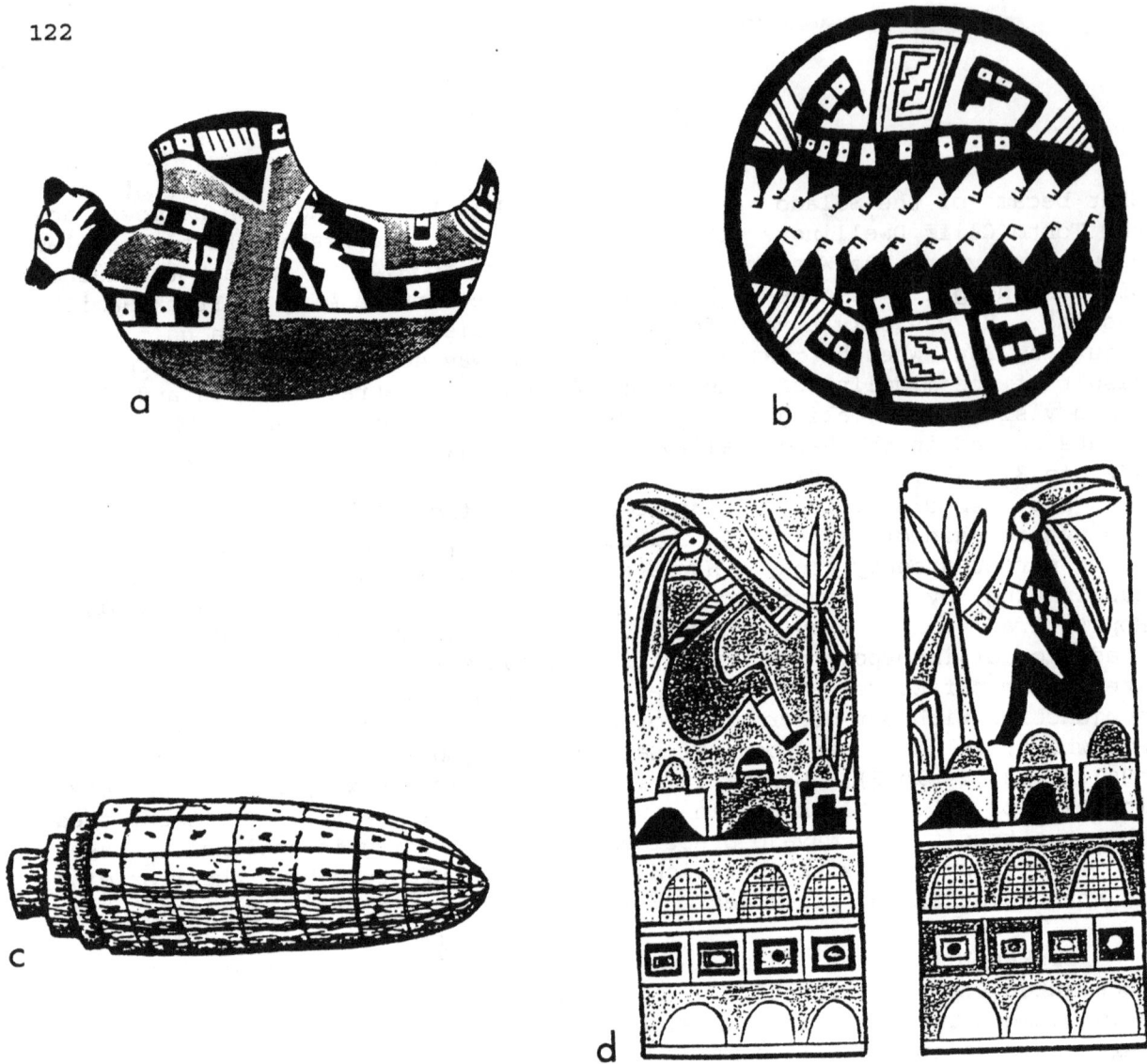

Figure 54. Corn Symbols.
a. Tonto Polychrome jar; Gila Pueblo (Young 1982; Figure 6f).
b. Gila Polychrom bowl; Kinishba (Young 1982; Figure 1).
c. Hopi corn-ear prayer-stick (Parsons 1936: Figure 18).
d. Hopi Flute altar tiles (Parsons 1936: Plate 22).

motif, which normally contained a black a dot in its center, in a single instance would omit the dot (Figure 56e). There are perhaps a dozen situations, such as the two just described, which reoccurred over and over again in the Salado polychrome sample. Because this phenomenon occurred with such frequency and because the imperfections were usually quite obvious and obtrusive, we are inclined to believe that they were made intentionally rather than inadvertently. And just as we see a continuum of the prehistoric Salado life line in contemporary Navajo practices, so also do we see a continuation of the prehistoric Salado practice of incorporating one or more intentional imperfections into the decoration of a ceramic vessel. We see

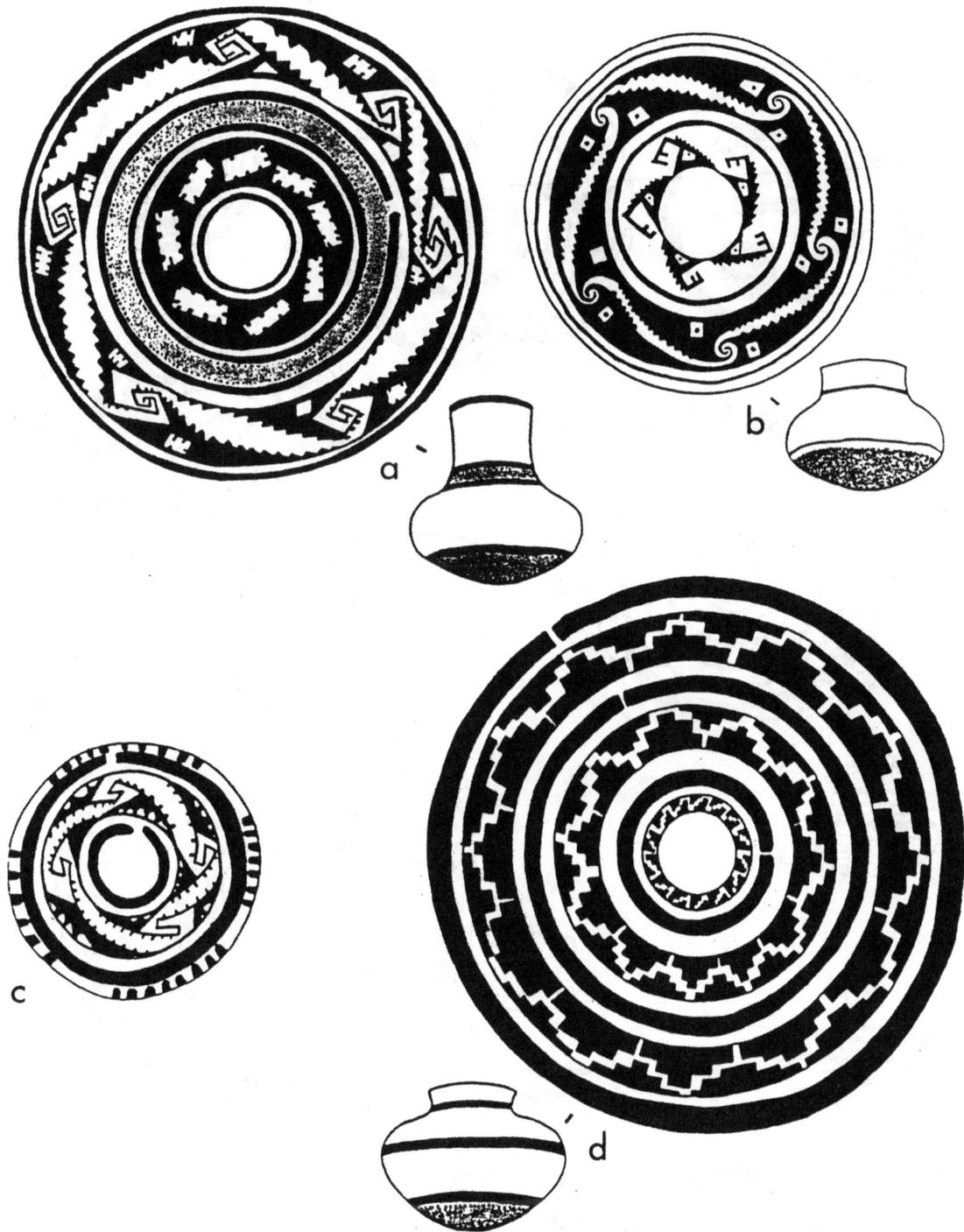

Figure 55. Life Lines.
a. Tonto Polychrome jar; Gila Pueblo (Young 1982: Figure 10g), diameter is 18 cm.
b. Tonto Polychrome jar; Roosevelt 9:6 (Young 1982: Figure 10e), diameter is about 14 cm.
c. Tonto Polychrome bowl; Anglers Inn (Young 1982: Figure 5a), diameter is 37.5 cm.
d. Tonto Polychrome jar; Gila Bank Ruin (Young 1982: Figure 5c).

124

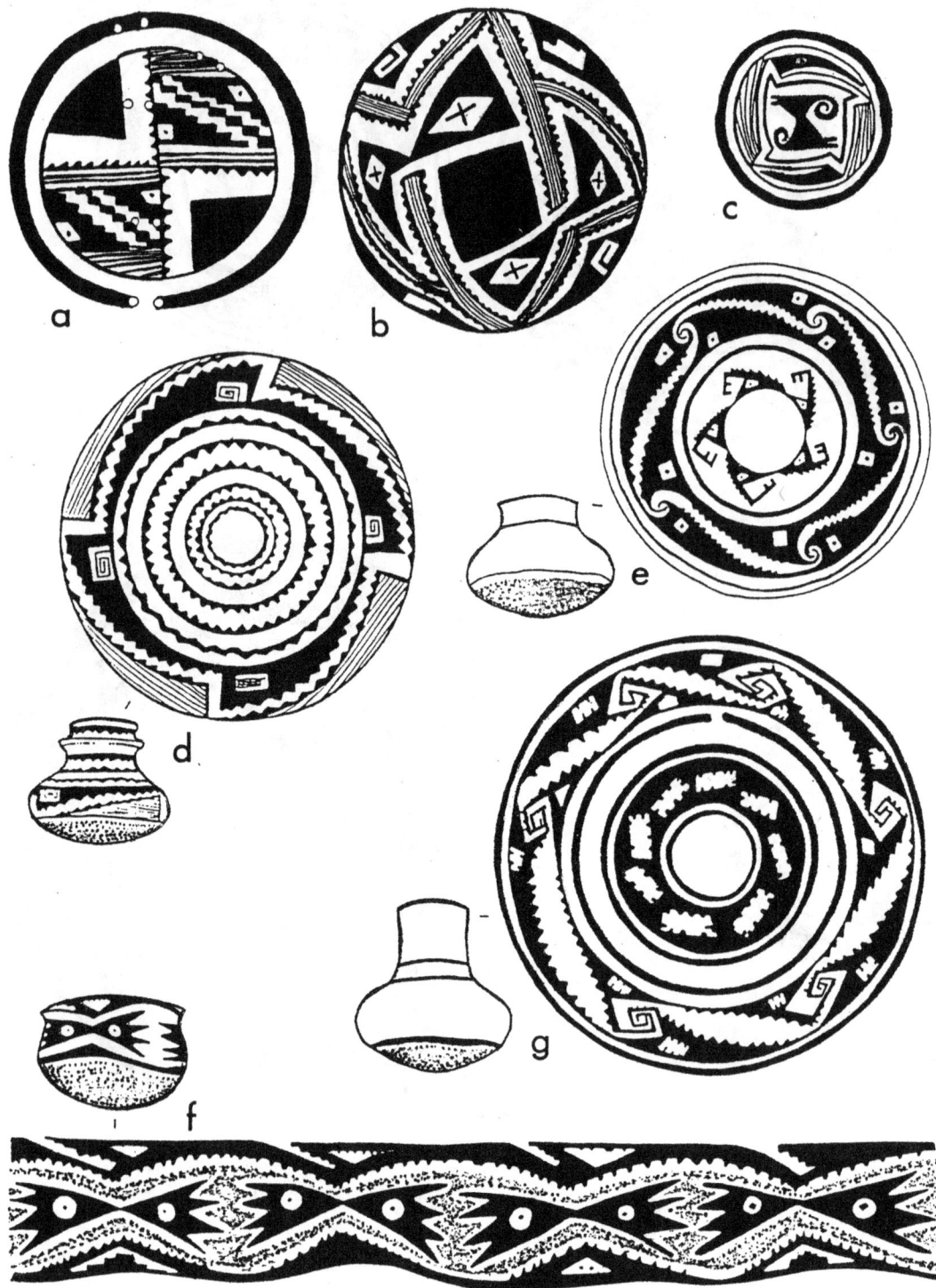

Figure 56. Exampes of the Presence or Absence of Apparently-Intentional Imperfections in the Execution of Designs on Salado Polychrome Vessels.
Scale: Diameter of d. is 18 cm.
a. Gila Polychrome bowl; Gila Pueblo (Young 1982:Figure 10a).
b. Tonto Polychrome bowl; Gila Pueblo (Young 1982:Figure 10b).
c. Gila Polychrome bowl; Anglers Inn (Young 1982: Figure 10c).
d, e, g. Tonto Polychrome jars; Gila Pueblo (Young 1982: Figures 10 d, e, g).
f. Tonto Polychrome jar; Kinishba (Young 1982: Figure 10f).
      a and b - no obvious imperfection.
      c through e - a single obvious imperfection.
      f and g - several obvious imperfections.

that continuation in the contemporary Navajo practice of incorporating one or more obvious imperfections into those sandpaintings that are not going to be destroyed before the sun has set on the day of their construction (Kluckhohn and Leighton 1962:306, Reichard 1936:160).

REFERENCES CITED

Anderson, J. E.
     1969   The Human Skeleton. The National Museum of Canada, Ottawa.
Anderson, Keith M., Gloria J. Fenner, Don P. Morris, Geaorge A. Teague, and
Charmion McKusick
     1986   The Archeology of Gila Cliff Dwellings. Western Archeological
                   Center, Tucson.
Baldwin, Gordon C.
     1965   The Warrior Apaches. Dale Stuart King, Tucson.
Beaglehole, E.
     1937   Notes on Hopi Economic Life. Yale University Publications in
                   Anthropology 15, New Haven.
Blalack, Carmen Mallory
     1954   Personal Communication.
Bradfield, Wesley
     1929   Cameron Creek Village. Monograph No. 1. School of American
                   Research, Santa Fe.
Brody, J. J.
     1977   Mimbres Painted Pottery. School of American Research, Santa
                   Fe.
     1978   Mimbres Painting and the Northern Frontier. In Across the
                   Chichimec Sea, edited by Carroll L. Riley and Basil C.
                   Hedrick. Southern Illinois University Press, Carbondale.
Brody, J. J., Catherine J. Scott., Steven A. LeBlanc, and Tony Berlant
     1983   Mimbres Pottery. Hudson Hills Press, New York.
Brown, Jeffrey L., and Paul Grebinger
     1969   A Lower Terrace Compound at San Cayetano del Tumacacori. The
                   Kiva 23:185-198.
Castetter, Edward F., and Willis H. Bell
     1942   Pima and Papago Indian Agriculture. University of New Mexico
                   Press, Albuquerque.
Castetter, Edward F., Willis H. Bell and Alvin R. Grove
     1938   The Early Utilization and Distribution of Agave in the
                   American Southwest. Bulletin No. 335, Biological Series Vol.
                   5(4). University of New Mexico, Albuquerque.
Castetter, Edward F., and Ruth M. Underhill
     1935   The Ethnobiology of the Papago Indians. Bulletin No. 275,
                   Biological Series Vol 4(3). University of New Mexico,
                   Albuquerque.
Colton, Harold Sellers, and Lyndon Lane Hargrave
     1937   Handbook of Northern Arizona Pottery Wares. Bulletin No. 11.
                   Museum of Northern Arizona, Flagstaff.
Cosgrove, H. S., and C. B. Cosgrove
     1932   The Swartz Ruin. Papers of the Peabody Museum of American
                   Archaeology and Ethnology Vol. 15(1), Cambridge.
Cosner, Aaron J.
     1956   The "Stone Scraper" and Arrow "Wrench." American Antiquity
                   21:300-301.
Crary, Joseph S.
     1989   Personal Communication.

References

Crary, Joseph S., Stephen Germick, and Michael Gollio
    1992   Late Mogollon Adaptations in the Upper Sonoran Desert. Paper
                presented at the 1992 Mogollon Conference, Las Cruces.
Creel, Darrell and Charmion McKusick
    1993   Prehistoric Macaws and Parrots in the Mimbres Area, New
                Mexico. American Antiquity 59:510-523.
Day, Jane S.
    1992   Aztec. Denver Museum of Natural History, Denver.
Dean, Jeffrey S.
    1990   Thoughts on Hohokam Chronology. In Exploring the Hohokam,
                edited by George J. Gummerman, pp. 61-149. University of New
                Mexico Press, Albuquerque.
Di Peso, Charles C.
    1974   Casas Grandes, No. 9. Amerind Foundation, Dragoon, Arizona.
Drucker, Phillip
    1941   Culture Element Distributions: XVII, Yuman-Piman.
                Anthropological Records 6:91-230. University of California,
                Berkeley.
Duffield, Lathel F.
    1963   The Strawn Creek Site, Navarro County, Texas. MS on file at
                the Arizona Archeological Center, Tucson.
Ellis, Florence Mae Hawley
    1928   Pottery and Culture Relations in the Middle Gila. Unpublished
                M.A. thesis, Department of Anthropology, University of
                Arizona, Tucson.
Euler, R. Thomas, and David A. Gregory.
    1988   Pecked Ground Stone and Polished Stone Artifacts. In The
                1982-1984 Excavations at Las Colinias: Material Culture, by
                David R. Abbott, Kim E. Beckwith, Patricia L. Crown, R. Thomas
                Euler, David A. Gregory, J. Ronald London, Marilyn B. Saul,
                Larry A. Schwalbe, and Mary Bernard-Shaw, pp. 299-317. Arizona
                State Museum Archaeological Series No. 162:4. University of
                Arizona, Tucson.
Ferg, Alan
    1988   Exotic Artifacts and Shrines. In Erich F. Schmidt's
                Investigations of Salado Sites in Central Arizona, by John W.
                Hohmann and Linda B. Kelley, pp. 206-218. Bulletin No. 56
                Museum of Northern Arizona, Flagstaff.
Ferg, Alan, Austin Long, Christine R. Szuter, Karen Adams, Karen K. Zadina,
and Kim Beckwith
    1993   Unpublished Student Reports at the Arizona State Museum.
                University of Arizona, Tucson.
Fewkes, Jesse Walter
    1898   Archeological Expedition to Arizona in 1895. Seventeenth
                Annual Report of the Bureau of American Ethnology, pp.
                519-714. U.S. Government Printing Office, Washington, D.C.
Franciscan Fathers
    1929   An Ethnologic Dictionary of the Navajo Language. Max
                Breslauer, Leipzig.

128

References

Fry, Gary F. and H. Johnson Hall
    1986   Human Coprolites. In Archeological Investigations at <u>Antelope House</u>, by Don P. Morris. National Park Service, Washington, D.C.

Fulton, William Shirley
    1934   <u>Archaeological Notes on Texas Canyon, Arizona</u>. Contributions from the Museum of the American Indian, Heye Foundation 12(2), New York.

Gavan, James A.
    1940   Physical Anthropology of Besh-ba-gowah. <u>The Kiva</u> 6:(3):9-12.

Gifford, E. W.
    1932   <u>The Southeastern Yavapai</u>. University of California Publications in American Archaeology and Ethnology 39:177-252, Berkeley.

Gladwin, Harold S., Emil W. Haury, E. B. Sayles, and Nora Gladwin
    1937   <u>Excavations at Snaketown</u>. Medallion Papers No. 25. Gila Pueblo, Globe, Arizona.

Green, Jesse (editor)
    1990   <u>Cushing at Zuni</u>. University of New Mexico Press, Albuquerque.

Griffin, P. Bion
    1967   A High Status Burial from Grasshopper Ruin, Arizona. <u>The Kiva</u> 33:37-53.

Haury, Emil W.
    1945   <u>The Excavation of Los Muertos and Neighboring Ruins in the Salt River Valley</u>. Papers of the Peabody Museum of American Archaeology and Ethnology Vol. 24(1), Cambridge.
    1975   <u>The Stratigraphy and Archaeology of Ventana Cave</u>. 2d ed. University of Arizona Press, Tucson.
    1976   <u>The Hohokam</u>. University of Arizona Press, Tucson.
    1988   Gila Pueblo Archaeological Foundation. <u>The Kiva</u> 54:1-71.

Hayden, Julian D.
    1957   <u>Excavations, 1940, at University Indian Ruin</u>. Technical Series No. 5. Southwestern Monuments Association, Globe, Arizona.

Hayes, Alden C.
    1964   <u>The Archeological Survey of Wetherill Mesa, Mesa Verde National Park, Colorado</u>. Archeological Research Series No. 7-A. National Park Service, Washington, D.C.

Hayes, Alden C., and James A. Lancaster
    1975   <u>Badger House Community</u>. Publications in Archeology No. 7-E. National Park Service, Washington, D.C.

Hayes, Alden C., Jon Nathan Young, and A. H. Warren
    1981   <u>Excavation of Mound 7</u>. Archeological Research Series No. 16. National Park Service, Washington, D.C.

Hill, Willard Williams
    1937   <u>Navajo Pottery Manufacture</u>. Bulletin No. 31, Anthropological Series Vol. 2(3). University of New Mexico, Albuquerque.

Hodge, Frederick Webb
    1910   <u>Handbook of American Indians</u>, pt. 2. Bulletin No. 30(2). Bureau of American Ethnology, Washington, D.C.

References

Hohmann, John W.
    1992   Through the Mirror of Death. Ph.D. dissertation, Arizona State
                University, Tempe. University Microfilms, Ann Arbor.
Honea, Kenneth H.
    1965   The Bipolar Flaking Technique in Texas and New Mexico.
                Bulletin of the Texas Archeological Society 36:259-267,
                Austin.
Hough, Walter
    1930   Explorations of Ruins in the White Mountain Apache Indian
                Reservation, Arizona. Proceedings of the National Museum Vol.
                78(13):1-21. Washington, D.C.
Irwin, Henry T., and H. M. Wormington
    1970   Paleo-Indian Tool Types in the Great Plains. American
                Antiquity 35:24-34.
Jeancon, J. A.
    1923   Excavations in the Chama Valley, New Mexico. Bulletin No. 81.
                Bureau of American Ethnology, Washington, D.C.
Keen, A. Myra
    1971   Shells of the Tropical Pacific. Stanford University Press,
                Stanford.
Kent, Kate Peck
    1954   Montezuma Archeology, pt. 2. Technical Series Vol. 3(2).
                Southwestern Monuments Association, Globe, Arizona.
Kidder, Alfred Vincent
    1932   The Artifacts of Pecos. Southwestern Expedition Papers No. 6.
                Phillips Academy, New Haven.
Kluckhohn, Clyde, and Dorothea Leighton
    1962   The Navajo. Doubleday and Company, Garden City.
Lange, Charles H., and Carroll L. Riley (editors)
    1970   The Southwestern Journals of Adolph F. Bandelier, 1883-1884.
                University of New Mexico Press, Albuquerque.
Lehmer, Donald J., and David T. Jones
    1968   Arikara Archeology: The Bad River Phase. River Basin Survey
                Publications in Salvage Archeology No. 7. Smithsonian
                Institution, Lincoln.
Lincoln, L. M. and D. Jacobs
    1990   Pedestals of the Roosevelt Platform Mound Study. Paper
                presented at the 63rd Pecos Conference, Blanding, Utah.
McGregor, John C.
    1943   Burial of an Early American Magician. Proceedings Vol.
                86(2):270-298. American Philosophical Society, Philadelphia.
    1965   Southwestern Archaeology. University of Illinois Press, Urbana
McKusick, Charmion R.
    1981   The Faunal Remains of Las Jumanas. In Contributions to Gran
                Quivira Archeology by Alden C. Hayes, pp. 39-65. Archeological
                Research Series No. 17. National Park Service, Washington,
                D.C.
    1986   Southwest Indian Turkeys. Southwest Bird Laboratory, Globe,
                Arizona.

130

References

Miller, Mary and Karl Taube
    1993   The Gods and Symbols of Ancient Mexico and the Maya. Thames
                and Hudson, London.
Mills, Jack P., and Vera M. Mills
    1969   The Kuykendall Site. Special Report No. 6 El Paso
                Archaeological Society, El Paso.
Moorehead, Warren K.
    1906   A Narrative of Explorations in New Mexico, Arizona, Indiana,
                etc. Department of Archaeology Bulletin No. 3. Phillips
                Academy, Andover.
Morris, Don P.
    1986   Archeological Investigations at Antelope House. National Park
                Service, Washington, D.C.
Olson, Alan P.
    1959   An Evaluation of the Phase Concept in Southwestern
                Archaeology: As Applied to the Eleventh and Twelfth Century
                Occupation at Point of Pines, East Central Arizona. Ph.D.
                dissertation, University of Arizona, Tucson. University
                Microfilms, Ann Arbor.
Parsons, Elsie Clews
    1936   Hopi Journal of Alexander M. Stephen. Columbia University
                Press, New York.
Pierson, Lloyd M.
    1962   Excavations at the Lower Ruin, Tonto National Monument. In
                Archeological Studies at Tonto National Monument, Arizona,
                edited by Louis R. Caywood, pp. 33-68. Southwestern Monuments
                Association Technical Series Vol. 2, Globe, Arizona.
Reed, Erik K.
    1950   Eastern-Central Arizona Archaeology in Relation to the Western
                Pueblo. Southwestern Journal of Anthropology 6(2):120-138.
                Reichard, Gladys A.
    1936   Navajo Shepherd and Weaver. J. J. Augustin, New York.
Reid, J. Jefferson, Barbara Klie Montgomery, Maria Nieves Zedeno, and Mark A.
Neupert
    1992   The Origin of Roosevelt Red Ware. In Proceedings of the Second
                Salado Conference edited by Richard C. Lange and Stephen
                Germick, pp. 212-215. Arizona Archaeological Society
                Occasional Paper 1992, Phoenix.
Reid, J. Jefferson, and Stephanie M. Whittlesey
    1992   New Evidence for Dating Gila Polychrome. In Proceedings of the
                Second Salado Conference edited by Richard C. Lange and
                Stephen Germick, pp. 223-229. Arizona Archaeological Society
                Occasional Paper 1992, Phoenix.
Riley, Carroll L., and Basil C. Hedrick (editors)
    1978   Across the Chichimec Sea. Southern Illinois University Press,
                Carbondale.
Ross, Kurt
    1978   Codex Mendoza. Productions Liber SA, Fribourg.

References

Russell, Frank
    1908   The Pima Indians. Twenty-sixth Annual Report of the Bureau of
                American Ethnology, pp. 1-390. U.S. Government Printing
                Office, Washington, D.C.
Sauer, Carl O. and Donald D. Brand
    1930   Pueblo Sites in Southeastern Arizona. University of California
                Publications in Geography 3(7), Berkeley.
Scott, G. Richard
    1981   A Stature Reconstruction of the Gran Quivira Skeletal
                Population. In Contributions to Gran Quivira Archeology by
                Alden C. Hayes, pp. 129-137. Archeological Research Series No.
                17. National Park Service, Washington, D.C.
Seltzer, C. C.
    1944   Racial Prehistory in the Southwest and the Hawikuh Zunis.
                Papers of the Peabody Museum of American Archaeology and
                Ethnology 23(1). Cambridge.
Shiner, Joel L.
    1961   A Room at Gila Pueblo. The Kiva 27(2):3-11.
Smiley, Terah L.
    1951   A Summary of Tree-Ring Dates from Some Southwestern
                Archeological Sites. Laboratory of Tree-Ring Research, No. 5.
                Tucson.
Spears, C. Duane
    1973   Test Excavations in Compound B, Casa Grande Ruins. Ms. on
                file, Western Archeological Center, Tucson.
Steen, Charlie R.
    1962   Excavations at the Upper Ruin, Tonto National Monument. In
                Archeological Studies at Tonto National Monument, Arizona
                edited by Louis R. Caywood, pp. vii-32. Southwestern Monuments
                Association Technical Series Vol. 2, Globe, Arizona.
Steen, Charlie R., Lloyd M. Pierson, Vorsilla L. Bohrer, and Kate Peck Kent
    1962   Archeological Studies at Tonto National Monument, Arizona.
                Southwestern Monuments Association Technical Series Vol. 2,
                Globe, Arizona.
Teague, Lynn S.
    1993   Prehistory and the Traditions of the O'Odham and Hopi. The
                Kiva 58:435-445.
Tschopik, Harry, Jr.
    1941   Navajo Pottery Making. Papers of the Peabody Museum of
                American Archaeology and Ethnology Vol 17(1). Cambridge.
Tuthill, Carr
    1947   The Tres Alamos Site, Southeastern Arizona. The Amerind
                Foundation, No. 4, Dragoon, Arizona.
Vickery, Irene
    1939   Besh-ba-gowah. The Kiva 4(5):19-22.
Vietmeyer, Noel
    1987   How a Bug Made the World See Red. International Wildlife
                17(2):42-47.

132

References

Wedel, Waldo R.
    1936   Introduction to Pawnee Archeology. Bulletin No. 112. Bureau of
             American Ethnology, Washington, D.C.
    1959   An Introduction to Kansas Archaeology. Bulletin No. 174.
             Bureau of American Ethnology, Washington, D.C.

Wheeler, Richard P.
    1965   Edge Abraded Flakes, Blades and Cores in the Puebloan Tool
             Assemblage. Memoirs of the Society for American Archaeology
             19:19-29.132, Salt Lake City.

White, Diane E., and James Burton
    1992   Pinto Polychrome. In Proceedings of the Second Salado
             Conference edited by Richard C. Lange and Stephen Germick, pp.
             216-222. Arizona Archaeological Society Occasional Paper 1992,
             Phoenix.

White, Theodore E.
    1953   A Method of Calculating the Dietary Percentage of Various Food
             Animals Utilized by Aboriginal Peoples. American Antiquity
             18(4):396-398.

Wood, J. Scott
    1985   The Classic Period in Southwestern Prehistory 1150-1400, for
             Prehistory of the Southwest, a class presented by the Arizona
             Archaeological Society, Phoenix.
    1987   Checklist of Pottery Types for the Tonto National Forest. The
             Arizona Archaeologist 21.

Woodbury, Richard B.
    1954   Prehistoric Stone Implements of Northeastern Arizona. Papers
             of the Peabody of American Archaeology and Ethnology Vol 34,
             Cambridge.

Wylie, Henry G.
    1975   Pot Scrapers and Drills from Southern Utah. The Kiva
             40(3):121-130.

Young, Jon Nathan
    1967   The Salado Culture in Southwestern Prehistory. Ph.D.
             dissertation, University of Arizona, Tucson. University
             Microfilms, Ann Arbor.
    1982   Salado Polychrome Pottery. Papers of the Archaeological
             Society of New Mexico No. 7:31-57, Albuquerque.

INDEX

134

Index

Index

Index

Index

White, Theodore E.; 85
Whittaker, John C.; 55
Whittlesly, Stephanie M.; 36
Windmiller, Ric; v
Wood, J. Scott; 1, 4, 101
Woodbury, Richard B.; 52
Wormington, H. M.; 58
Wylie, Henry G.; 58
Wyoming; 55
Xipe Toltec; 118
Xiuhtecutli; 118
Yavapai; 106, 113, 115
Young, Jon Nathan; 121-124
Yucca; 40, 55, 91-92, 97, 102
Yuma Indians; 40
Zuni; 28, 97-98, 121

www.ingramcontent.com/pod-product-compliance
Lightning Source LLC
Chambersburg PA
CBHW081647270326
41933CB00018B/3375